MW01595275

Cover Design

Courtesy of Creatspace.com

ISBN-13   978-1503049451

ISBN-10   1503049450

Dedication

To my first husband, Bob who was killed in an accident at work in 1987, and my brother Larry, they both laughed when I mentioned I could write a book. Yes, I began my journey in the mid 1980's. Well, finally here it is.

To my husband Tim, who encourages me to just do it. See, I told you I was going to do it this time.   To my friends who kept encouraging me. Thanks to you all.

CONTENTS

Still

Loving

You

By

R.E. Laurel

CHAPTER 1

"What did you say?"

"I said that I was shocked to find out that Matt is leaving for the Navy."

Stacy's hands white knuckled the edge of the kitchen counter looking with stunned disbelief at her mom. "No! I don't believe it! *I won't believe it! He-he never told me a thing about it and if he never did then it isn't true!"*

Her eyes glistened with unshed tears at the news regarding her best friend, Matt Sadler. With an agitated swipe of her hand through her hair, she spun away. Hurrying out the back door she jumped down the four steps, landing on the grass to run to the refuge where together they made a lifetime of fun and good memories.

Her mother Beth followed stopping on the back porch. Her hands grip the metal railing. "Stacy! Come back here!" She

frantically called, helplessly watching her disappear among the rich northern Pennsylvania fields, thick with colorful, swaying wild flowers, then to the woods beyond.

Stacy wildly ran on the dirt path until reaching the neighborhood swimming hole. Plopping hard onto a large flat rock that protruded over the water, she sat crossed legged. Gasping to catch her breath, her chest heaved as she took deep gulps of air as anguish erupted from deep within until the cries changed to soft whimpers while dashing the tears from her face and eyes.

The over abundant chorus of cheerful chirping of the many birds along with the droning buzz of the different insects serenaded her. The breeze was warm for this spring day gently blowing through the branches of the many trees. A day filled with beauty of cotton ball clouds aimlessly floating in the bright blue skies, constantly changing formations then slowly drift away, to fade into white puffs of nothingness.

But nature's beauty being so elaborately displayed, went unnoticed by seventeen-year-old Stacy Cannon. She sat cross-legged, her elbows resting on her knees. Her face cradled on her fists as she mutely stared at the babbling water, watching as it fed into a large opening of the swimming hole. Through tear filled eyes she stared mesmerized to the reflection of the bright sun glistening with sprite like sparkles.

Hopelessness draped over her. She blinked while tears ran unchecked down her cheeks. All she wanted to do is fade away into blissful oblivion, so much like those lucky clouds. She hated changes and today the bombshell of all changes fell from the sky and threatened to hit her hard.

Feeling the loss, she wearily wiped a hand over her eyes, brushing away the most recent round of torrential tears as she fought to calm down. Believing she finally gained some sort of control over her heart broken emotions, her thoughts drift to Matt and the dams burst forth with renewed powerful force.

Her life is in a total shamble. Her boyfriend of four months, Dan Black, demand more from their relationship; more than she is willing to give. She told him that she isn't ready for the commitment of sex but he's growing tired of waiting. He's nineteen and becoming impatient with her childish ways. Oh yeah, that's what he called her, childish.

"Boys were so much easier when they had cooties," she muttered.

And now, she discovers that her neighbor and best friend, whom she spent practically every day with since she could remember is leaving home, leaving her, to join the Air Force and those planes that he so much loves. The news came as a complete shock.

Matt Sadler, the brother she never had is also two years older. His long, wavy dark brown hair reached past the nape of his neck and his expressive sky blue eyes were surrounded with long lashes. She considered his smile alluring, crooked, where the cutest dimples would erupt on his cheeks. His laughter proved so lighthearted and infectious. Whenever he'd let loose with a good dose of his humor, everyone around couldn't help but join.

They grew up playing the games that children played, from cowboys and Indian to schoolhouse. Bike riding to roller-blades. The neighborhood held daily games of baseball bringing all of the children together. As he matured and his interests changed to girls and cars, he still let her tag along with him and his friends, who didn't mind.

She and Matt had a unique friendship. He had an older brother and she an only child, he always referred to her as the little sister and was very protective. Coming from a family where his father served as a war pilot, his interests followed to the vast sky. He loved airplanes and longed to fly. At the age of fifteen, he received his pilot license.

Maturing into young adults, they shared a lot of secrets, except for this one. He often hinted about joining the Navy but that was as far as it went. And she had to hear from her mother and as young hearts go, it devastated her. Tilting her head back, her gaze went to the open skies. Her blurred vision followed the fading white trail of a jet and she wondered what could be so great about them? What could being up there, be so fulfilling, that it would lure a young man away from home?

"What am I going to do without you?" Her quivering voice cried to the wide space around her. The damn happy chirping of the birds answered. "Oh, shut up."

She made a nasty face to the trees as she roughly brushed away more tears. In the distance she heard the familiar sound of his trail bike. She made another face of disgust, knowing that he was in search of her. Too soon, she'd have to face him. Too soon, and she didn't care to at the moment. An overwhelming emptiness filled her. She had the feeling she was losing a part of herself. Maybe it was being immature and greedy, but, she didn't want to let him go!

She remained motionless, sitting cross-legged with her elbows resting on her knees as her closed hands cradled her face. She closed her eyes, giving up, permitting the tears to freely drop onto the rock. Her eyes closed tighter when the sound of his bike sounded louder to roar down the dirt trail through the woods, leading him to her.

* * *

Matt approached the swimming hole, slowing his bike, stopping at the end of the trail when his gaze fell on the tiny figure sitting on the rock. Beth said how upset Stacy got when she mentioned he was leaving and he hurried in search of her. He needed to explain why it happened so fast. Next problem, how?

She looked so damn disappointed and he couldn't blame her. He killed the engine, pushing the kick stand down to lean the bike on before he went to her. Nervous, his hands rubbed on his thighs before being shoved into his back pockets. His chest puffed out by the deep breath he inhaled, then released. Determined, he locked his gaze on her before taking steps nearer.

Her brown, shoulder length hair was loose, flitting about in the gentle breeze. Her tanned legs were bare from the cut off denim shorts, the hem badly raveling from the many machine washes. The dark blue T-shirt she had on was far too big on her, hiding her thin figure. He noticed her shoulders trembling. He paused, sucking in another deep breath. He wasn't good with girls, especially girls in tears.

"Stace," he softly spoke her name. His answer a loud heart wrenching cry to escape from her before her hands covered her mouth trying in vain to hide it.

With lips twisted in a smirk, he plopped next to her, mocking how she sat. He couldn't help but notice how fast she turned away, showing her stiff back to him. He grimaced and released a long sigh while rubbing a weary hand across his forehead before his splayed fingers combed through his hair. He braced an elbow on his knee to place his chin in his hand as he patiently looked at her trembling back. He leant over, nudging his shoulder against her back.

"Hey."

Her back rose and fell from her sigh.

"Stace?"

"Hmmmmm."

The reply was quick. Her voice wavering.

"Are you going to be okay?" He wondered, watching her head quickly shake back and forth along with a shrug of her shoulders. "I'm so damn sorry that I didn't tell you."

Her head snapped up to look over her shoulder as her tear filled eyes angrily glared at him. He gasped at the brightness of her dark brown eyes. Her long dark lashes were etched together from her tears. Her cheeks showed traces of where the tears flowed. He remained silent as she turned her body to face him.

"Why didn't you? I suppose that Sandy already knows!"

His eyes rolled with her accusation but the truth be known, he didn't talk to Sandy any longer. Since he broke things off last month, he rarely saw her, which is fine with him.

"You know that I broke up with her."

"Yes. I thought we meant a lot to one another! But no! I have to find out from mom that my best friend is leaving me to join the Navy!" She accused as more tears began flowing.

"I didn't know how to go about telling you..."

"*You know me Matt*! You of all people should know how to handle anything when it concerns me!"

But I don't! Not with you! Lately you confuse the hell out of me!

"Come here," he gently demanded, reaching for her. His arms suddenly felt awkward as he reached out to wrap her in them. Her body was stiff but soon she yielded to ease her shuddering body against his. His other arm went around her waist, feeling how fragile she felt as he placed his chin on the top of her head. They remained silent as he held her, gently rocking her as a parent would with an upset child. He felt her fingers clutch his T-shirt, pulling him closer as she buried her face into his neck to release more of those nonstop tears.

"I never knew I meant this much to you," he tried teasing but her reply further confuses him.

"You mean the world to me," she cried into his neck.

His eyes rolled heaven ward. How often had he tried to get her to go on a date, had constantly been on her case about it but she always refused with the excuse of them being too good of friends to risk ruining it. So, he had to remain her best friend and it killed him watching as she went out with others. Finally, he accepted her words and settled into the best friend, older brother routine and not liking it.

"You need to quit crying like this. I mean, you don't want me to remember you with red swollen eyes, do you?" He again teased. This time she shook her head. He grinned. She's taking him so serious.

She tipped her head back, her lips close to his cheek. The softness of her breath tickled his skin when she spoke, "Do you really have to go?"

Matt looked down at her very pretty face, a face he'd never forget. Her glistening brown eyes looked at him, holding such sadness that it broke his heart. Her lips trembled in her sorrow. He was used to seeing her always happy and it hurt him to know that he's the reason for her behaving this way.

"I tried college and it wasn't for me. You know there isn't much here for a man to do to earn a decent living for a family and besides, I don't want stuck in a corporate office job. I want to see the world."

"Why do you have to go to see that world? Can't you just turn on the *Discovery Channel* or something?"

"Stace," he scoffed, lovingly gazing into her stubborn face. His hand gently cupped her cheek, feeling her press her face deeper into his palm.

Her lips pressed tightly together, trembling as she bravely fought to control her distraught emotions. But she was powerless as slowly, the tears began filling her eyes.

His hand moved, his fingers lightly touch her lips, surprised when she placed a soft kiss on his fingertips. He stilled his hand, her touch sending a tingling sensation to flow over him, ending as a knot in his loins. Pausing, he soaked this moment into his brain to never forget. He looked long and hard at her lips, mere inches from his, constantly thinking about them; wondering if they would be soft pressed against his; thinking that he'd like to give his best friend a kiss.

"You're beautiful," he murmured seeing the look of wonder on her face.

His hand moved to her jaw, cupping her chin as he slowly dipped his face to tentatively press his lips against hers, tasting the salt from her tears. He was equally surprised when she kissed him back. It was a light sweet kiss. Her meek gesture silently urged him on. His other hand slid through her hair, gripping onto the back of her head. His lips slant over hers in a long, languorous kiss, parting her lips as the kiss deepened, engulfing into a flame of hunger.

Words weren't spoken as he slowly, eased her back on the rock. He lay next to her. His mouth still covered hers. His nervous hand slid down her waist, embracing her to him. He felt her arms wrap around his shoulders, holding him tight to never let go. His lips left hers to press kisses down the delicate arch of her throat.

An inward gasp escaped from her parted lips. Stacy was stunned with these new strange sensations coursing through her body, to her feelings! Her soul. Suddenly she felt alive! Nothing close with Dan as he kissed her and tried to advance his intentions on her. She always stopped him but with Matt it was different, she felt different. She felt special in his arms. She tried to fight her emotions but nothing mattered. Surprising herself, she realized that she needed, wanted Matt Sadler to make love to her and it wasn't a mistake as she hungered for his touch.

"Don't leave me," she frantically whispered.

"I have to," he returned. His lips pressed against her slender neck, suddenly wishing he never joined.

Matt's feelings erupted inside his soul like he never before felt with anyone else. Being like this with Stacy was everything he dreamed of. Slowly, his trembling hand trailed beneath her T-shirt and behind to fumble with the snap as he tried to undo her bra.

With a light yank, he pulled the material from her tiny breasts to cover with his hand to lightly he caressed the quivering flesh. As he pulled her shirt higher, he dipped his head his mouth covering a hard nipple, teasing with his tongue and tugging with his lips. His actions got such a nervous gasp from her that he looked onto her unsure face causing reality to hit home.

"This isn't right," he whispered while slowly backing from her. But his body screamed out that it was. She was always on his mind as he wondered what it would be like with her.

Stacy wanted this more than anything else, except for him to stay here. The tender touch of her hand on his stopped him when she felt him cover her breasts with her shirt. No, she was going to see this through. It felt right in his arms.

Laying on his side, he took her into his arms. His eyes widened when he felt the innocence of her lips on his neck. Then the brief, unsure touch of her hand sliding down his stomach. She didn't know what kind of repercussions her kisses were doing to him; or that her touch drove him mad beyond reason. If he didn't stop now, then there would be no turning back.

"Are you sure about this?" He wondered, his answer a nod and a nervous grin. "Really?"

"Definitely. Matt make love to me."

His eyes held hers. The feeling was stronger as his desire mounted. He didn't want to stop. He wasn't going to. Determined, he undid the metal snap of her shorts to impatiently tug them from her slender hips. His thoughts remained persistent with it not being right, but it felt right.

Soon her leg was free of the one opening. Quickly, he reached a hand to gently stroke between her thighs, feeling her legs clamp tight together with her innocence. Slowly, uncertainly, his fingers slipped beneath her panties, touching her most sensitive spot. He continued, his fingers sliding into her virginal wetness, hearing a quivering cry on her lips and feeling her pelvic raise to meet him, grinding against his hand. His mouth covered hers, pushing his tongue past her lips to dart into her unsure mouth. He moved, his knee easing her legs open. With his free hand, he reached to release himself.

Stacy was absorbed with her new, erupting emotions. She couldn't believe these feelings Matt stirred inside of her and wondered why she always refused his dates. Suddenly, she felt more like a woman than a teenager. This was foreign to her, yet felt so comfortable; natural.

A cry of pleasure escaped from her gasping mouth, "Matt. This feels so good," she whispered. She felt the first, tentative touch of his hardness pushing for entry, she reacted with her legs tightening about his hips.

"Relax darling," he whispered against her quivering mouth before tenderly kissing her.

Her hand gripped the length of his hair at the back of his neck. She knew he was beyond stopping and she didn't want him to. With a nervous swallow, she relaxed her legs, opening them to permit him to enter.

Her head broke the contact of his mouth on hers. "Ahhh!" She lightly gasped.

Matt gazed into her face to find her expressive eyes open, watching him. Eyes locked together, he pushed again, seeing the slight grimace crossing her features. This time he achieved his goal as he completely entered her. He lay for a moment to permit her to get used to him. He never had a virgin before. The few other girlfriends were experienced.

"Oh God, Stace," he whispered into her ear, "I didn't realize," he added before placing gentle, reassuring kisses on her neck, face and nose until he found her lips. Slowly he began to move.

As she relaxed, she moved with him, and it felt heavenly. Her hips pushed against him, welcoming his hard plunges. Too soon, a strange feeling swirled from deep inside of her. She felt her muscles tightening before the onslaught of her release. Her body shuddered with convulsed spasms, tingling from her legs down to her toes. A loud moan of pleasure escaped from her parted lips.

He gasped into her neck, erupting his release deep inside of her, feeling her take him all. Bracing his body on his elbows, he held his torso up to gaze into her precious face. Looking at her closed eyes, he saw a frown form on her lips. He mistook that look for being ashamed for what happened.

Quickly, he withdrew from her comforting heat to rearrange himself. His concerned gaze kept darting back to Stacy who now drew her legs together, her hands holding her long shirt down to cover herself. Politely, he turned his back, listening as she stood to get dressed. He prayed that he didn't hurt her. He never dreamed that she'd still be a virgin, especially dating Dan.

"Uh, I'm sorry Stace..."

She looked at his broad shouldered back. A back she clung to with new found ecstasy. And her world reeled with her the realization as she knew her true feelings.

She loved Matt Sadler.

She didn't realize it until the news that he was leaving. Now she knew why she behaved so sad, she realized she really did love him and it was too late to tell him.

"I didn't hurt you, did I?"

"No," she muttered, thinking, only her heart.

Not knowing what he should say. He shook his head, "I'm sorry, Stace," he repeated, as the feeling of remorse about what just happened fell over him. Her words surprised him.

"I'm not, Matt. I'm glad that you were my first," she truthfully answered vowing to get strong. She gave him a lame excuse of a smile.

He looked over his shoulder at her, "Let's get back. Do you want a ride?"

"I'll walk, thanks."

Matt bit at his lower lip. Squinting he looked to the water, at the ripples as it sparkled beneath the bright shining sun. A decision was made. After what just happened he felt a strong urge to get away. He felt a strange feeling of remorse mixed with a deep craving from the core of his heart that he wanted more of Stacy Cannon. It couldn't happen again, he needed to steer away from the ladies and concentrate on his career, his future, his life.

"I'm leaving this evening," he softly said.

His words caused her to slowly look at him. "Oh, I thought we'd have a week together but I guess I understand." She managed to answer.

"I was leaving tomorrow but I got a call. They want the new recruits to report tonight," he lied.

"I guess this is good bye. Keep in touch."

He nodded.

She remained silent, understanding it was the life path he chose. After a quick hug, she watched him walk away, listened to the bike start and then fade in the distance. He's nineteen and knew there wasn't anything here in the tiny area of Rose Hollow, Pennsylvania for him. Jobs were scarce. Good paying jobs that could keep the next generation here weren't around. He didn't care to go to a college and be stuck in the classes so he joined a branch of the arm services and that is where he is going; to his future.

Stacy arranged her clothing and slowly walked the dirt trail through the fields and woodlands back to her home. Funny how much she changed in this short time spent with him. She needed time alone to get her turmoil thoughts under some form of control. A tremor swept over her as she released a sad sigh, not believing that she made love with Matt and how good it felt to be in his arms.

Matthew Gregory Sadler left for his destination. He left never knowing the secret remaining behind with Stacy Cannon.

CHAPTER 2

Twelve Years Later

It was loud, roaring, the disturbance causing those on the ground to look to the heavens. The noise was so violent that it shook the hangars at the airport and out buildings at the Forrest Sherman Field Naval Air Station of Pensacola, Florida.

With a low, deafening rumble mixed with a high pitch squeal, the F/A 18 Hornets zoomed past in a blur of blue metal before executing a left break spin turn only to disappear into the clouds. Two more MIG's followed in close pursuit. The F/A 18 returned, doing a few distinguished swaying side swings to abruptly, effortlessly, swoop straight up before maneuvering a loop.

The intent eyes narrowed beneath the brim of his Naval hat as his head tilt back, watching the display of uninhibited maneuvers being shown by his top flier. Bracing his hands on his hips, he released a long breath, trying hard to control his mounting temper. He knew he needed to get that young man grounded before he killed himself and any others.

He released a long hissing groan. His eyes locked onto the MIG watching the outlandish, unheard of show. The one doing the deathly, fancy flying was flight Commander Major Sadler and he of all people should know better than to do such dangerous stunts like this.

"What the hell is he doing?" Chief Baker gruffly demanded while he stood outside the doors of his office watching the so called professional maneuvers and supposed training of the new Blue Angel Pilots.

The shorter Captain Smith stood nearby, mute, also closely watching the wild maneuvers. He shrugged in response.

Chief Baker's eyes never left the Number 7 jet as it continued with the wild angles and sharp break a way. He noticed that his top flier, Captain Matt Sadler, hasn't been himself for the past two months and today it showed with his uninhibited, sloppy performance and training of the up and coming young guns.

Filled with dread at the flight patterns, the Captain could only watch until he finally managed a response. "I don't quite know, Sir but I'm saying the Sneak Pass."

"I know. Well, it's time I had a good long talk with him. When Captain Sadler does finally get his ass back on solid ground, you send him to my office, pronto." He ordered before brusquely turning on the heels of his polished boots to disappear inside.

"Yes Sir," Captain Smith echoed to his retreating back, his eyes still on the jets.

Matt smoothly landed his air craft. He shut down the engines, remaining in the cockpit working to get his thoughts in order. He knew he just did some sloppy, hell, dangerous flying out there. Obviously the worse since he began his career and he knew that the repercussions would soon fall on him. He took a quick breath, wishing he could manage to keep the necessary concentration on his job instead of the news from home.

"Stace Cannon, what the devil have you done to me?" He muttered, raising the glass roof to climb out.

His thoughts centered on his best child hood friend. The last day spent with her being forever etched into his thoughts and the memory of her tears still broke his heart. Her mournful words, do you have to go, still haunted him too.   But it was their lovemaking, that one and only time, that he kept close and dear to his heart. He never knew of a woman to ever get beneath his skin and stay there like she has. And now, that damn letter from his mom was burning through to his soul and the pictures enclosed of a boy shocked him.

Also with the help of his mom, he knew how beautiful the woman Stace transformed into. With her long dark hair, dark brown eyes outlined with long dark lashes. A sensuous smile that could bring a man to his knees. And damn it, he couldn't help it if his heart melted each and every time he looked at those pictures.

"Stace, what the hell did you do to me?"

His flight partner, Captain Mike Darcy, remained silent while collecting his bearings. He slowly shook his head at the unbelievable wild ride Matt just gave them. He glanced at Matt, noting that he remained in his seat.

Mike climbed out, standing, he slipped off his helmet, holding it under his arm as he turned to patiently look up at the jet, waiting for Matt to emerge. He remained quiet, watching as Matt climbed out while he removed his yellow helmet.

"I don't know what the hell this Stace has done to you but you've actually made my head spin," Mike answered.

"Fuck you." Matt quipped.

"What the hell?" Mike returned, not missing the glare. He needed to find out what was going on with him? Mike decided that his top priority would be to get to the bottom of things before he ever agreed to climb in the cockpit with Matt again.

Mike was of a medium height and easy going until shit like this happened. It never bothered him to confront anyone who crossed his path and did stunts that he never believed in. His thick barrel chest led to a hard muscled stomach to tiny hips. He and Matt joined up at the same time and made fast friends. Both were interested in becoming a Blue

20

Angel and helped one another with the testing and rigorous training that involved becoming one of the elite.

Matt turned, not missing Mike's pissed off stance. Keeping his focus forward, Matt stomped past his partner to hit the showers. He didn't want to discuss anything about his private life. Not at the moment anyway.

Mike's head turned to watch his somber friend walk away.

"What the hell were you doing out there?" Mike demanded, taking fast steps to catch up to Matt as he hurried through the door.

"Checking to see if Number 7 could do the Sneak Pass."

"You know damn well it can. Fess up."

"I don't care to talk about it..."

"I think you better. You know that you'll be sent to the oval office for this one."

Matt came to a fast stop. Shit, he knew he'd be summoned to the Command Master Chief's office, otherwise nicknamed by Mike as the Oval Office. He turned to look into Mike's light brown eyes, noticing the concern in them.

With a reassuring smile, his dimples erupted on his clean shaven cheeks. "Don't worry about me."

"I do. You haven't been yourself this past week. What the hell is going on?"

Remaining stubbornly silent, Matt pinched the bridge of his nose between his finger and thumb as he moved away towards his locker. Mike, ever being the persistent, concerned friend, was close on his heels. He waited as Matt reached into his locker to take out his wallet. Opening it, he flashed the picture inside.

Mike grasped onto it to take a better look of a boy about ten years old, giving the camera a mug shot. "He's a good looking boy. Nephew?"

Matt pressed his lips together with that one word.

"And Stacy," he added, his interest peaked. "Whoa baby. She is one fine looking woman."

Matt turned the wallet around to look at whom Mike drooled over. It was a latest picture of Stacy standing sideways from the waist up, wearing a very form fitting black crop top that helped to emphasize her full, round breasts. Her back was slightly arched with her hands on her flat stomach. Her long brown hair nearly brushed her upper waist. She wore a seductive look, her lips barely parted and eyes sensuously looking to the camera. He opened the door of his locker where the same photo hung only a bigger size.

Matt gave him a level look, answering, "My brother's fiancée, Amy, took it for her."

"Compared to the other pictures I've seen, it doesn't look like her. You left something like that back home to fly planes? Man, you *are* insane!" Mike released another long whistle.

"Never mind," Matt muttered, reaching his hand inside of his locker. "Here, check out these two pictures. Tell me what you think." His finger went back to the pictures of the boys.

Lightly he tapped on the images of the dark hair, blue eyed boy with the lopsided grin.

"Sure does look like you. He's got the same eyes and face shape. Nephew?" he repeated, his gaze going back to Matt.

"No," Matt took the wallet back. With a long sigh, he studied the smiling face. His thoughts went to Dan Black, with blonde and blue eyes. "Do you think that these two pictures resemble one another?"

"I told you yeah. And Stacy is a whistle blower too."

"My best friend..."

"Oh yeah Stacy, the best friend," he repeated the name.

"Yeah. He's her son. So, you really think that he looks like me? And by the way, that other kid is me at the same age." Matt repeated his earlier question, looking harder at Mike.

"I said yeah...whoa," Mike paused. "Holy shit," Mike's eyes widened as the implications of all of these questions finally sank in. He gave Matt a long look. "Your son?"

"I don't know. But the older Greg is getting, mom is seeing things and implying. She sent me these photos and a letter." Matt returned his wallet inside of his locker then began stripping out of his blue flight suit.

"Wait a second. You had sex with your best friend?" Mike asked, his interest now going to this mystery.

Matt shot him a long look, "Once."

"That's all it takes, stud," Mike teased, giving him a punch on the arm.

Clamping his mouth shut at Mike's words, Matt grabbed a towel before brushing past to the showers. He turned the water on full force, letting the sprays hit him on the back. Turning, he braced his hands on the white tiled walls, the hotter water slamming him in the face and chest. The muscles on his shoulders tensed as his hands tightened into fists to gently tap them onto the wall.

"Stace, why didn't you tell me?" he whispered.

He could feel his frustration and anger mounting with this situation then he quickly calmed down. He couldn't let his thoughts run so wild with the implications. They'd only do him more harm than good. These emotions would get him no where except careless with his job and the last thing he needed was to be grounded. He didn't know for certain if Greg was his, but everything indicated that he could be no one else's, except for Dan.

"Christ all mighty," he softly swore as he turned to let the pulsating water sting his tensed shoulders, the steam filled the showers to the effect of thick fog as he stood feeling so helpless.

He finally emerged, the white towel hung low on his trim hips as his feet prints followed on the floor after him. Glancing around, he wasn't surprised to find the Gunnery Sergeant patiently waiting for him.

"Captain Smith," Matt greeted, stopping in front of him.

"Captain Sadler, the Chief requests you in his office, S.T.A.T."

* * *

Chief Baker looked up at the light knock on the door before Matt entered. After saluting he speculatively eyed Matt, noting the extra quietness surrounding him. He also noticed a tenseness in how he held his body. Normally he'd be so calm, relaxed, always ready with a smile but now there was a certain rigidness about him. His brows were drawn together and the lips were a tensed line.

"Captain Sadler, have a seat."

Matt did as ordered, laying his hands on the arms of the chair he look into the older man's face who, at the moment was studying reports placed in front of him.

When he looked up, his gaze held Matt's in an angry, perplexed glare. Silently, he noted Matt returning with an even, confident glance. He reached for a cigarette to take a long drag then huffed the blue smoke into the air. Stalling, he wasn't sure how to begin. With a series of jabs, he snuffed the cigarette out in a nearby amber glass ashtray. He rest his forearms on the desk, placing his folded hands on the top of the calendar ink blotter.

In a monotone voice, he began, "Captain, just what the hell were you doing up there?" His authoritative voice kept cool as his eyes remained firm on Matt's face. He was in search of Matt's emotions, hoping to find them steady.

"Sir, I'm sorry sir. I've been slightly distracted."

"I have noticed. Hell, we all have noticed. You can't afford to be distracted. You know that one slip and you could be killed so Sadler, what's going on?"

Matt pressed his lips together before speaking, "Sir, I've received a letter from home."

"I hope that it isn't bad news?"

"I don't believe so, Sir."

"That's good but why the distractions? I've been watching and you are not safe at the moment. Hell, you could've killed someone out there today, not to mention yourself. You're near to retiring from the Blue Angels and I'd sure hate to lose you over some silly, irresponsible mistake that you, my commander pilot, has made."

"Yes sir," Matt quietly spoke, looking apologetic.

Chief Baker shook his head, giving Matt a long, hard look and found that even now, as he was speaking, that Matt's thoughts were straying. He could tell by the furrowed brows and the way his eyes were shifting instead of the usual steady, confident look he always received from him.

"As friends, Sadler, what's going on?"

Matt took in a cleansing breath before beginning. "Well, I recently discovered that I may be a father."

Chief Baker's mouth dropped open. Quickly, he composed himself. "You haven't been conducting yourself in an un officer manner have you?"

"No Sir, this happened just after I enlisted."

Chief Baker swore that his mouth dropped open even further before he blurted out with, "And you never knew?"

"I still don't know for certain but the pictures I'm receiving from home are strongly indicating that I may have fathered a son, Sir."

"Do you have them on you?"

"Yes sir."

"May I?" His hand reached out for the photos in question.

Matt shifted in his chair to remove his wallet from his back pocket, opening it he handed it over and showed the pictures. He waited as Chief Baker shifted his eyes back and forth between the picture and then to Matt a few times.

"Who's this woman?"

"That's Stacy, Sir."

"Ah the one."

Matt pressed his lips together then blurted, "Christ does everyone know?"

"She *is* the one you know. Why else would you be carrying her picture in your wallet?"

"She's my friend..."

"Of course, the friend story. How long has it been since you've been home? I mean really home for a long, easy, forget about your job vacation?" Slowly Baker closed the wallet to hand back.

"I don't know. I was back, briefly, maybe five years."

"That's it? It isn't any of my business but why?"

"She wasn't there so I returned."

"Are you seeing anyone?"

"No sir. My career comes first to me."

"There isn't any special lady in your life? Except Stacy?"

Again, Matt pressed his lips together. He could see where Chief Baker's slight lecture was leading. "No sir. I haven't located one to share my dreams."

"You love no one?"

Matt stalled, remained silent, giving him an even look before briefly shaking his head. Chief Baker returned with a grin. He knew the stories about the few ladies in Sadler's life and how he always seemed to be comparing them to a mysterious lady from his past. Now that he saw the picture, he understood why.

"You know Sadler, a lot of men have both a marriage and a career. You should be no different. I find this wanting to be putting one hundred percent in your work very uplifting but I don't understand why you never closed this important chapter in your book." He grumbled.

"We were best friend's sir. She told me that was how it would be and nothing else."

"Women can change their minds too, God knows my wife does enough of that to keep me on my toes," he muttered as Matt laughed out. "Captain Sadler. I want you to take a month or longer leave and get this straightened out. You are far too important to lose. You're my top man, my top trainer, and my top flyer and I need you here but not when you can't concentrate on your job. Since we're doing a show near your hometown, you fly your jet out and we'll ship your bike in the Fat Albert. That way you can get some flying time in to keep your skills in top notch form between finding out the truth. Precision flying is important to keep all of you men alive. No one needs to be put in jeopardy just because you can't concentrate at the moment."

"Sir, what if I don't get this figured out in the time off?"

"We'll cancel shows of course but I have a feeling things will work out for the best between you and the lady."

Matt gave him a grateful smile, "Yes Sir. Thank you."

CHAPTER 3

The rumble of the yellow school bus as it stopped then blowing its horn caught Stacy's attention.

"Damn," she hissed, glancing to the wall clock then watching out the window as the bus moved on. "He missed it again. What am I going to do with him?" She pushed the skillet to a back burner before hurrying through the living room. "Greg! You're going to be late for school!" Stacy impatiently shouted. She stood at the bottom of the stairs, looking up to where she hoped her son would soon emerge.

Placing an arm on the wooden railing, she patiently tapped her French Tipped, manicured fingers while waiting for a response from her soon to be twelve-year-old.

"Today and I'm not going to tell you again!" she loudly added the threat.

Her eyes curiously narrowed at the sound of metal hitting together before he appeared on the landing. Wearing a pair of favorite faded denim jeans and baggy black T-shirt, his sky blue eyes beneath dark, furrowed brows, gave her a look of irritation. In his hands he held a pair of metal airplanes he'd been playing with before her shouting interrupted him.

"Do I have to go?" He questioned in his high voice.

"Yes, you do. You only have a couple of weeks remaining this school year. I mean, I know that it's going to be tough on you and I know that if you should apply yourself and concentrate real hard, you can do it," she teased, catching the scowl forming on his cute face. The dimples erupted with the flex of his lips as he pressed them together.

"Aw, come on Mom. There's a show on this afternoon about the Blue Angels and I wanna watch it..."

"Sorry bud, school comes first."

"Aw mooommm," he drawled the word, his blue eyes darkening as a scowl formed a crease on his forehead.

Recognizing that look of having a total, all out argument, Stacy rest her chin in her hand. "You go to school and I'll record it for you. Deal?"

Greg let go with a long, extra loud sigh before answering in a not so happy tone, "Deal."

"Now put your airplanes back on the shelf and I'll set the DVR and I'll have to take you to school because again, your bus is already here and gone."

She watched as he spun around and disappeared. With a disbelieving shake of her head, Stacy turned to the living room to do as she promised. Honestly, she couldn't believe where he got this infatuation about airplanes and pilots. That word sent her memory to Matt.

Matt Sadler.

His memory entered her mind daily, be it because of Greg or how they had parted without closure, she really didn't know but he's constantly there. She recalled when he left, how it tore her apart. In retaliation and with high hopes to try to get his gentle touch out of her thoughts, she went to her boyfriend, Dan, and gave to him what he'd been trying to get for months, herself.

Eagerly with fumbling hands he did the deed and instantly became irate with the fact that she wasn't the virgin she maintained herself to be. That led to a huge brawl and then he left for college vowing to never want to see her deceitful face again!

With Dan gone, she realized to her disgrace and huge upsetting disappointment, having sex with Dan just didn't work. Matt and his tender lovemaking was burnt into her skin. Then came the day that she skipped her period. Talk about a major upheaval in her life! In her haste to get it over with Dan, they didn't use a condom either! For nine months she had to wonder who fathered her child. Surely with the first look she'd know but she quickly discovered, to her dismay, that babies, newborn babies, all look alike. Cute, pink and cuddly with blue eyes and round faces. Some had hair, others didn't.

As the years went past, Sam and Marge Sadler, Matt's parents, kept her up to date with his life. From his first frightening combat battle to the day he made it as a Blue Angel. Matt loved his planes, and his life. And through it all, she never mentioned anything to Greg about the best friend she had.

Keeping her secret, she was happy with the letters read to her from his parents and equally happy that Matt succeeded with his life dream and passion.

No doubt, Samuel Sadler had to be where Greg heard the stories of the planes which gained his interest. Samuel is a tall handsome, rugged looking man with brown hair sprayed with shades of gray. He had a smile to match his son's, always quick and easy. The years made his once tall, lean body now slightly soft. His sky blue eyes were still bright and alert and he always had a story for Greg.

She grinned.

Samuel took a fast fondness for Greg. From the time she announced her pregnancy to day one of Greg's arrival, he would often visit her and bring gifts of tiny planes for Greg instead of the usual stuffed animals.

Now, Greg's bedroom had models hanging throughout and his wall paper had blue angel fighter plane border about the top and his walls painted a sky blue. On the day she painted it, Greg watched, sitting on a stool in the center of the room, gazing at it with amazement. She'd been so engrossed with the chore that she barely looked at her accomplishments. Then Greg spoke in his tiny voice.

"Mom, it's like the sky."

She stopped with the papering to step back and look at it. And he was right, it was like the sky.

Sighing, she shook away the thoughts of the past while grabbing for the remote, and began the journey through the one hundred fifty plus channels on the cable to locate the program in question. She put it on the History channel, checking the guide. With a relieved smile she came across the program. As she set the timer, the familiar sound of heavy footsteps clomping on the stairs, filled the house. With a hateful grimace, she turned away, hoping and praying he would keep going.

Yes, it was Dan Black, he returned from college begging for her to take him back and like the fool she did. He released a loud yawn as he hurried down the stairs. He was running late and he could only blame it on her.

"Stacy!"

Her shoulders hunched upwards at the harshness of his voice brought her back from the past. Her lower lip began to tremble, hating this not knowing what to expect next in life. She reached a finger to her lips, lightly touching the cut on the corner and the tenderness of the bruise on her cheek.

She often wondered how and why they ever got back together. She didn't love him as she pretended and after last night, she came to the conclusion that he had to get the hell out of her home. He wasn't good for her. In the beginning they were happy, at least she thought they were, but as the years rolled by, he became violent towards her, especially after he consumed quite a few beers.

"Jesus Christ, woman!"

She flinched. Any sentence out of him that began like that could not be good. Standing, she followed him into the bright airy kitchen where the morning sun cast the warm, welcoming rays through the windows.

"Where's my damn coffee?" he ordered, standing next to the coffee maker filled with the hot brew.

"I'll get it for you."

She scurried past to quickly retrieve the cup from the cupboard so she could serve him as he moved to take a seat at the table. After placing the filled mug in front of him, she hurried to get his packed lunch from the refrigerator.

"I'm already late for work. Why the hell didn't you wake me?" He growled as he grabbed a morning pastry.

"You have nothing to worry about, you're the boss," she carelessly snapped.

"Yeah, and don't *you* forget it, either."

Stacy heard the undertone of his threat. She stopped to catch her breath. Stop it! She had to stop running around like a scared rabbit! Taking a breath to compose herself, she calmly answered.

"I shook you quite a few times but you wouldn't budge..."

"You should've tried harder," he accused with narrowed brown eyes over the rim of the cup as he took a sip.

"You shouldn't have been drinking so much last night."

"Well, maybe you shouldn't have fought me last night when I wanted to fuck you," he sneered.

She could feel her eyes tear up. "You're so crude," she hissed, hatefully glaring at him before turning away.

She braced her hands on the counter top as she gazed outside the window to the cheerful morning. Looks could be so deceiving. She blinked, pushing her tears back. The last thing that she wanted was for him to see how he had browbeaten her down.

"All I wanted was some last night. Some attention from you. You should never say no. I meant to get it."

"Is this going to be another worthless, useless, getting nowhere fight?"

"If you want it to be and we both know who will win, like I did last night," he added with a chuckle.

Stacy nervously clasped her hands in front of her as she wondered how bad things had become in her life. How did it all happen? Or still, when did it all happen? Her nervous fingers played with the diamond ring he gave her two years ago. Since he began drinking he became so angry, so unpredictable. She didn't want a man like that. She wanted a happy life like her parents and she knew there were men out there, somewhere.

She had to tell him.

Turning, she faced down the black hearted monster she thought she once loved. His dark blond hair was still wet from his shower and plastered against his head. His white T-shirt snugly fit his hard body. Fearfully, she eyed those muscles. He was so damn strong and liked to flaunt his strength, especially wherever she was concerned. He seemed to get off displaying his power.

She wasn't so sure how he would react and she feared another back hand would come her way, but it had to be ended. Finalized. She wasn't about to live her life as a man's punching bag.

Clearing her throat, she began, "Dan. I think its best that we stop this so called thing of a relationship."

"So called thing?" He repeated, glancing at her.

She nodded, a hand going to her lip.

"If it's about that cut and little bruise on your face..."

"*Little bruise!*" she surprised herself with the strength of her voice as she yelled back.

He stood his medium height to stalk across the room to stand in front of her. His callused hand reached out to touch her injury, catching how she flinched. A crooked smile shaped his lips. His friends were right, it was best keeping the women in control.

"It isn't that bad."

"Dan, we cannot go on like this. *I* will not go on like this," she began, her hand again twisting at the diamond she wore on her left hand. "I am not settling with you. I am not happy. I want you out of my home and out of our lives, today. I expect your clothes and other belongings gone by this evening," she bravely added, finally tugging the ring free from her finger. "And you can begin with this."

He stared to her opened hand at the engagement ring she held in the palm. He bought it for her when he moved in. Back when things were great and he was happy, they were happy. Yeah, he'd been expecting this. Things were getting worse between them each day and that kid of hers wasn't making it any easier.

When they dated in high school and she wouldn't give any sex to him. She denied him stating she wanted to remain a virgin until she married. Oh man, he scoffed, recalling when she was by far the virgin she claimed to be. He'd been played a fool. She strung him along as he patiently waited for her to agree. What a laugh that was when she becomes pregnant. And to top the story off, she refused to tell who she thought knocked her up!

He instantly broke it off with her. Still bitter, still angry, he went off to college but he still couldn't get Stacy Cannon off of his mind. Four years later, when he graduated, and he returned home, he came back around beginning slow with casual dates. He decided to forgive her and took her back.

They remained a steady couple finally living together for the past two years. That was when the things began spiraling downwards. It started with every time he looked at Greg and saw nothing that resembled him. That jealous monster always crept to the surface as he wondered who dared to touch his girlfriend. Even worse he wondered what was so damn special that she would let a man she didn't date have her for the first time. Damn it, she was his girl!

His thoughts came back to the present. His gaze slid to her beautiful face, seeing that look of determination as she stared him down while she held the ring in her hand. He reached out, tightly gripping her wrist, giving it a twist.

"Ahh, Dan please!" she cried out fighting the tears of pain filling her eyes.

"Why are you doing this?" He whispered.

"Why are you? How do you expect a woman to love a man who treats her so brutally. How do you expect a woman to love a man who doesn't respect her? How do you expect a woman to love a man who doesn't even show this so called love to her! Who stays away for a week at a time without calling? Who returns home with the smell of another woman's perfume on him? We're only engaged, how do you expect me to marry you knowing my life will be nothing but a damn lie anyway?" she rambled, tensing as she he reached up to grip her by the back of the neck.

Sucking in her breath, her eyes widened and nostrils flared, but ignoring his threatening gesture, she bravely rattled on. *"How can you love me like you say you do and treat me like...like shit!"* She screamed before lashing out to give his cheek a healthy slap, stunning them both.

Dan's eyes narrowed. She never dared to raise a hand to him before. "Woman, you don't hit me..."

"Well Dan, it's called self-defense. Whenever I think you are going to strike me, you'll get one too." She felt his hand slightly tightening.

"Now you listen to me..."

"No, you listen to me. You will never ever touch me again you no good piece of shit."

"Mom?"

Dan jerked his hand away when Greg's voice filled the room.

"I'm coming Greg! By tonight," she strongly added, placing the ring on the counter before moving away. "Come on Greg. Let's get you to school," she ordered, her arm draping across his shoulder to turn him away from that scene.

"Are you all right?" Greg asked, the concern in his voice strong.

"Better than you can imagine," she truthfully answered, hoping Dan would listen to her and be away from them today.

"Did you set the recorder..."

"Yes," came the irritating reply as she ushered him outside to her 4 door Jeep Wrangler. With a final, hateful glare in Dan's direction, she loudly slammed the door shut.

* * *

They rode to the school in a tensed silence. Greg fought the grin on his lips whenever his mom would now and again shake and flex her fingers of the hand she used to slap Dan.

"Does it hurt?" he finally asked.

Stacy gave him a quick look before glancing back to the road. Her hand touched her lip. "Maybe a little."

"I meant your hand. Does your hand hurt?" he repeated, nodding to her hand. "I saw the hit you gave that old bastard."

"Greg, no swearing."

"All right."

"And, yes, it's stinging."

"Good. That means you hit him hard and hopefully knocked some sense into that bastard's head."

"What did I just tell you about swearing?"

"Sorry." He grinned.

"It isn't how I raised you!" she loudly added.

"I said I was sorry!" he loudly repeated.

"Besides, your dad wouldn't tolerate any of it either," she muttered, not knowing why that came to her mind and quickly praying he didn't hear that remark.

"What?"

"Nothing. It was nothing," she strongly repeated, giving him a long look. She couldn't miss his thoughtful expression. "I told him to get his stuff packed and out of our house, by this evening. Soon, Greg, we'll be back to ourselves."

"Mom, is Dan my dad?" Greg wondered, his blue eyes gazing at the traffic ahead of them.

Stacy grimaced, knowing one day that question was coming but prayed it wouldn't be for a long, long time. And, once she opened the door with an answer he would want the truth.

Sighing, she responded with, "No, thank God."

Greg's smile broadened with the relief he felt. "Good. I don't like him."

"Well Greg, he is out of our life now. I'm never taking him back again," she vowed, feeling better saying the words.

"Good but mom, if he isn't then who is my dad? The guys at school tease me, pick fights and some call me a bastard."

A chill fingered up her spine wondering what to say. She wished that children wouldn't repeat what parents talk about. It had been twelve years! She realized that the majority of these parents of Greg's classmates were her classmates, many who began ignoring her even whispered whore when she'd walk past.

They came to a stop sign. Stacy braced her elbows on the steering wheel, covering her face with her hands. A long moan slipped from her mouth. She knew Greg would be looking at her and wonder at her reaction to his simple question. She also knew she should answer, but how?

"Sweet heart," she slowly began, struggling for the right words. Leaning back in her seat, she straightened her arms, hands tightly gripping the black leather steering wheel cover. Her eyes stared ahead. "Oh God. It's so complicated that I don't think I can tell you yet."

"Why not? Is he a spy with the underworld?" he excitedly asked, his eyes widening with his words.

She gave him a get real look, "Oh come on Greg. Listen to how ridiculous you sounded."

"I know. Does he love me?" he wondered, surprising himself with that question.

Her vision blurred with tears. "Oh Greg, I know that if he knew you existed, he would. He's a kind, generous, fun to be around, caring man. And, I know that if he knew you were here, he'd never miss a day with you. I'm just so sorry that I haven't told him, or anyone for that matter," she softly said praying her words would appease his curiosity for now. She grimaced with his next words.

"Well, why didn't you ever tell him? Are you ashamed of me?" his worried eyes looked at her.

Her mouth dropped open with his shocking words. She never realized how he felt about not knowing his father and today certainly stunned her.

"Oh no! How could you ever think such a thing! You're my pride and joy. Every day I thank God that he gave you to me," she cried, her hand lightly gripping his chin, another soon to be reminder of Matt.

Each day more of his characteristics were emerging from Greg and she prayed his parents wouldn't see it. It was difficult to live in a small community as an unwed mother. When her pregnancy advanced, those damn speculations were cast about. But, she remained silent. Even to this day, few people still wondered.

She just wished that people would forget about her past discrepancy. She wasn't the only one who had ever gotten pregnant out of wedlock. Those few others that she knew were happy and others enduring a life of unhappiness. The men had felt captured, trapped and as they grew older, regretting it. Regretting that they married so young. She knew they were unhappy, the advances she received from them was a sure sign for her. She grinned, maybe she was better off than they were after all.

* * *

At the loud slam of the front door, a feeling of empty finalism fell over him. Dan felt his heart break, drastically rip out of chest. He leant his buttocks against the kitchen counter, slowly rubbing his hands over his face. The silence of his life shrouded him. He didn't care for this tomb like stillness. Dropping his hands, his tired eyes aimlessly flit around the kitchen before falling on the Wrangler as he watched them drive away.

How had things gotten so out of sync between them? They always got along until lately; especially with Greg growing she devoted all of her extra time to him. He heaved a lengthy sigh at the resentment he felt with the deceit his life had been for these past twelve years. Once again he wondered who fathered that little bastard. At first he thought that it could have been him but lately, he highly doubted it. Who had sex with his girl, getting her pregnant? The more he thought about it, the angrier he became and he was having a tough time dealing with it all.

He reached for the telephone to let his secretary know he wouldn't be in today. Slowly, he walked up the stairs to begin the hateful task and do as she asked, silently vowing he'd change and win back her love.

CHAPTER 4

Beth Cannon dropped the damp, wadded dish towel onto the counter top to slide the last plate of the breakfast dishes in its place on the shelf. Adam, her husband, left moments earlier for his job at the car dealer where he worked as the head salesman. At the sound of an engine shutting down, she peered out the kitchen window, surprised to see Stacy especially since she knew that she had photo shoot to do this afternoon.

As the kitchen door opened, Beth turned wearing a large, greeting smile. She loved seeing her strong willed daughter. On the day that she told them that she thought she was pregnant it devastated them. But they vowed to stand behind her on whatever decision she made about the baby. Her decision to keep the baby didn't surprise them and are so glad they did. Greg was the joy of their lives. With Stacy being involved with Dan for what seemed like forever and engaged, they were certain there'd be a wedding and another grandchild to arrive.

That is until her gaze fell on Stacy's lightly battered face. Beth's mouth dropped as an angry squeal filled the room. She hurried to her. With arms outstretched, Beth took her into her arms, surprised to find that Stacy wasn't in tears. She felt the quick embrace. When she pulled away, there was a smile on her lips.

"Good morning mom," she brightly spoke then stepped away to get a glass of water from the refrigerator to pour in a glass.

"Stacy?" Beth turned to watch her.

"What?"

"What happened to your face?" she demanded, reaching a hand to touch the crack on her lip then to her bruised cheek. With an angry glare, her eyes shifted to Stacy's.

Stacy sipped her drink, her finger touching her lip and cheek. "Oh that..."

Beth braced her hands on her hips. "What do you mean by simply saying, oh that? Did Dan hit you?"

"Yes and he is, as we speak, packing his shit and getting out of my...h-home," she ended. Her tough exterior finally crumbling and the tears broke through.

Beth wrapped her arms around her, holding her tight. "How long has this been going on?"

"I don't know, maybe the past three years..."

"And you never told us?"

Stacy moved from her mother's arms to take a few steps away. "I know how dad would have handled the situation." she said, wiping away her tears.

"You better believe it, with a shotgun!"

"And I didn't want that to happen. When it began, I thought it was only from the stress from his job. You know, he had it rough for a while when he went out on his own in the construction business but it kept getting worse."

"And you stop making excuses for him. Nothing is that bad to make a man beat on his woman. And he states he loves you," she scoffed. "Love is not hitting."

"I know mom that's why I ended it this morning."

"Why did it take you so long?"

"I don't know. Deep down I knew that wasn't the real Dan. I guess I was hoping that it would stop. You know, it all began

rather sudden. He was never that way until then."

"Oh honey. I'm so glad that you broke it off with him. There was something about Dan that we never cared about and that went way back to your dating in school."

Stacy was tired. Tired of talking about it; tired of thinking about it. At the tone of her mother's voice, she closed her eyes. She wasn't in the mood for a lecture but knew it was coming.

"You didn't glow like a woman in love usually does. Instead, you became withdrawn from us and your friends. Your whole personality changed. We all noticed."

Stacy's eyes opened with those revealing words. With a nod, she wiped the tears from her eyes. It must have been even more obvious than she imagined since mom saw it too, saw that change in her.

"We should have never even been together. Can I hang here for a while? I don't want to be there when he is," she asked, changing the subject.

"You don't have to ask me. You're always welcome home."

"I know. I'm just not thinking very straight and I have to take some prom and pictures and Little Leaguer this afternoon and pick Greg up at school. Oh, so much to do!" she muttered while walking to the living room.

Beth gave a warm smile to her retreating back. "I can get Greg for you!" she called out, still smiling as the happy answer came from another room.

"That would be great! Thanks!"

Beth turned back to her kitchen sink when a knock on the back door stopped her. Glancing through the window, she saw Randy Sadler politely waiting. "Randy, good morning! What are you doing here?"

"I saw Stacy pulling in. I need to talk with her."

"You don't need to stand on the porch like a stranger. Come on in."

Randy opened the door, strolling inside. He stood medium height with dark brown hair and blue eyes, a lot like his younger brother Matt. Where Matt had the tendency to be the serious type, Randy was more playful.

"Randy wants to see you," Beth sweetly, loudly announced while giving him a charming grin.

Randy returned the grin.

Stacy sat on the couch, her feet curled beneath her. Her face formed a grimace. How can I face him looking like this? With an extra sweet voice, she called out, "What do you want, Randy?"

Randy strained his neck, trying to get a look at her. "I have some money for you for doing our wedding pictures! I missed you at home!" he called back, giving Beth a look of uncertainty. "Is it okay to yell in your house?" he teased.

With a gentle sway of her hand, "We always do," Beth loudly shot back.

Randy nodded as he turned back to the direction where Stacy's voice came, "Where do you want me to put it?" he yelled while smiling at Beth.

"I'm sorry Randy," Stacy emerged from the next room as she decided she wasn't going to hide. I can take..." her voice trailed off at the stunned look on his face.

"What the hell?" He began.

"Dan. It isn't the first time. He's moving out. I broke it off with him," she simply answered giving him a grin.

"But, no one ever knew. Damn Stacy, you should have let me know. I'm across the road! That son of a bitch!" Randy reached out, gripping her chin in his hand. He gently eased her face to the side so he could take a closer look. "That no good son of a bitch," he repeated.

"Believe me. The less who knew the better it was for me," she explained lifting her chin from his grip.

"Jesus, girl. If he bothers you please make sure to get a hold of me, a.s.a.p. You promise me." He grasped her hand in his giving light squeezes to emphasize he meant it.

"I will but God willing, I won't have to."

"Amen to that," Beth added.

"Okay, well any how Amy will be over later for her shoot," he offered, giving her a quick hug.

"It had better be the last time," Beth added. "Maybe some makeup would help until it heals."

Later that afternoon when Stacy went home to see if Dan left. Slowly, she unlocked her backdoor. Entering the mud room, her eyes scanned the room. The house was very silent. She had Greg stay with her parents until she discovered if the coast was all clear and so far it appeared it was. She kicked herself for not grabbing her photography equipment this morning. She needed to get to the job.

With a quick look around their bedroom, she relaxed to find his clothes gone and that he left the place orderly. She believed that in his anger and resentment, he'd trash the home. Quickly she hurried to her studio located in the basement to retrieve her gear before going to the school.

* * *

Stacy labored for what seemed like an eternity to get the small, rowdy group of ten year olds to pose for their Little Leaguer team pictures. Finally, she had everyone in their places and smiling her way.

"Okay guys, look alive!" she ordered looking at the back of the camera she had on a tri pod. "Smile!" she cheerfully called out fighting a laugh as one stood with arms crossed while wearing a serious expression. "Tad. Come on Tad, give me a smile," she softly coaxed with a smile of her own as she waited.

Slowly, a grin erupted, showing two front teeth missing as the area in question formed a very prominent black gap against his pale skin and slightly freckled cheeks. She fought her laughter. Raising her hand in the air she ordered, "Okay everyone look at my hand and hold this pose. I'm going to snap a few of them then I'll get your individual shots."

The deep rumbling sound drew nearer as a blood red and gleaming chrome *Harley Davidson* appeared on the side street. Just as she pressed the shutter release, a few heads turned to the bikes direction. She released a loud, impatient sigh. All of her work shot down the tubes all because of a loud engine. She turned to watch the main attraction as he drove past, not missing that he was looking her way as he slowed his bike.

* * *

Home.

Matt cruised down the highway towards the small community he had grown in. Has it really been twelve long years? He moved his head from side to side, taking it all in of tree lined streets, black iron light posts spaced along the cement sidewalks. Flowers were planted in raised beds, too.

Gotta love the Flower Garden Club, he thought. His thoughts held the one person that drew him here. He kicked himself for never phoning her but once at the training sight, time was scarce for him and the fact that he dove into the books, studying, hopefully to quell his feelings. Also, the years went by and he was ashamed with himself for putting things off.

Just when he believed that he succeeded to get her out of his mind the scenario replayed over and over, especially in his dreams, waking with a strong urge to want to see and hold her. He dated quite a few women, a lot who were a touch on the wild side. Quickly, he realized that all they wanted was a free travel guide. Good ol' Mike brought to his attention was they all had the same coloring as Stace.

His wandering thoughts came back to the present. The place looked smaller than he remembered, but it was all here. The drive inn restaurant still reminiscent of the nineteen fifties, a great place to have car cruises. Along the way the drive in theater once stood. Good memories there, he smiled, gassing his bike. His eyebrows shot up when he approached the elementary school and high school.

Since he left, more buildings and fields were added. A group of children wearing baseball uniforms were impatiently standing as a curvaceous woman wearing denim shorts and a white tank top worked at positioning them for a group photograph. He sat at the stop sign, his bike smoothly idling as he watched how patiently she maneuvered them, placing shorter ones in a line and the taller in front kneeling.

Knowing Stacy was a photographer, he instinctively knew it was her and rather enjoyed discreetly being able to watch her in her natural environment of photographer. He watched as she would point to this one and then that one before she went and placed her hands on those in question to catch their attention. He chuckled when one would finally stand still, the other would move and so on, causing her to have to start all over.

Still grinning, he watched as she stood behind the tripod, ready to take the photo when suddenly the car behind him impatiently tooted its horn. He revved the engine, the roaring sounding louder before he slowly drove on. His gaze was still on the scene in the field as she seemed to turn his way giving him a look of disgust. Laughing he twist his wrist, he zoomed off towards home. He didn't want her to know he was home just yet as he looked away.

Matt was anxious to see his family and friends, wishing he'd kept in better contact. His mom more than made up for that little problem by the many phone calls and letters. The most surprising information he received was the news of Stacy being pregnant. That totally blew him away. Well that and the fact that he was her first.

Sure, he had photographs that his mother sent to him but they only managed to make him want to be with her and he knew he couldn't do that. He was certain that she would mature into a knock out. Another surprise is she never married the man who fathered her son. In his letters he'd ask his mother, hopefully sounding uncaring, if she married and always received the same answer of no.

But, it was this last letter along with another photograph that set his thoughts spiraling into another direction. Maybe he was being dumb or just never wanted to believe that Stacy could become pregnant with their one-time union.

He took in a long breath before releasing it. Wow, she had a son; she's a mother and maybe he's a father. That was a really bizarre concept for him. In his heart, she would always be his best friend. The kid sister he never had. As he turned down the tar and chipped road where his suburban two-story home was, he swore that he could feel the little boy emerging. That same little boy caused his share of mischief in the neighborhood along with his kid sister.

* * *

Sam and Marge Sadler worked in the back yard, weeding a garden and planting flowers. Sam's white button down shirt had the sleeves rolled back, exposing his tanned forearms. He was busy with the roto-tiller between the rows of vegetables. Marge wore yellow Capri shorts and a plaid blouse. Her shoulder length hair was pulled back in a bun as she busily plants flower seeds among the border. Each stood with a look of wonder as a rumbling of a rather loud engine shut off in the drive way.

"I wonder who that could be?" Marge tugged the blue floral gloves from her dainty hands. Her eyes went to the side of the house where she could see a motorcycle parked in the driveway.

"Don't know. Let's check..." Sam's sentence faded on the breeze when their son strolled from the back door of the house. "Good God," Sam muttered with disbelief as a huge smile spread his lips. "It's Matt."

"Matt? Matt!" Marge cried out, rushing as fast as she could in his direction. Her arms were spread open wide to take her youngest son in a clinch and hold onto him to never ever release him again. She felt Matt wrap her into his strong embrace, holding her tight. It's been so long since he's been back. The few times they flew out to see him had been too long in between.

"Lord, I missed seeing and hearing you," he stated, amazed at how strong her tiny arms were as she refused to release her baby.

Matt stood, straightening his body, smiling down into her pretty, tear streaked face. Her hands pressed tight along his cheeks, holding him steady.

"You are still handsome," she cried. Standing back, she added, "So tall and proud." She grinned at the slight blush rising in his cheeks. "And you still get embarrassed with compliments too I see."

"Share him Marge," Sam demanded as he eased his wife away. "Matt," he whispered giving him a salute. He waited for the return then took him into his arms in a tight embrace.

When they finally pulled apart, Matt's tears filled his eyes. "You two are making me cry," he said with a wipe of the ball of his hands across his eyes. "So, where's Randy?"

"He's at his house doing some painting," Sam said.

"Why didn't you tell us that you were coming home?" Marge

playfully demanded as her hand gave his cheeks light slaps.

"I didn't know for sure myself. I have a leave of absence."

"For how long?" Sam asked as they turned to enter the house.

"One or two months," Matt answered, draping his arm across both of their shoulders as he walk between.

Marge looked into his face, "That means that you can stay for Randy's wedding! Oh, he'll be so happy!"

"We're not going to want to let you go," Sam added as he gave him a hug.

Matt bent to retrieve his duffel bag that he placed in the doorway. He moved to the stairs. "I think I'm going to lie down for a while. I flew my jet into Harrison Airport and they flew my bike in for me."

"Harrison? That's about an hour and a half away."

"We're having a show soon there and this way I can do my practices. But there's a lot I want to do here, too. Mom, how is Stacy?" He stopped on the bottom stair, giving his mother an anxious look as he patiently waited for an answer.

"She's fine."

"She grew into quite a beautiful woman," Sam added with a wink.

Matt laughed. "The photos showed me that and I sure can't wait to see her. But right now I'm fighting to stay awake and I need to freshen up. Do you have iced tea?"

"I sure do," Marge answered.

Matt changed his direction to the kitchen, his parents following behind. He grabbed a glass and retrieved the best sweet tea from the refrigerator. Plopping onto one of the wooden chairs, he added, "Mom, dad, sit down. I want to talk with you two before I grab that nap."

"Okay but I have to go to the market and get some fresh steak for supper. I'm going to make all of your favorites."

"Mom, just a few minutes first, please?"

Sam sat across from him, not missing the seriousness of his voice. "What's wrong, son?"

"Seems I'm having some difficulty concentrating on my flying because of the letters from mom."

"Oh?" Marge batted her lashes in feigned innocence.

"Yes mom. So fess up. What all do you know?"

"About what."

"About Stacy's son."

"What are you getting at?" Sam wondered.

"Well, no one knows for sure. It's a well-kept secret but I see you in Greg. He's such a handsome boy and there have been rumors here and there but not only about him."

"Hmmmm."

"What are you going to do?" Sam wondered.

"I don't know yet." He emptied his glass with three gulps. "I'm off to get some sleep before I confront her."

"And I'm going to give Randy a call and give him the good news," Marge happily exclaimed between the claps of her hands.

"And tell him not to tell anyone I'm here just yet."

CHAPTER 5

"Oh my good Lord! Randy told me about your face!" Amy cried out, taking closer steps to look at the discoloration on Stacy's cheek. She just arrived for her wedding portrait taken but her gown was temporarily forgotten about when she saw the bruise and cut on Stacy's face.

"Dan hit me."

"Why? What happened?"

"Long story short, I don't know but I kicked his ass out this morning. Now, let's get your pictures taken." Stacy wanted the conversation ended regarding Dan. He was gone, out of her life and to her, there is no sense in talking about him.

"Maybe you should see a doctor."

"Amy, it's done. I don't want to talk about it."

Sighing, Amy went to change into her gown. Thirty minutes passed. While Amy changed, Stacy got the lighting on; the drop cloth down of a pretty slate grey with mauve swirls background and was ready to go. All she waited for is the model. Stacy's brows furrowed at the silence. She looked to the room used as a dressing room wondering about Amy.

"Are you all right in there?" She called out. Her gaze held concern, wondering if Amy passed out and fell, hitting her head. Turning, she looked at the closed door separating them. "Amy?" She again asked, cracking the door to peer inside.

Amy stood in front of the full length, oval mirror. Her eyes were wide, staring at her reflection. Her chest rose and fell at the long, deep breath before expelling.

"Holy shit, oh wow. I am wearing my wedding gown and fill the urge to cry."

"Is that all," Stacy laughed.

"I made a pledge that I wouldn't cry but now when I look at myself," she released another long sigh. "I look positively heavenly," she added, fingering the pearl halo perched on the crown of her dark blonde head. "What do you think of this hair style?"

"It's regally beautiful."

"Is that a word?"

"If it isn't, it is now."

Amy went to the hair dresser and had her hair arranged in curls among the finger-tip lace veil, also edged in tiny pearls. She lightly turned her body back and forth, eyeing her slim waist in the strapless white gown and the pearls and sequins pattern on the breast. The long train trailed behind her. A light cry escaped from her lips.

"I have been waiting on this for a long time and cannot believe how quick it's coming."

"Brides have the right to cry on their day and, before. You and Randy are perfect for each other."

"Thank you. You're the bestest friend anyone could ever ask for."

Amy wrapped her arms around Stacy, receiving a hug in return.

"Let's get this done." Amy put the finishing touches of her pale pink lipstick on her lips and led the way to the studio.

Stacy positioned her in different poses, her head shaking in disbelief. "What a difference an up sweeping hair style could do to change one's appearance. You are so beautiful and Randy is going to have a tough time taking his eyes from you."

Stacy knew how important this day was for Amy. She and Randy dated seriously for five years and this was all Amy ever spoke to her about, marrying Randy Sadler, the man of her dreams and having his children.

Stacy shook her head. "You are a beautiful bride," she wistfully repeated while blinking back her tears.

Amy twisted her fingers together, her nervous laugh matching her gestures, "How are you going to take pictures of the ceremony when you're crying?"

Stacy laughed, "I'll manage. I just can't get over how much you glow, and it isn't even the wedding day."

"Do you really think so?"

"Yes."

"Stacy, this is what I've wanted for so long; to be married to Randy. He's so good for me. He has made me so happy."

"I've heard this story a million times over the last years. I'm so happy for you, for the both of you," Stacy answered, turning to retrieve a camera.

A sudden sadness fell over her, wishing things had been different in her life. Many nights she lay awake wondering where Matt was, how he was and if he ever met anyone. If he did, was he happy in love? She knew that it was insane on her behalf but she wished she would've spoke up that day he left. So much needed to be said. If she ever got the chance, she vowed to make amends with him. First she needed to find a way to ever tell him about his son.

Her lips formed a wry grin. Listen to you, acting as if you would ever have that chance. He never kept in touch and Randy said he wasn't coming home for his wedding. Quickly, she shook that empty sadness away, to tuck deep into her heart. Turning to face Amy, the bright smile formed on her lips.

"Come on, let's get started. Is he home?"

"I don't think yet."

"Good, grab your bouquet and then let's go outside first for those shots in the yard. We don't want him to see you in your gown."

* * *

Matt lay on his twin bed, his fingers laced behind his head. Feeling restless, he squirmed this way and that, trying to find a comfortable position.

"How the hell did I ever sleep on this thing?" Sitting up, he reached to the nightstand for his wallet to look at the pictures he carried. A finger lovingly traced the one he looked at the most. Stacy was in her ninth month of pregnancy. He didn't know why but he loved it and how she glowed as her hands protectively rest on the large swell of her abdomen. Then he flipped it to Greg when he was ten years old. He was quite the handsome looking boy.

Closing it, he lay back down, clasping his hands behind his head. He released a long sigh, feeling his body going into total relaxation. It felt good to be home. He stared at the ceiling, painted white. His eyes followed the swirled pattern before shifting to the walls, also painted white. He grinned, amazed at how nothing changed. His model planes were still on the wooden shelves. Following their trail, his eyes narrowed noticing that he was minus a few. His gaze locked on a picture in a wooden frame perched on his tiny wooden desk. His lips curved in a small grin as he picked it up.

It was of him and Stacy taken during a neighborhood picnic. They were fifteen and seventeen and sat on the ground, both with huge smiles on their faces. He had an arm draped about her shoulder as he lightly squeezed her by the neck, pulling her to him. Their heads were tilted, touching as they mugged a face for the camera. Setting it back in its place, he turned to leave his room. Suddenly he wasn't feeling as tired. After grabbing a shower, he knew what he was going to do. He was going to find Stacy's home and surprise her.

"Mom?"

Marge stood in the kitchen making cookies. She spun, surprised to see him. "I thought you were going to lie down?"

"I can't. I'm too anxious to see Stace."

"Ohhh?" A knowing grin formed on her lips as she replied with raised eyebrows.

He shot her a level look. "And just what is *that* supposed to mean?"

She pressed her lips together in a, whatever look. "Oh, I don't know," she stared at him. "So, are you seeing anyone?"

Normally, his response was that he wanted to wait when he would be able to give one hundred percent to a relationship and at the moment, he was giving one hundred percent to his job. Meeting, getting to know and choosing a mate for life took a lot of time from his already busy days and he always felt that he couldn't do both at the same time.

"No," he quickly replied as he picked up an apple to take a bite. The fresh fruit crunched as he spoke. "Where does she live?"

"Across the road from Randy. I still cannot believe that you never kept in contact with her. It's such a disgrace!"

He chewed on his apple as he nodded. He managed to answer before swallowing. "The same old story mom. You promise yourself that you will. The first year was constant letter writing, then they all together came to a stop. I moved around a lot and I guess I never took the time to write and ask what was going on. I assumed that her letters never caught up to me."

"Matthew that's a sorry excuse if I have ever heard of for never keeping in touch with your best friend. Have you ever heard of the invention called a telephone? How about that thing called E-mail? How about those cell phones? I think you were more afraid..."

"All right, mom. I get where you're coming from."

"She's a beautiful woman," Marge repeated with an extra sweet smile. "A giver and a hard worker too."

After getting directions, Matt returned her extra sweet smile with his own before answering. "Well, I'm off to surprise her. See ya later."

"Be home for supper!" she ordered as he left with a quick wave of his hand.

CHAPTER 6

Stacy finished Amy's portraits twenty minutes earlier and was in her office going over the proofs she downloaded on her computer and loved them all. She enjoyed working with someone who took directions so well and quickly. Being happy in love helped too with the finished products.

"She is so photogenic," she softly stated.

Being so engrossed in her work and choosing the best shots to edit and getting ready to send to her lab that the chimes of the doorbell caused her to jump.

"Oh great," she muttered, wishing she had the foresight to lock the door. "It better not be Dan." Pressing save order, she jumped from the wooden chair to cautiously walk up the stairs. The chimes again sounded. "I'm coming!" she called out, putting on a friendly smile for the possible customer.

Matt discovered his stomach tightening into a swirling, continuous mass of knots. His chest rose when he took in a long breath, held it then released as he pushed the doorbell. Then he heard her voice and for some odd reason, he found his throat seeming to go bone dry, making it difficult to swallow. He wondered if she remembered him. He grinned as the sultry sound of her voice called out an answer to the second chime. It was raspy, richer than he remembered. One could even say, on the verge of being very sexy. Then he heard her light steps hurrying on the stairs. He licked his dry lips then took in and exhaled a deep, ragged breath. Nervous! He could not believe how nervous he was!

His gaze softened and a pleased smile curved his lips when she came into his view and yep, she is who he briefly watched at the ball field. He looked directly into the face of an angel. Why had he been so negligent in keeping in contact with her? Her dark brown hair parted in the middle, reached midway down her back. Somehow he knew in soft luxurious waves. Long bangs brushed her high cheeks. Her almond shaped, dark brown eyes were framed with equally long dark lashes beneath delicate, winged eyebrows. And her wide, friendly smile were framed in lips brushed a pale pink.

Then he noticed what could be a discoloration on her jaw and cheek. He thought it appeared she was covering a bruise with makeup and he also didn't miss the slight cut on the corner of her lip and he felt his anger bristle.

Stacy faltered in her steps when she caught the sight of a very attractive man standing at her door. His mirrored, aviator glasses shielded his eyes from hers at they rest on a short but straight nose and his crooked smile appeared unsure, yet familiar. His dark brown hair was long on top and short on the sides and back. Then he smiled showing white teeth and to die for dimples.

Her eyes narrowed as she briefly studied him. He slid his hands into his back pockets his already tight pale blue, short sleeve shirt showed off his well-defined muscular body. She glanced at his tanned forearms, noting the strength they held as he easily stood there. His long, muscular looking legs were covered in denim jeans. Her gaze returned to his rugged, charming face.

"May I help you?" she asked through the screen on the door, "I know you." The name Matt instantly coming to her mind.

His body shook as a tingle swept over him when he listened to the rasping softness of her voice, like a fragrant blossom loose from its stem to aimlessly float on a breeze. He liked how she sounded. Then he spoke and he believed that he'd have to perform mouth to mouth on her.

"Hey Stace. How have you been?"

With a surprised gasp, Stacy slammed the door shut. Leaning against it for support, she swore she was about to pass out. Stacy felt the blood rush through her body as she began to swoon and her mouth formed an oh. "Holy shit!"

Turning, she peered through the oval swirled lead glass design at his stunned expression. She looked long and hard at his face. A very handsome face that would be easy to look at every day. Her hand reached out to grasp the door frame, hoping to brace herself. Stace? Only one person ever called her that.

Slowly she opened the door as his long fingers gripped a leg of his sunglasses, slowly removing them to reveal dreamy ice blue eyes, surrounded by long dark lashes. They were eyes she often dreamt about and whenever she looked at her son, she saw them there, too. She felt her breathing labor; felt the rapid pounding of her heartbeat rise to her temples as his name instantly came to her lips.

"Matt?" She finally managed to speak.

He grinned again, "Well, that's a good sign that you haven't forgotten me," he laughed waving a hand to the door. "What was that about?"

"Ohhh, how could I forget you," she softly stated as she eased open the door to step outside. "I'm sorry about slamming the door, I um am a mess."

"Far from it."

Matt stepped back to give her room to join him on the back porch. His gaze slowly roamed her body, taking in her gentle curves, tiny waist and rounded hips before falling on her engaging, exquisite face. He couldn't believe how great she looked. Her pictures didn't do her any justice. In fact, the flesh and blood was far better.

Stacy's hands reached out, not sure whether she should touch him, take him in an embrace or shake his hand. Oh my God, he seemed to have grown taller since he left and oh my heaven help me, he definitely filled out. He matured into quite a stimulating, intimidating specimen of the male gender. His parents often said that his time was tight and that as the reason he never came home. Even Randy had been upset when he thought that Matt wouldn't be here for his wedding.

Her whirling thoughts thread in many directions as she thought of the child they made. Should she mention anything about him? No! Don't be foolish. Now wouldn't be the time to say, 'I'm fine and by the way, so is your son.' How would he handle such earth shattering news? Surely, his parents and Randy told him she had a child, wouldn't they? But, they didn't know who the father is. Breathing a light sigh, she decided to play it all by ear.

"I sense your uncertainty. And I can't blame you, I mean, for me to suddenly show up on your doorstep after a twelve year absence. Hell, I'd probably act the same way."

"Oh yeah. You've definitely caught me off guard."

"I'm sorry but you look great, Stace," Matt made the first move to take her into his arms. His hands slipped around her waist and a sense of comforting coming home overwhelmed him but the ringing of the telephone stopped him and disengaged the feeling as it broke the nervous tension.

"Come on in while I get the phone," Stacy ordered, turning out of his almost embrace to rush inside. A slight breath escaped from her nervous lips. Oh sure, she didn't miss the tingling warmth she felt from the brief contact of his hands on her. She sensed his overwhelming virile maleness as his strong presence filled her home.

"Hello?" she breathlessly asked, turning to study him as his gaze curiously glanced around the studio wedding room props. She watched as he looked on a picture of Greg and a smile formed on his lips. The gesture caused her heart to skip a beat.

"Hey Stacy. What are you doing that you sound out of breath?"

Amy teased, wishing that Stacy wouldn't be so serious all of the time. It was something she was noticing more and more with her.

"Oh, I have company," she gently answered, giving him a grin.

"Is Dan there harassing you?"

"No. Nothing like that. It's better."

Amy's brows furrowed. "Don't forget about tonight," her light voice filtered through the telephone.

"Yeah, I'll meet you. I have a lot to tell you."

"Since I left thirty minutes ago?"

"Oh yeah. I'll see you later."

Matt shoved his hands into the back pockets of his jeans. Their eyes never broke contact as she hung up the telephone. He couldn't believe that he stood in the same room with her, speaking with her, looking at her. He mentally kicked himself over and over for never keeping in contact but always assumed the father of her son wouldn't necessarily care for another man writing to her. He sure as hell knew that if the cards were turned, he wouldn't care for a strange man writing to his wife.

Then her eyes glistened as the tears formed. That took him back to the day he left; and his heart broke all over. Sliding his hands from his pockets, he slowly approached to wrap her into his embrace. He felt her curvaceous body melt against him as her arms wrapped around his neck. Her body trembled in his arms.

His eyes closed as she began to cry. Her arms tightened about his neck, holding him to her. Bending, he laid his cheek on her head, savoring the feel of her very female form against him. His hand slid up her back ensnaring through her long hair, feeling the silky softness glide through his fingers. Twelve years quickly dissipated as the feeling of being apart felt like twelve days.

Stacy couldn't understand what made her behave like this. She always thought of herself as a strong woman, but now, she wasn't so sure. Maybe it's the tension filled sadness that her life has been. Dan's temperament constantly kept her on edge but when Matt's arms went around her, it seemed like the worry, any worry, was lifted. Even if it would only be for a brief period, and it felt so relaxing, calming.

Matt pulled her closer. "Hey. What's with the tears?"

"Oh God. I have missed you," she whispered, feeling his arms tightening as they slowly rocked back and forth.

She clung onto him, never wanting to let him go. All of her life was a struggle from being a single parent and the talk associated with that. To raising a son to dealing with Dan and his abusive treatment. But when she felt Matt's strong arms wrap around her, his strength bonded to her and she felt she could deal with anything so much easier with him next to her.

"I've missed you, too," he muttered, hesitating in releasing his hold to take a step back. He reached a hand to her cheek, wiping the tears away. Along with it came her makeup, exposing the bruise. His eyes narrowed as his anger instantly rose. "Who hit you?" he demanded, the protective older brother quickly, easily emerging.

Gasping, her hand shot up touching her face. With wide eyes she stammered in her answer. "It..it was nothing."

"Who the fuck dare to hit you," he ordered, the Military Commanding tone surfacing.

"It was nothing," she strongly repeated then stubbornly clamped her lips together. She raised her chin while shooting him a silent dare to speak any more about it.

Matt nodded, remembering the trait. When she didn't want to discuss an issue, she gave him that look. The eyes never wavering look. "Never mind. Sorry I brought it up."

The tension was evident at the strained moment.

"So, I see that you have your own business. Photographer huh?" he asked, changing the subject, his gaze glued to the discoloration.

"Yeah. It's great. I meet a lot of interesting people. I love it," her finger delicately touched the bruised area on her cheek. "That makes a job fun. Not the same boring routine."

"That does help." Reaching out, he picked the picture he looked at earlier into his hands. "I hear that you have a son too. Is this Greg?"

She faltered with her answer, realizing that Marge had to be the one keeping him up to date with her life. Casting her gaze to the picture, "Yes. Yes, that's him."

Matt looked long at the recent photo seeing a resemblance. He just had to be his. "He's a good looking boy."

"I'm very proud of him. He's quite the little man."

He returned the frame to the stand. "I'm sure he is. You glow with pride," he stated grasping her by the hands to hold them to the side as he stepped back to slide his gaze over her slender figure. She wore denim shorts and a loose fitting white tank top but he could see the female body that lurked beneath and it was a very tempting, very curvaceous one. "Stace, you're beautiful despite that damn bruise and cut."

Stacy felt the heat of the blush on her cheeks with the compliment as he freely looked at her before his eyes locked onto hers sending an amazing wave of desire coursing through her and surprised at the emotion. Grinning at her unease she shifted her eyes away then back to his captivating face.

"Still can't take compliments either," he laughed.

"Not very well, no," she returned, "Especially when you bring up the colors on my face."

His concerned gaze focused on the bruise on her cheek and lip. It bothered him. No man has the right to hit a woman, especially this special woman. "Who hit you?" he wondered, seeing the stubborn woman arriving with her even stare and pressed lips.

An expression of disbelief crossed her features. "I can't believe how forward you are." She gently tugged her hands free of his warm grip as she evenly glared into his eyes. "That's a rather personal question, don't you think so? Matt, you haven't been around for a long, long time."

"I know but..."

"So what gives you the right to ask me that?"

Her condescending words reverted him back to the young adult teenager; to the times when they'd argue about the relationships they were in and how they'd put down the others boy or girl friend. But they were now adults and hoped they knew a bit more about life and the ups and downs that went along with this wild ride.

"Stace. You didn't let me down. Still as temperamental as you used to be."

"Some things just *don't* change."

"Maybe I've been away from you but the moment I laid my eyes on you my protective instincts materialized."

Stacy relaxed, grinning, feeling like they'd never been separated. She watched as Matt slid his hands into his back pockets and tapped a booted heel on the carpeted floor.

He heaved a long sigh, "You're right. I apologize. I never expected to see something like that on you...I just wanted to protect...I'm sorry," he stammered, grinning as she stepped closer, standing on tip toes, to press a kiss on his cheek.

Stepping back, she reached a hand out to wipe away the lipstick mark left there.

"Thank you big brother," she teased, seeing a strange look enter his eyes with her words.

"You know, speaking of big brothers, I need to go and see mine. I'll call you later. We'll go out to eat somewhere."

"I have plans tonight."

"I'll be in contact. It's great seeing you Stace," he added, placing a hand on her cheek, feeling her press her face into it.

Again, he was transformed to their encounter so long ago. Try as he might, he couldn't erase it from his memory. He'd done a lot of wild, impulsive things in his life to hopefully erase that heated moment of her soft, yielding body. The time he made her a woman, but those other ladies and the many meetings with the bottles didn't help.

She spoke, breaking the silence. How long are you staying?"

"However long that it takes." He grinned.

"I'll see you around," Stacy cautiously added wondering about his devilish grin and what the it could be.

"I want to meet Greg," he added.

"You will."

She followed him outside. She watched as he sat astride his motorcycle before starting it. With a quick wave he coasted it across the road to where Randy lived. Heaving a sigh, she went inside. Her gaze went to Greg's picture. The same one that Matt smiled at. It was of Greg and her father Adam and of Matt's father, Sam, during one of many fishing trips. Her body shuddered at the delicious memory of his arms wrapped so tight around her. He still felt good, she realized. The sound of her mother's car in the driveway shifted her attention. She smiled when Greg bounded out followed by her mother.

"Did you tape it for me?" he instantly demanded.

"Hello and of course I did. Go and get your clothes ready. You're staying with grandma and granddad tonight." Her eyebrows shot up when he came to a skidding stop on the sidewalk. He glared at her as he

66

slid his hands to his back pockets. "What's wrong?"

"Do I have to go?"

"We'll have a good time Greg," Beth said as she stopped next to him, draping her arm across his shoulders.

Stacy caught that stubborn stance of his, knowing that he wanted to talk to her, privately. With a smile, she said, "Yes you have to go. I'm not going to be home tonight," she said changing her look to Beth. "Mom? I'll bring him over. He

wants to watch his Blue Angels program. And, I think he wants to have a word with me. Children," she laughed.

Beth gave him a hug, "I'll see you later."

With a nod and a quick wave, Greg hurried inside, casting a searching glance around the room. Stacy followed. "Is Dan gone?" he wondered as he slowly approached the stairway.

"Yes he is. Didn't I tell you that he would be?"

CHAPTER 7

Night already fell when Stacy arrived at a local tavern. She found the party already starting. The filled to capacity dance floor swayed with the crowd, lured by a mixture of rock and country, not that hip hop rap stuff. The dim lit room flickered with bright lighting from the flashing lightshow the disc jockey provided. Advertising signs of various beer companies hung on the many walls. Stacy grinned, waving at the abundant greetings aimed her way from her friends.

"Stacy! Save me a dance!" a male voice shouted.

"Me too! I hear you ditched Dan!" Another yelled, waving a beer bottle to salute her.

Her brows rose, astonished as she waved back. "Wow, word certainly spread fast," she muttered.

Truthfully, she didn't desire a man in her life. At least not right now. The constant answering to the immature demands of Dan bellowing, putting down her thoughts; imagination; ideas took its toll. Besides, she had her son to deal with. Her gaze shifted to a corner where a couple of flames from lighters waved back and forth. She laughed as Amy held one in each hand. Slowly she weaved through the maze of round tables, her hips pivoting and swiveling.

"Hey Stacy!" Amy cheerfully called. "It's about time. I was beginning to wonder if you were going to show!"

Stacy plopped onto a wooden chair, resting her forearms on the table in front of her as her chest rose then fell when she heaved a sigh of relaxation.

"I'm sorry. I had a time with Greg. He didn't want to go to mom and dad's. I actually had to bribe him," she laughed.

"I can't wait for a problem like that," Amy wistfully replied. "So, what's it like being Dan free?"

"It hasn't completely sunk in yet but I love it so far." Leaning closer, she added, "You cannot believe who was at my house this evening."

"Did Dan come back?"

"No..."

"Matt," Amy added with a knowing grin. "I met him this afternoon. Randy is so excited especially when he told Randy he couldn't make it home and here he is!"

"I'll bet he was and yes, it was Matt and my God he looked great," she softly answered as a waitress placed a pitcher, a bottle of Tequila; some salt and cut limes in front of them. Stacy stopped talking as the concoction caught her attention. "What's this?"

"I've always heard of these. Tequila shots and Kamikaze. I've decided that we shall get wasted tonight. It's my semi bachelorette party."

"Oh really? Well, are you certain about these?"

"No problem. We're going to have a great time!"

"Then, do we have a designated driver?"

"Randy is but a phone call away."

Stacy glanced around, "Where's the other lady of the bridal party? Your sister," she sneered with obvious dislike.

Amy ignored both that look and tone. She knew Stacy didn't care for her sister, Sandy. She never understood why and for all of these years, she chose not to ask either.

"I don't know where she went. She said she was off to the ladies room and I haven't seen her since. Let's get started without her."

"I haven't done this for such a long time."

"I don't think that you've ever done this and that's because you turned into a mother at such a young age. Come on, live it up for me tonight," Amy pressured, pouring each of them a shot, adding, "I think this is how they do it. Lick the salt, chug the drink and suck on the lime."

Stacy's unsure expression changed to interest. "Well, since Greg *is* at mom and dad's this evening...and it has been a long time since I let myself go..."

"And have a good, carefree, unthinking time. Ou, I know. You also need to celebrate Independence Day."

"Amy. Need I remind you that this is May?"

"I mean your independence from Dan. What you did took guts especially with the way he's been treating you." The sound of glass scraping on wood met her ears as Amy slowly slid the shot across the scratched table to rest near Stacy's hand. "So, let's get busy."

As the revelation of her freedom swept over her, an adventurous feeling engulfed her. A smile of daring shaped her lips as she touched the cold glass, wiping at the moisture on the outside before picking it up. Amy joined. The rims of their glasses lightly tapped together.

"Here's to a night of wild, indulgence." Amy began.

"And not looking back," Stacy added.

Bringing the glasses to their lips, they tipped their heads back, chugging the liquid, feeling it turn down their throats to the depths of their stomachs. Releasing a long breath, they plopped their glasses onto the table, rapidly blinking their eyes to stop the watering.

"Wow, that's good," Stacy slowly said.

"It sure is. It went down real smooth," Amy gasped with wide eyes watching Sandy return through the crowd only to sway away from them as she caught the sight of someone.

"Let's have another," Stacy suggested but Amy already had another round poured.

Matt and Randy sat on the stools at the bar getting caught up with their lives. After going home for his steak dinner, Randy told Matt what Amy was doing so they decided to go out. They spent the past hour sharing stories of the missed years between them, laughing until tears ran from their eyes.

"I can't believe that you actually borrowed a chopper to pick a lady up in another state for a date," Randy gasped, wiping at his eyes with the palm of his hand.

"Well, after I asked her out, she got transferred to another base and she was visiting with her family," Matt defended his actions.

"What kind was it?"

"A Blackhawk."

Randy's mouth dropped open. "I've seen those on television, a lot. Christ, could you imagine the looks on her parents face when you sat the thing down in their yard?" he added with renewed laughter.

With a nod, Matt took a long swig of his beer. Swallowing, he added. "Yeah, it was funny and she loved it especially since she enjoyed being the center of attention."

"After pulling a stunt like that, I hope you didn't get caught *and* that you got lucky."

"Well, I had permission and I did, but hell, I already forgot about her..." he trailed off as his fingers grabbed a handful of mini pretzel sticks in a nearby dish to shove, one at a time, into his mouth.

The distant tone in Matt's voice immediately caught Randy's attention. Quietly he studied Matt, noting a mood of listlessness bordering on boredom. Could it be that tight-lipped Matt is hung up on a lady? Both, e-mails and calls home never mentioned anyone. His lips formed a loving grin as he noted the thoughtful look on Matt's face as he sipped his beer.

"So, you never met anyone special in the Navy?"

"Nah...well yeah but in the end, they couldn't compare."

"To who?" At the blatant ignoring of his question, Randy changed the subject. "Man, I still cannot believe that you're home. You being home to share my wedding day has made it all complete."

Matt grinned at the light brotherly punch he received on the arm. "I wanted to surprise you. I didn't even tell mom and dad."

Matt returned a punch.

"Oh, so that's how you managed to keep it so hush hush?"

"Sure did." Matt began, stopping at the soft touch of a female arm draped across his shoulder. Turning his head, he looked into the green eyes of Sandy, a past girlfriend.

"Matt? What a sweet surprise!" Sandy loudly declared before placing a solid kiss on his stunned lips.

Matt's hands firmly gripped on her upper arms to ease her away. He looked at her flushed face, noting that she is drunk. "Hello Sandy."

"Oh, isn't that sweet? He didn't forget me!" she squealed, wrapping her arms so tight around his neck that he swore it would snap like a dried twig. She leant closer, pressing her rounded body against him as she coyly ran a finger down his arm.

Matt coughed a gasp, his breath hampered by her attention. He wrapped his fingers around her wrist to unwind them from him, easing her away. At Randy's laughter, he shot him an agitated glare. He wasn't in the mood for Sandy. Their brief time spent dating had been tumultuous filled with accusations from her of him cheating. Tired of the arguments, he broke it off.

"Hey Sandy, is Amy here?" Randy asked.

Sandy blinked, focusing her blurred vision on her future brother in law. "Randy! You're here too?"

"Yes I am. Is Amy here?" He repeated, struggling with his laughter.

Sandy's hungry gaze locked onto Matt as she loudly answered, "Yeah, she's over in the corner sitting with Stacy."

Matt perked up. Glancing about the room, he eased Sandy away. An opening on the dance room revealed the treasure he searched. His eyes found her sitting at a corner table chugging shots with Amy.

He looked to Randy then tilt his head in their direction. Both watched them put salt on their hands, licked, chugged, sucked on a lime then drink a shot from their pitcher for a chaser. The sour faces they made were well worth the watch. After a few more drinks, they weaved their way onto the dance floor to join the others.

"This ought to be interesting," Randy muttered, turning to get comfortable to watch the show. "She isn't a drinker."

"It's been great seeing you Sandy but Randy and I are having an important discussion. I'll see you around," Matt suggested. Placing his hands on her buttocks, he lightly shoved her away. He sat like Randy, his interested gaze rest on Stacy and her wild, drunken sensuous moves. Stacy's eyes were wide and on her lips she wore a broad smile.

"Oooh mmmyyyy but I am feeling noooo pain," she giggled. Holding her arms out, she used them as a beam trying to help steady herself. With a wobble she gripped onto Amy's arms.

"Actually, I'm not feeling much of anything. Ame? Can you feel your legs?"

"What legs?" Amy snickered before a loud guffaw escaped from her mouth.

Swaying, they leant into each other, covering their mouths with their hands to help hide their exaggerated merriment. A loud bump and grinding song played and they relaxed, swaying with the beat. Stacy turned feeling Amy's hands grip onto her hips. Standing behind, they moved, sensuously bumping and grinding with the music. Their drunken voices joined in, singing at the top of their lungs as Sandy joined them.

Matt watched, amused, at the drunken' display as they danced extra close to one another.

"Oh my God," Randy muttered, resting his back against the bar as he crossed his arms across his chest. "Wasted, big time."

Matt narrowed his eyes, his voice teasing with sarcasm, "Oh really? How can you tell?" His eyes remained focused on Stacy's tight, low riding jeans and short tight red top helping to give him a glimpse of her midriff. He uncomfortably discovered that her choice of attire helped to emphasize her curves.

"Easy. She's singing and Amy doesn't sing. And Stacy doesn't drink anything stronger than a Fuzzy Navel. And that, dear brother, is not what's in that pitcher," Randy easily explained not missing where Matt's eyes were glued to. "What's going on, Matt?"

Matt shrugged, "I just need to find out the truth about a few things."

"Such as?"

"Those damn curve balls that life sometimes sends," Matt briefly explained, not missing the confused expression Randy gave to him before turning his interested attention back to Stacy.

Stacy couldn't believe the lighthearted way she felt. It'd been quite a while since she let her defenses down. Whenever she and Dan went out with friends and she'd begin to laugh and have a good time, he'd always give her a hard nudge and tell her to behave herself. It happened so often that she actually forgot her real personality. But tonight it all came back. Hips slowly gyrating, she turned and then turned again as she believed she noticed a familiar smile. Her gaze found Matt's handsome face as he sat next to Randy, watching her.

His smile was slight perhaps a bit of amazement but enough to curve the ends upwards and she didn't miss his head slowly nod with the beat of the song. Emboldened with the alcohol, the normally quiet, shy female felt alive. That heated expression Matt wore didn't help either. Flirt. It's been so long since she felt this way. With wide, over emphasized swaying hips, she sashayed towards him. Her gaze held and locked onto his. With a look of tossing a dare she crooked her index finger in a come here motion.

The appreciative smile spread on his lips. Keeping his relaxed pose, Matt silently watched, enjoying the smooth, catlike gracefulness in her moves as she approached. His eyes shamelessly raked up and down her sensuous body then he watched her arm raise, feeling her hand on his shirt front, gripping; tugging as he easily stood.

"Matthew, dance with me, now!"

His hands encircled her waist, feeling the warmth of her bare skin. "No, really, I'm fine sitting here." With a gleam in her eyes, she naughtily lean closer, barely touching her lips to his.

"Come with me Matthew. I won't bite," she teased, stepping away, her hand clenched onto his shirt.

At the feel of her hot breath on his lips and the smell of her exotic perfumed body, his smile faded. To his dismay those lips now so temptingly close were constantly on his mind and the package that went along with them were equally desirous.

"Go on!" Randy urged giving him a light push to get him started. "Have some fun!"

With her hand refusing to disengage the grip on his shirt, she turned, tugging him along behind. Relenting to her demands, he permitted her to lead him onto the dance floor. Cheers and applause erupted from his old friends. He waved a hand in the air then felt her arms lightly drape over his shoulders as she turned to face him. Glancing onto her upturned face, he didn't miss the mischievous glint hovering in her eyes.

Quickly he found out about that look as she seductively, lightly brushed her body against his, moving with the beat. He gasped, feeling the dormant fires deep inside as they sparked to life to burn, the heat of the flames spreading from his groin to the pit of his stomach until it engulfed his body. Exhaling, he glanced to her hips, then back to her face. Hesitant, his arms slipped around her waist, feeling the warmth of her skin against his forearms. He slid his hands on her rounded buttocks, feeling her move.

An uncomfortable sigh slipped from his mouth as he felt the gentle touch of her lips pressing kisses on his neck then down his chest. Though he knew she was inebriated and doing things she would normally never do, at least what he thought she would never do, the simple gestures sure started his blood to boiling.

"Is it hot in here?" he asked.

"No. It's perfect," she muttered between her kisses.

"Stace," he murmured. Her smile was angelic when she looked into his face.

"What's wrong Matthew?" she asked, adding an innocent smile of crimson red painted lips.

He took in her flushed features, not daring to speak the words of what he really wanted to. At his silence, she turns in his arms, showing him her back. Her arms swayed in the air as she sensuously brushed her buttocks against his groin. The spark was instant. His arm slide to her waist feeling the flatness of her stomach beneath his hand.

He heard the gasp slip from her lips when his other hand lightly brush against her breast as it moved around her waist. Not able to stop, he pressed his lips on her shoulder giving slow, passionate kisses towards her neck. Matt tried hard to fight the temptation and how her body stirred his blood, but the combination of his drinks, her drinks, and the way she moved with the music stimulated him.

Tilting her head to the side, she whispered, "Ohhh yeah."

Closing her eyes, she melts further into him, savoring this moment of gently being held in strong, loving arms and feeling his tender lips on her skin. No one else was in the room, no one else mattered except for she and Matt.

* * *

Dan sat at the bar, slumped in his seat. Hearing Stacy's name, he sat up, his alert gaze watching her. Today's argument and her demands shocked him. She's been constantly on his mind since. He decided the best thing to do would be to keep his distance for a while, hoping she'd calm down, then he'd approach and ask for forgiveness. But for now, he'd have to be content watching her.

His calloused fingers gripped onto the long neck bottle, raising to his lips to sip at his beer. His eyes narrowed, angered at this dude pawing all over his woman. The sips changed to chugging. His eyes remained glued to the pair and he couldn't stand it any longer. The extra hard tapping on his shoulder caught his attention. Matt looked up to see a blonde hair man with blood shot eyes glaring at him. He wasn't as tall as him but had a barrel, muscular chest and corded arms. Matt released his grip from her waist as he took a step back, eyeing the stranger up and down. Quickly, he came to the conclusion that he wasn't much to contend with. He looked familiar but he couldn't place who he was.

"Excuse me but do you have to have your hands all over my woman?" He wondered in a gravelly voice.

His woman? Dan? Christ, did he change! And more than likely he was the bastard that placed those bruises on her face. His eyes hatefully narrowed at the creep.

"The lady in question has failed to mention anything about a poor excuse of a man such as yourself for a boyfriend," he scoffed. Matt slid his arm to her shoulders to smoothly guide her behind him.

Stacy heard the familiar angry tone of Dan's voice instantly taking her back. Fear filled her as Matt lightly shoved her away from them.

"Well, I do happen to be her boyfriend," Dan shot back, standing his body as tall as he could to hopefully intimidate this stranger.

Anger seethed through her with his insolence. Stepping from behind Matt's protective shield, Stacy braced her hands on her hips. *"No you are definitely not!"*

"You be quiet!" Dan ordered.

"You make me!" she snapped, adding, "I told you we're done and I mean it!" Her hand tightened into a fist as she drew her arm back to take a swing at him.

Matt's quick reflexes grasp onto her attacking arm, spinning her into a circle. She swung at the air, missing her target.

"Hell, it sure didn't take you to damn long to find someone else. Maybe we are better off being through especially since you seem to be falling into a category of whore!" Dan sneered.

Matt sent the man a glowering stare.

"I have been done with you for a couple of years, just didn't know how to end it until today."

"I don't give a damn what you say, whore!"

"Apologize or regret it," Matt growled.

"Hell no. I ain't apologizing to that whoring bitch."

Retaliating with a right hook to Dan's jaw, the impact instantly knocked the half tanked man sprawling backwards onto the floor. Matt stood, flexing his fingers, his legs straddling over the prone body waiting, hoping that he would stand up.

Stacy's mouth dropped open at the lightning speed Matt displayed. She loved the way he easily laid the so called, tough guy Dan out with one punch. Definitely a huge turn on. Then it dawned on her, Matt defended her!

"Ohhh my," she breathed in a voice quivering with emotion. Her gaze locked onto Matt's muscular form.

With a loud groan, Dan's head slowly moved back and forth.

Seeing the argument and fists fly, Amy hurried to join them, leaning her swaying form against Stacy, her arms lightly draping over Stacy's shoulder.

"Yeah! That serves you right you arrogant jackass!" Amy loudly stated.

Still stunned, Stacy looked at Amy, her brave words spurning her on. She looked back at Dan as he slowly propped himself on his elbows. "Yeah! Come on! Stand up! Do you want some more of him?" She added.

Matt looked at her, amused to find them both precariously dancing on the balls of their feet. Stacy held her hands up like some prize fighter, gesturing with wiggling fingers, trying to coax him to get up. The picture of how they all looked filled him, and it was quite hilarious.

"Let's get you home," he suggested trying to refrain from his laughter.

"I...don't...want to go...just yet!" she whined in her loud, drunken voice.

"Well, I do."

"Awww, are you sure?"

"Oh yeah. Come on," he took her hand in his. With a slight tug, he gently eased her along behind him, still fighting his laughter with her words of refusal.

"But Matthew, I want to stay and fight him some more!"

"Correction. I think that you mean me to fight."

"Whatever it takes to get the job done!"

He stopped at the table. When he looked to her, he notice that her body was weaving and her vocals came louder. The drinks were beginning to hit her harder now, he thought, still wondering how she was standing.

"Here's her purse and keys," Randy stated, handing the items to him as he plucked Amy from where she stood to hoist across his shoulder. "Good luck," he added, watching as Matt wrapped an arm across Stacy's shoulder to help steady her.

CHAPTER 8

During the ride to her home, her slurred chattering faded as she finally passed out, or fell asleep. He wasn't quite sure which. After parking her Jeep in the garage, he went to her side. Opening the door, he studied her, smiling at the soft snore.

"Stace? We're home."

His fingers lightly tapped at the flushed cheeks on her face to hopefully waken her. No movement, no reaction. Nothing at all except a soft snore. Sighing, he simply scooped her into his arms to carry her inside. Her head fell back and each step he took, her hair swayed and her arm limply hung open.

Easily, he opened the front door, entering. His steps were light as he went up the stairs, peering into a couple of bedrooms until he found what he guessed to be hers. Careful not to hit her head on the door frame he entered her bedroom. With an extra tenderness, he laid her on top of her huge cannon ball style bed. Stretching, he reached to turn on a tiny lamp on the night stand then straightened, gazing onto her flushed face then his eyes slowly followed her well-endowed chest, tiny waist and rounded hips, traveling down her legs before back to her face.

His brows rose, surprised when somehow she began to move. Her soft groan met his ears as she slowly struggled to an upright position.

With her eyes still closed, she proceeded to tug at her shirt, straining to remove it.

"What are you doing?" he wondered. His eyes glued to her bared stomach and red lace bra. He muffled a laugh when her shirt got stuck on her head. Her arms tugged to the sides when her balled hands got wrapped in the material.

"Undressing. I can't stand clothes on while in bed," she loudly complained then continued stripping.

"Oh good lord, that meant she slept naked," he muttered.

His eyes followed the shirt as it flew through the air to land on the floor across the room. Swinging his head back, Matt pursed his lips at the incredible sight of the most perfect female form he ever laid eyes on. Dumbfounded, his voice froze in his throat. She slowly slid to the edge of the mattress to stand her swaying body up.

Then her hands went to her waist, fumbling to undo the snap of her jeans. His breath caught at the slow, strip tease as her jeans slid then paused on her hips. When she presented the little wiggle to help them down, he breath caught and held. Damn, they didn't move. Exhaling, he soaked in her delicious body, memorizing every minute detail of the precious angel in front of him. His eyes narrowed when he first noticed the pierced belly button diamond glimmering in the light.

"Matthew, help me," she whined, her eyes opening into slits to focus onto his shocked face. She blinked. "What's wrong? Are you not feeling too good?" she weakly breathed, suddenly feeling tired.

Frustration swept over him. Sexual frustration, causing his irritation to surface. Contemplating his next move, he pressed his lips together. Well, no use denying it. The slow, sexy way she began disrobing caused an instant response of his body. Hell, it seemed everything she did caused him to react. Desire soared through his veins. It was a strong desire, a need he has been fighting with since he left her so long ago.

"Oh God. I want to be more than a brother," he dared to whisper.

His hungry gaze watched as she staggered nearer, again wiggling her hips, trying to yank her jeans off. His hands reached out to capture her face.

"I didn't mean for this to happen," he added in a hoarse voice before his lips slowly, deftly took firm control over hers. His kiss was lazy, taking his time, enjoying the feel of her lips on his, welcoming him home as he completely covered her mouth.

And God help him, it did feel like coming home.

His head spun from the blissfulness and excitement of holding Stacy so firm in his arms and kissing her so sound. His heart reveled in the unconditional way she responded to him as she just as slowly kissed him back. So open, refreshing, pure, giving. Passionate.

And he didn't want to stop.

Her mind travelled to a pleasurable haze. This is the best dream, Stacy thought. The warm feel of his hand as it cupped her face then the hunger touch of his lips on hers sent the irrepressible shiver to erupt from deep inside of her until she didn't have control over her body. Then, she felt herself relax, taking pleasure when his kiss softened; in his gentle touch when his arm wrapped around her shoulder and waist to pull her nearer.

It felt so good.

She let her arms slip around his waist, holding him as she tentatively respond to his gratifying attention. She felt his mouth slant over hers then, opening her mouth, his tongue slide inside dancing with hers, deepening, lengthening the kiss.

"Oh God," he whispered against her giving mouth. Matt felt himself come to life. He straightened, her lips moving to his neck. "I need to stop this now."

Matt eased away, his hands still helplessly entangled through her hair. He gazed at her soft face. His chest rose and fell from his labored breathing as he pressed his forehead against hers, fighting to control his tumultuous emotions. Slow down, remember, she is drunk. Tilting his head back, he looked into her wide, slightly glazed bright eyes, seeing confusion in them. Then a euphoric smile spread on her lips.

"Matthew, do you want to know something?" she asked with a sing song voice.

"What?"

"I think that you are the mostest handsomest man I have ever known," she confessed before her mouth opened in a lazy smile.

"Thank you and you are completely drunk out of your mind," he politely answered.

"Phffft, no I am not!"

"Oh yes you are."

"Am not. But, it's true Matthew. You are handsomest," she declared with a seductive pout then leaned in to brush her lips to his in a sloppy kiss.

He quickly ended the kiss. Lightly easing her away, he kept his grip on her upper arms, helping to steady her.

Giving him a naughty, sideways glance, she added, "Ya know what else?"

He grinned. "What else," he fought the chuckle as she made the cutest face of her eyes squinting shut and mouth pursing as if debating whether she should tell him. Her hand caressed his cheek then lightly patted him.

"I love you," she snickered, embarrassed with revealing a deep dark secret. "To the moon and back, for real."

"Sure you do and I love you, too," he answered, grinning at her half crying expression. Then her eyes watered and it appeared like she was about to cry.

"Awwww, that's so nice to hear."

"Now, I think the best thing for you to do is to get to sleep. Believe me, after what you've drank, you'll need it." His eyes widened with her response.

"I think I need you," she helplessly muttered turning away to finally succeed dropping her jeans about her ankles. Gingerly she managed to step from the material without falling on her face before she turned towards the bed.

His gaze fell onto her rounded, upside down, perfect sized heart-shaped derriere, not missing the matching red lace thong revealing bare skin to his hungry eyes. She may appear as the motherly type on the surface but what he looked at was anything beyond. Revealing red lace underclothes, belly button piercing, what else was she going to expose?

Good Lord, but he wanted nothing more than to follow that tempting body to her huge bed, hide beneath the covers and make slow, passionate love to her. He lifted his hands to cover his face as he took in a deep, shuddering breath to regain his emotions. When he looked back she stood, facing her bed, debating about getting in.

"That's a good place for you," he muttered, taking a backward step feeling the deep urge to get some distance between him and her tempting body. Pausing, he couldn't miss how quiet she had become. Matt watched the exaggerated way she swung her hips. She wobbled, slightly losing her balance. Her hand reached, gripping onto the foot board before slowly, methodically, climbed into her bed.

"I'll get you a couple glasses of water, that'll help with the hangover." He turned to the bathroom.

Ignoring him, Stacy lay on her back. The smile was still on her lips. This was some dream. It was so realistic. She felt her head slowly begin with the swoon as the room began to spin. She didn't know if the cause was from her dream man's kiss or the alcohol. With a nod, she slowly rolled onto her side, snuggling deep beneath the covers.

"The kiss."

She brought a trembling hand to touch her lips where moments ago her dream man, Matthew kissed her. The thought sent a tremor through her.

Matt returned with the glass of water to pause at the edge of the bed, resting his hands on the footboard he watched as sleep quickly over took her. The battle had been tough on him but he won the impulse to strip himself down to join her in that spacious bed. He released a long, weary sigh before he shut off the light. With a shake of his head, he turned away to search for a bed. He approached a nearby open door. Flicking on the switch brought a bed side lamp to a glow. His eyes widened. The room was lined with rows of shelves where a different airplane was proudly displayed. He took slow steps inside, his hand lightly touching a F/18, perfectly detailed like those he mainly flies.

Glancing about, his eyes fell onto a few picture frames. Picking one up, he grinned to see a bright blue eyed boy with a crooked smile being hugged by an equally beaming Stacy. Sighing, he removed his clothes to his boxers before he lay on the double bed. He braced his hands beneath his head as he glanced about at the wall paper border of planes. He grinned, imagining the energetic Greg and his enthusiasm for aviation. Reaching out, he turned off the lamp before rolling over to fall asleep, that vixen in the next room on his mind.

* * *

Matt woke to the very familiar sound of someone retching their guts out. Looking at the clock, it was after nine. He made a nasty face when he heard her cry out in pain before releasing another round. He knew he should've forced that water down her throat last night. Slipping into his jeans, he hurried down the stairs to the kitchen where he fixed her a fresh pot of strong coffee. he knew from personal past experiences that this would be her best friend, well that along with a cold compress and aspirin.

He returned to her bedroom to find her lying on top of the covers displaying those luscious curves to his starving eyes while she tightly gripped the blankets over her face. Gently, he placed the tray that held the carafe of coffee and cup on the nearby night stand.

"Shhhh," her muffled voice was smooth, gentle, lightly reprimanding.

Matt grinned as he slowly lay next to her. He lounged on his side, his head resting in his hand. Easing the covers from her face, he couldn't help but burst out with laughter at the sight that met his eyes. She lay on her side, her hair in wild disarray being held by her arm over her face shielding her closed eyes from any form of sunlight.

"Didn't I tell you shhhh?" she softly asked before slowly gliding the covers back over her face.

He pulled them back down, pushing her hair back so that he could see her, his hand cupped her cheek. She grimaced with the mild movement. "How badly is your head hurting?" He whispered.

"I swear that the throbbing is so loud that every blood vessel in my brain is about to burst," she meekly cried.

"That bad huh?"

She vaguely nodded.

"I got you some coffee." His voice was as soft as a whisper.

"Oh...yippee."

"Aspirin too."

"Good."

"And a cold cloth for your forehead."

"What about a noose so that I can hang myself? Or maybe a tourniquet to stop the blood flow to my head."

Snickering, he asked, "Just what *did* you drink?" He placed the cold cloth on her forehead, grinning at her soft sigh. His hand stayed on her face, a finger outlining her lips as she talked.

"What's that song by the Eagles about a sunrise?"

Matt began thinking then his eyes widened, "Tequila? You were doing Tequila shots?" He asked in a louder voice.

"Shhh, please. But, I guess so. And what's those planes that fly into boats to blow up?"

He made a thoughtful face before answering. "Tequila *and* Kamikaze? Christ, you're going to be such a mess today darling."

Stacy's brow furrowed. Did she just hear him correctly? Did he just name her darling? Struggling, her one eye painfully opened into the merest of a slit to look at him. He lay on his side, his elbow bent resting his head in his hand. On his muscular bicep he had a tattoo of Eagle with spread wings over the flag and initials U.S.N. Her one eye fanned to his chest, noting his equally, muscular torso was bare.

Definitely not a dream.

She noticed his eyes follow a finger from his hand as he traced the features on her face. She felt the light touch as he dare to glide it between her breasts to her stomach then retrace his path back to her face. She swore that every nerve joined forces to go towards that lone finger, each wanting to be touched by it. Suddenly she realized he was touching flesh.

"Where are my clothes? Did you remove them?"

"No. That's another interesting moment from last night. Thank you for the show," he chuckled, noting her furrowed brow. You were sensuously adorable," he added with a naughty chuckle.

"I don't remember a thing," she meekly offered.

"That's a shame. I'd love to see a repeat performance of the strip show."

"Strip? I stripped?"

"You sure did." He let out a low whistle.

"I'm going to ignore that. But what are you doing?" she whispered with a shaky voice. A gasp slipped from her mouth at his simple, ordinary, like he had every right to reply.

"Touching you."

"Why?"

"Because I can and I want to. You're tensed. Close your eyes and just relax," he gently commanded.

Slowly she did as he said, closing her eyes, feeling his hand gently brush her neck and top of her shoulder where he proceeded to rub. He was right, she was tensed and oh, his touch was magic.

"Ummm, this is heaven," she murmured. "I have so much to do today. I told Greg we would go to the museum this morning but I feel so lousy. I have to do a wedding this afternoon..."

"I'll take him," Matt offered.

Stacy's breath caught. The mere idea of Matt and Greg together set her pulse racing. Removing the cold cloth, she slowly managed to sit up as Matt's hand fell to her stomach. She gave him a long hard look into his eyes, his weak spot where she remembered she could tell if he were lying to her. She saw sincerity there.

"You'd be willing to spend your free time with a child? Mind you, not just any child, but one that is energetic, inquisitive and intelligent?" She softly asked, the disbelief showing on her face.

Matt's hand cupped her chin. With a reassuring smile, he answered, "Sure. I love kids. I hope to have some of my own one day."

Her heart began an unmerciful fluttering in her chest with his unexpected words. *You already do!* "But Greg is different than others. He keeps to himself a lot. He'd rather read, watch documentaries than be with kids his age. Sports are okay for a while but he gets bored with them. He's very mature for his age."

"We'll have to change that, won't we." He gazed into her eyes with a fondness he never felt for any woman before. He wanted to take her into his arms and kiss her but knew if he did he may not stop.

Being with her, so near like this would have to do for the moment and he was enjoying this. Slowly he leant in, placing a kiss on her forehead. His knuckles lightly brushed along the side of her face, feeling the warm smoothness beneath. As he moved back, he read a look of need in her eyes.

Words failed her as she only nod in response as her headache now throbbed harder. A short time later, after making sure that she would be fine, Matt left. The Harley was loud as it roared down the road, past Beth's car as she returned Greg home.

* * *

Sam watched Matt hurry inside and up the stairs, taking them two at a time. He opened his mouth to speak but before he had the chance, Matt disappeared. He raised his eyebrows with wonder for certainly he didn't miss that huge smile his son wore.

"Was that Matt?" Marge asked as she joined her husband in the living room. She carried a wooden serving tray with two glasses of iced tea to set on the coffee table.

"I think so. He ran past so damn fast that I couldn't tell," he complained as they heard the water from the shower spray.

They took a seat on the couch, "You know he didn't come home last night," Marge said with a long sigh. "I'll never stop worrying about him."

"I know. I won't either. He is our youngest. Well, have you talked to Randy?"

"Briefly. He said that Amy and Stacy had a bit too much to drink last night and Matt took Stacy home."

"I like that girl. I just don't know why those two never got together," he muttered before sipping his iced tea.

Marge shot him a wizened look. If only he knew, she thought. She nodded with agreement as Matt hurried back down the stairs. He still wore his smile but now was whistling as he hurried towards the kitchen, giving them a quick wave.

"You just like her because she sits with you and still listens to your war stories." She teased with a grin.

"Nah now. That ain't it. I just like little Stacy. She's like the daughter I never had. Always here eating breakfast or any meal she happened to be here for. Never was shy about asking anything. She always helped you, too."

"Ah huh."

"Matt's girlfriends that he brought around were all a bunch of worthless extra baggage in my book."

"Oh Sam!" she squealed, surprised to hear those words coming out of him.

"Well it's true!"

"What's true?" Matt asked taking a seat to join them with a sandwich in one hand and a glass of iced tea in the other.

"That..." Sam began.

"It's nothing Matt. We were only reminiscing, that's all."

"What about?"

"About your old..." Sam once again started.

"About when you were still at home and your girlfriends and wondering why you didn't come home last night. That's all. What are you up to today?" She innocently rattled off.

Matt gave them a look of wonder. They seemed to be acting a bit strange. He had his mouth full, chewing on his ham sandwich, noting they curiously looked at him. Then, there it was. The look, not just any look but *the* look. His mom wore that familiar, all too well, knowing what he was up to look. Her eyebrows were raised, head lowered and eyes pinning him where he sat. Her lips were lightly pressed together, trembling, as she held back some sort of news or laughter. It was a look that always seemed to unnerve him as a child and young adult to now. And his dad quietly waited for an answer.

He swallowed his food now managing to speak, "Just what all do you know?" He carefully asked.

"That you spent the night with Stacy," Marge quipped.

"Nothing happened."

"Pity. I like her," Sam declared, his words getting a pinch from Marge and a choking cough from Matt who was taking another bite of his sandwich.

Matt shifted his gaze to his mother who still looked at him in that same way. He spoke, "I'm taking Greg to the museum this afternoon..."

"You've met Greg!" Marge loudly interrupted, her shrill voice causing him to jump in his seat.

"Not yet. Why, shouldn't I take him?"

"I'm sorry. You surprised me, that's all."

"He's a good boy. I really like him, too. Calls me Grandpa Sadler."

Matt's alert gaze shifted back and forth between the pair. They weren't telling all, he realized as he once again wondered about the parentage of Greg Cannon.

"Well, I gotta get moving."

"Are you staying with her tonight?" Sam asked with a wink, getting a light slap on his hand from Marge.

"Dad. Really. We've haven't seen one another for..."

"Twelve years. That's too long to be apart," Marge complained, nodding her head.

"Apart? Mom, we were never together, remember?"

"Yes, and that's too bad," she lightly answered with an extra sweet smile.

"You guys are acting crazy." He stated, a look of concern crossed his face. Slowly he stood, "I need to get going. I don't know when I'll be home this evening."

"Take all night if you have to!" Sam yelled with a loud guffaw, getting another painful pinch on the arm.

"Oh and Matt? About Greg? I think he is," Marge called out.

Matt paused in the kitchen looking towards the living room and his mom's voice. With a grin he exhaled a long breath as he slowly shook his head still not believing their conversation.

CHAPTER 9

Beth and Adam followed Greg inside to find Stacy sprawled on the couch. A partially filled cup of coffee rest on her stomach and a cold compress pressed across her forehead.

"What happened to you?" Beth wondered taking a seat next to her. Concern constantly filled her that maybe Dan returned and hit her.

"One to many drinks," Stacy muttered.

Adam's eyes darkened as a serious expression appeared on his face. "Looks more like a lot to many drinks. Did you take anything?"

"Yes..."

"Mom is Dan here?" Greg loudly demanded, entering the living room with his bed pillow firmly held in his hands. His shrill question caused her to wince in pain.

"No why?" she softly asked.

"I smell a man's cologne on my pillow," he stated giving the object mentioned a rough shake in the air.

Beth gave Stacy a new look then shifted to Adam who was also looking amused.

"Matt was here last night," Stacy began as Greg plopped on the edge of the coffee table. She gave her parents a glance, "He slept in your bed Greg!" She loudly defended only resulting in the pounding in her temples to throb harder.

"Who is Matt?" Greg demanded. With Dan gone, his instincts to be the one to take care of his mother returned.

"A good friend of mine. He's going to take you to the museum today, is that okay with you?"

"I don't even know him. Why have you never mentioned this dude before?"

Removing the cold cloth from her eyes and forehead, she shot him an impatient long look while taking in the overnight maturity he displayed. Smoothly she replied, "I have darling. He was my best friend. He's come home for Randy's wedding and he wants to meet you. Since I have a wedding to do today, Matt has kindly offered to take you with him."

"You'll like him Greg," Adam added, receiving an angry glare from him.

Looking back to his mother, "Are you crazy? You're going to let me go with a complete stranger?" Greg asked with amazement.

Stacy pressed her lips together for once wishing he wasn't so perceptive with what all she taught him. Her voice came stronger, "All right. Matt is an old friend of mine. We were neighbors, growing up together."

"What does he do?"

"Greg please! You'll have a good time. He'll have a lot of great stories to tell you."

"Like what?"

"I don't want to spoil the surprise, okay?"

Greg recognized that tone of voice so he knew when to back down with his questions. He stubbornly crossed his arms in front of him. "Okay, sure. I'll have fun."

He spoke with such sarcasm that Stacy lost her temper. Despite her raging headache, she set the cup of coffee on the table then swung her legs from the couch and sat up to look him in the eyes. Her tone was angry and even, knowing she would have his total attention.

"Now you listen to me young man. I don't ever want to hear *that* tone of voice coming from you when you speak to me! Do you hear and understand me? And yes, you *are* going with Matt. He'll show you a good time, I promise!" Her fingers vigorously rubbed her forehead. "What *is* your problem?"

Greg's eyes narrowed in an angry glare. He wanted desperately to tell her, I just thought that with Dan gone we'd be left alone for a while! I won't have to worry about a man hitting on you again! Instead, he remained silent, staring out the window. "Okay. I'll go but I'm not going to particularly like it," he angrily muttered. The angry stomping of his feet faded as he went outside.

Stacy watched him stride away before snickering caught her attention. Her gaze pivoted to her mother then to her father who also tried to not laugh, "What am I going to do with him? He's getting so protective, demanding to know everything that I do?"

"He's being the man of the house," Beth stated giving her a comforting smile. "He may have seen or heard more than what you think," she suggested as she stood to leave.

"I hope not."

"We'll leave you to your rest. Call me."

As they drove away, Beth and Adam waved to Amy who was sitting on her front porch enjoying the mid-morning breeze. Amy pulled her sun glasses down to keep the bright glare from cutting into her eyes as she walked across the road. She watched Stacy emerge from her house to sit on a chair and decided to join her. Greg sat on a step, his hands bracing his chin.

With mild interest, Stacy watched Amy's slow progress across the paved road then through the green grass of the front yard and finally slowly maneuver the steps. She lightly gave Greg's drooping shoulder a pat before slowly taking a seat in a wicker rocking chair. She released a long sigh when she relaxed.

"I see you're still breathing," Amy began, resting her head back on the thick green and white floral cushion.

"Barely," Stacy answered as the deep rumble of a bike came nearer, adding, "He certainly didn't waste much time." She smirked at the glare Greg cast over his shoulder. Then he changed his direction to the motorcycle.

The distant rumble brought Stacy's nerves to erupt, but her eyes widened as the now familiar Harley Davidson stopped in her driveway. Trying to catch her breath and with a nervous swallow, she watched Matt get off. As he approached, he swiped a lean hand through his short hair, recognizing it as one of his nervous gestures. His strides were long and easy as he walked to the porch where she sat. She shifted her nervous gaze to Greg who was speechless with this tall man walking his way then he looked at the motorcycle. His head pivoted to give her a stunned look before looking back at Matt.

Matt's tanned arms were bared to the sun. The black muscle shirt fit his rock hard body very well, she thought. He wore his mirrored, aviator sun glasses.

"Good morning Stace, Amy," he spoke as the smile she loved and missed formed. "I see you survived last night, too," he added with a laugh.

"But it's a last time," Amy answered.

"Matt, hi," Stacy haltingly spoke. She sat with her hands pressed together, her fingertips lightly touching her lips. A nervousness engulfed her at the realization of a father meeting his son and they didn't know it.

How often she sat and thought about when this day would happen. "Matt, this is my son, Greg. Greg this is Matt. I was telling you a bit about him."

Still grinning, he looked at Greg who was staring at the tattoo on his upper arm of the Navy emblem. Greg's eyes widened. He definitely recognized what it was and meant. Removing his sunglasses, Matt stuck his arm out, his hand opened waiting for a handshake. "Greg Cannon? I'm Matt Sadler."

Slowly, Greg's hand went into his father's, getting lost in the vast hugeness as he received a strong handshake and returned one. Stacy fought back a cry at the sight of the two touching for the first time. She bit her tongue, denying the urge to blurt out, *'Yes! Yes! I made a mistake. I should have told you as soon as I knew it! You are father and son!*

And dear God, they looked more alike than she ever imagined! As they released their hands, Greg stared into Matt's eyes seeing a warmness there. "Are you really a pilot?"

"I sure am."

"And are you for real a Blue Angel?" Greg added, his eyes widening further.

"Yes."

"Whoa, that is totally awesome." He breathed believing he was about to pass out from talking with an honest to goodness pilot.

Matt released a rich laugh, "I couldn't mistake that you like airplanes?" He asked, taking a seat on the steps next to him, straightening his long legs out in front.

Greg quickly mocked Matt's seat as he stared at this stranger with a new respect. "Oh yeah. They're awesome."

Matt glanced over Greg's head to Stacy who still sat with her hands to her lips. A slight grin curved her lips as she watched them.

"Awesome," he repeated.

His words causing her to laugh out before nervously biting at her lower lip. She rapidly blinked back her tears.

Matt shifted his gaze to the battery control airplane sitting in the yard. "How does she fly?" he asked Greg as he looked at the young man. Greg opened his mouth to speak but Matt filled his words for him. "Awesome, right?"

Greg laughed, "Cool."

Matt again laughed, "Care to show me?"

"Yeah, come on!"

Stacy released a long, shuddering breath, beaming at the pair as they walked towards the airplane.

"Aren't they cute. Two boys playing with airplanes," Amy giggled, watching them.

Pressing her hands now in a tight clasp her eyes remain on them. "It's awesome," Stacy repeated her son's words.

"Look at them. That's amazing, simply amazing. You see that? They have the same walk, hair coloring. And look at their hands. Both have them in their back pockets...and *Oh my God!*" Amy squealed with excitement, her tone of voice causing both to wince before looking with wide eyes at Stacy.

"Oh my God, what?" Stacy calmly repeated, giving her a look with what she hoped to be with indifference.

"Stacy, is Matt Greg's father?" She dared whisper the question.

There it was. The question had finally surfaced between the best friends. Stacy leant closer to her and with a warning look, she whispered, "Don't you even dare breath this to a soul. Yes."

"But, you and Matt?" Amy said, still not believing it.

"What about it?"

"Unreal. It's all so unreal. No one would ever think that because you two were buds."

"Buds who had sex one time and she got pregnant," she added with a sour voice.

"Does he know?"

"No."

"Are you going to tell him?"

"I'm not sure how."

CHAPTER 10

Matt hurried home, silently cursing that he rushed out forgetting his wallet. He spent a good half an hour talking with Greg, getting him to relax and when they were about to leave, he realized what he did. He hated to leave Greg so soon, but it's easier to leave him at home instead of having him on the back of the bike while racing to get his wallet.

"Matt? It *is* you!"

He glanced to the neighboring house, smiling to see Beth Cannon standing on the porch wearing jeans and pink pullover shirt. She had her arms crossed in front of her and wearing a wide smile. He could see where Stacy got her appreciative looks from.

Beth closely studied Matt, seeing more resemblances of Greg in the man. The day he left burnt a painful memory into her heart as she dealt with the near depression his leaving caused with Stacy. "I knew it," she whispered.

A grin shaped his lips.

"Mrs. Cannon, how have you been?" he happily asked going to embrace her in a warm hug.

"Fine. We've certainly missed you!" she exclaimed as he took a step back. "Look at you," she breathed. "You've grown into quite a handsome man." She laughed when his face reddened with her compliment. "So what brings you home?"

"Randy's wedding for one and there's something that has been on my mind for quite a while that I need to get figured out."

"Oh, I hope it isn't anything serious?"

"I don't really know yet. I'll come over and talk but right now I'm off to take Greg to the museum. I left without my wallet," he explained.

"That's right. I heard about that. You be careful with my grandchild." She playfully warned.

"You bet. He's a pistol," he added as he hurried away.

She watched, noting how anxious he was to get back to Greg. He'd be quite a good father.

* * *

Greg constantly paced in and out of the house anxious for Matt to return. His eyes kept going from his wristwatch to the wall clock before going to the window to look up and down the road. Frustrated, he hurried to the photo studio where Stacy prepared her equipment for the wedding.

"Mom, are you sure he wasn't lying about taking me?"

Stacy grinned with his impatient words, "No he wasn't lying. He isn't that kind of man."

"Wow. It's totally awesome isn't it? I mean, he's a pilot, and a Blue Angel at that."

Her hands stopped what she was doing. Lifting her chin, she looked into his face. Grinning when she noticed that he beamed all over. "You're not afraid to go with a complete stranger?" she teased.

"No! I can't wait!"

"That's why I didn't want to mention who he was because I know that Grandpa Sadler has mentioned him hundreds of times. Believe me, Matt will have some stories for you. Did you know that Matt had his pilot's license at the age of fifteen?"

"Wow. Awesome. Do you think I can ask him questions and I won't upset him?" His anxious expression changed to concern.

Stacy couldn't miss it so she remarked on it. "I think that would be fine. Greg, why are you worried about upsetting him so easily?" He looked the other way, pretending with getting interested with a camera of hers. "Greg? You can talk to me."

He looked at the bruise on her face. His anger flared as he recalled how she got it. "Dan got mad easy when things didn't go right or he was asked things that he didn't want to talk about."

She rolled her eyes to the ceiling. She hated to hear him speak like that. It appears that Dan's nasty temper affected both of them. "You'll be fine with Matt," she reassured giving him a hug.

The rumble of his motorcycle filled the house. Greg jumped away to hurry up the stairs. "Yes! He's here!" He yelled, his excited voice filling the room.

Stacy hurried after him. Not on a motorcycle! Her fear of Greg on a bike surfaced. She burst up the stairs to find Matt already standing at the front door with Greg as he patiently listened to the list of questions. He wore a smile as Greg rattled off questions.

"Where are we going? Are we going on the bike? Did you really have your pilot license at fifteen? How long did it take to become a Blue Angel? What's your rank? How much practicing and air time do you do a day?" Greg excitedly asked.

"Whoa now. One at a time okay?" Matt laughed as he placed a hand on Greg's shoulder. Matt looked up, his eyes going to the main object of his desire. Her cheeks were still flushed but she looked far better than she did earlier. True, he thought about her all of the time but he blamed that on his own stupidity of leaving without speaking to her and getting some form of closure.

Now, since he saw her again it was very evident to his heart that oh yes, he was very, very interested in Stacy. He knew he also needed time to speak with her and hoped she'd accept his advances. Well, no sense in putting things off any longer.

"Matt, hi..."

Matt leaned in to swiftly brush his lips on hers, not missing how she jumped from the unexpected smooch. He stood back, looking into her wide eyes.   "You're definitely looking a lot better than when I left this morning."

Stacy curiously looked at him as the feel of his lips on hers sent her heart racing. What is he up to? A slight, unsure smile formed on her lips, liking his gentle attention. "Yes, I do feel better. Thanks. Uh, are you taking the bike?"

"Yeah, why not?"

"Yeah, why not?" Greg repeated with an unsure grin. He didn't miss the kiss.

"Isn't it dangerous?"

"Stace, since when have you been afraid to ride on a bike?" Matt countered, fighting the grin. "Remember the good times we had on my bike?"

Her face reddened with those memories, "Well, that was before my son would be on it," she quickly defended her statement.

"Awwww mooommm," Greg loudly complained.

"Yeah, aw mom," Matt repeated, placing his protective arm about Greg's shoulders.

She rolled her eyes heavenward with their statements.

"Her defenses are weakening," Matt knowingly said.

"I know," Greg happily added.

She pressed her lips together as they stood watching her, two pair of pale blue eyes giving her a long look, patiently waiting for her approval. Finally, she asked, "No wheelies?"

"On a Harley?" Matt countered.

"Well, knowing you, you could do it," she laughed. "How about obeying the speed limit."

"Always."

"Don't let him coerce you into driving it."

"You did it to me and I let you drive my trail bike. Now, there's a story Greg."

Greg's eyes lit up.

"Don't you dare say a word. Have a good day you two," Stacy quickly said as she gave Greg a fast hug.

For the first time, he seemed bashful to receive attention from her.
"Do you have to do that?" he muttered the complaint as she pressed a kiss on his cheek.

"If you don't want one Greg, I'll take one," Matt said with a teasing light in his eyes as his gaze met and held hers. His smile broadened as she stepped closer to him. He wrapped an arm around her waist, pulling her to him.

She tenderly placed her hand on his chest as she stood on tip toes to place a slow kiss on his cheek. "Thank you," she whispered before moving away from his loosened grip.

"For what?"

She wanted to tell him for Greg; for being a friend; for making her heart beat and her life feel more complete with him being here but for now she only shook her head.

Matt's hand went to hers, clasping it to bring to his lips. He placed a kiss in the palm, closing it after. "See ya later. Have a good time today at work."

Stacy pressed her lips together. She wanted to ask him again, what he was up to but Greg was paying extra close attention to them. Now is not the time to discuss any private emotions that may be blossoming. She followed them outside to watch as they drove away. She noticed how slow Matt drove but once out of sight, she heard the motor race louder before quickly fading.

Releasing a sigh, she turned to get a shower when she noticed a van pulling into her driveway with the information of a local floral business painted on the side. An older woman slowly approached carrying a lovely bouquet of pink carnations, white daisies and a single red rose in the center of the arrangement.

"Miss Cannon?" she asked, stopping on the porch.

"Yes. Are those for me?"

"Yes and aren't they beautiful?"

"Oh my, yes," Stacy returned her hands taking the flowers from her. "Thank you," she added reaching for the card. Opening it, her eyes hatefully narrowed. 'I love you and will do anything to win your heart, Love Dan.'

The delivery woman was on the last step when the bouquet flew past her head to land in a loose heap on the front yard. She spun about to see Stacy tear the card in half then toss it in the air before she disappeared inside. Her brows rose upwards, "I see *that* didn't work," she muttered with mild amusement before leaving.

* * *

Matt took Greg to the local Wal Mart before getting on their way.

With his arm draped across Greg's shoulder, they entered side by side. He noticed how Greg slowed his pace when three boys the same age as him, all turned to look.

"Who are they?" Matt asked, his gaze following Greg's.

"Three assholes from school."

"Don't swear," Matt kindly reminded him, adding, "They friends?"

Greg looked back at him with a smirk. "I just said they were assholes how can they be friends?"

"And I just said, don't swear. I was joking too. Why are they looking like that at you?" Greg nonchalantly shrugged his shoulder, casting his gaze to the ground. Matt didn't miss the pained expression in his eyes. "Come on. Talk to me," he coaxed, giving his shoulder a brief shake.

Before Greg had the chance to answer, the one boy shouted out. "Greg, who's that with you?"

Matt steered Greg in their direction. With a warm smile, he reached his arm out, his hand opened for a handshake. "I'm Greg's father. Pleasure to meet you," he answered giving the main speaker a hard, jerking, handshake. He had to fight the laughter as the youngster rolled his shoulder a few times.

Greg rolled his eyes to Matt, a broad smile on his mouth. That would be awesome if Matt were his dad. He really liked him, a lot.

"You are not. Greg's a bastard," another one added with a snicker.

"No he isn't. I am his dad and I would greatly appreciate if you three gentlemen would conduct yourself in a polite manner and never call my son that ever again."

"Yeah? Or else what?"

"Or else there is going to be hell to pay," Matt replied with a slight grin.

The main speaker balked at his words. His eyes roamed back and forth between the pair before he turned his attention to Greg. "Well, he does look like you. What does he do that he hasn't been around?"

Greg stood straighter, boldly eyeing him down. "He's a Blue Angel Fighter Pilot. He's been to war and working hard to protect our country."

Matt grinned, "Pardon us, we have got to get going. Nice meeting you," Matt interrupted, his arm steering Greg beside him.

Later, they journeyed down the highway, going towards the bigger city where the museum was located. Pulling to a stop light, Matt's eyes read the billboard of the baseball games. There was one scheduled for today. "Ever been to a baseball game before?" he asked over his shoulder to Greg.

"No," Greg replied, playing with his new aviator sun glasses that Matt purchased for him.

"Would you like to go to one?"

"That would be awesome. Mom hates baseball."

"That's where we're going," Matt added changing directions towards the stadium.

Matt bought seats in the top. Few others were there including those who were daring to do the outlandish outfits. Greg's eyes were fixed on two very overweight, shirtless men. Their bodies were painted bright blue, the color of the home team, with numbers of their favorite players on their chests. On their heads they chose the fashionable hard hats where cans of their choice beverage, this time beer, could rest in mesh holders on the side with straws circling towards their mouths.

As Matt and Greg took their seats, Matt couldn't help but stare too. These two were quite different out for a day of fun times and making new memories. The pair did the wave together and yelled obscenities to the opposite teams and mascot. Matt's chuckle caught Greg's attention.

"You see those two?"

"Yeah."

"That's today's entertainment."

Greg shifted his gaze to Matt, a smile forming on his lips.

He is a lot different than Dan ever was. Dan would be telling those men to shut up before getting into a fight.

Matt looked to Greg. He didn't miss the sadness that Greg carried and the stubbornness. "Tell me, what kind of things do you like to do? Do you want a foot long?"

"Yeah."

"How about a beer?" he added seeing Greg make an odd face. "You're probably right. Your mom would skin me alive if I brought you home with alcohol on your breath."

Greg frowned. "You got that right..."

"I was only teasing you. Greg, you're too damn serious," Matt said, giving his leg a playful pat.

Greg looked down at his hands, his fingers enter-twining as he pressing his lips together. "That's all right. Grandpa Cannon says the same thing."

Matt grinned, motioning to a hawker for sandwiches and pop.

"Well, I really like airplanes," Greg began.

"I've noticed that. What brought that interest around?"

"Mom says that Grandpa Sadler gave me model airplanes instead of stuffed animals. She blames him," Greg said with a giggle.

A sad smile formed on Matt's lips. He wished he was able to be here for her when Greg was born and would've loved to see his dad fall all over a baby.

"Yeah, dad was always one for not giving toys like that to boys. Those were the kinds of things girls should have, boys needed men toys like army cars, cowboy guns and stuff like that," he lovingly mocked.

"Did you really have your pilot's license at age fifteen?" Greg asked before taking a bite of his foot-long. His vision locked on Matt's face.

"Oh yeah. Dad had me interested in airplanes at a young age too. Did you know that he flew in the war?" He asked.

Greg nodded, his mouth full of food.

"Man, whenever he would tell me those war stories, I sat on the edge of my seat waiting for the climax of the battle as I envisioned him in that pilot seat facing the enemy."

"Those are totally awesome stories," Greg agreed.

"You ain't kidding."

"Do you really fly an F/18?"

"Yep. Among others. There's a show nearby in a week, I'll get passes for everyone."

"That would be awesome!"

"I thought you'd think that. Actually, I train the new guns coming in, but I still fly the shows."

"What's your rank?"

"Captain..."

"Cool. How many hours of flying do you have?"

"Over three thousand." Matt gave him a grin, enjoying these questions and answers.

"Why did you tell them that you are my father?"

Matt felt his stomach tighten. Releasing a sigh, he answered, "In my opinion, every boy needs a father if not, then a father figure in their lives and well, I believe that if the asshole who is your real father won't step forward and take the responsibilities then I'd like to," he proudly declared giving Greg a smile, then quickly adding, "That is if it's okay with you."

"Oh yeah. It sure is and don't swear," he teased giving Matt a matching slightly lopsided grin.

"Yes son."

Greg studied him, watching as he took three bites of the hotdog followed with a chug of *Coke*. He really liked him and also noticed how more fun and carefree his mom had become since Matt arrived on the scene. And he sure didn't miss that kiss. Before he realized, Greg spurt out a question.

"Matt? What are your intentions with mom?"

Matt stared straight ahead, wondering what the hell to tell him? Well, Stacy warned him that he was an inquisitive child. Clearing his throat, Matt slightly turned in his seat. Sliding his sunglasses on the crown of his head, he looked long into Greg's face.

"That question deserves an answer."

"A truthful answer," Greg replied, mocking Matt as he slid his glasses to the crown of his head.

"Ah, of course. Truthful." Matt pointed a finger back and forth between them. "This is between me and you, one on one, pilot to co-pilot, all right?"

Greg grinned, "All right."

"I have loved your mom since we were teenagers..."

"Is this going to be mushy?"

"Hey, you asked so quit interrupting. She didn't love me the same. When we had our problems we went to each other to talk them out. Christ, the stories I could tell you."

"Go ahead," Greg blurted, anxious to know more about his secretive mom.

"Sorry. I promised her, no. We were best friends, soul mates but when I left for the service, my heart stayed here, with her and I couldn't get her out of my mind. So, I've got some time off and wanted to see her and..." he paused, his hand going in a circular motion as he tried so hard to choose the right words. "...hopefully see if she's softened towards myself."

Greg wore a distant look on his face at those words. Mushy, he thought, "So, can I call you dad?"

"Sure," Matt quickly answered, along with a long sigh of relief, glad that little speech was over with.

"Awesome."

"She isn't seeing anyone is she?"

"She just kicked Dan out a couple of days ago."

"Oh yeah, Dan. What an asshole he is," he scoffed receiving a laugh from Greg.

"Hey, does your mom still like flowers?"

"I don't know..."

Matt retrieved his cell phone to place a couple of phone calls.

CHAPTER 11

It was late when Stacy returned from the wedding and reception. Soft voices fell on her ears. Listening, she found they came from the living room. Setting her camera bags on the hardwood floor, she followed to find Matt sprawled on his back as he lay on the couch, fast asleep. He only wore his jeans, his shirt tossed across the back of the rocker. His leg was bent, resting against the back of the couch, his other straight, resting his heel on the floor. An arm flung over his face, the other across his well-defined flat stomach. The soft voices were coming from the television.

She grinned, sniffing at the single red rose that she carried. He had it delivered to the wedding reception. The bride and groom loved the fact that a flower was sent for the photographer. When she read the simple message she felt her heart melt.

'We wish that you were here with us, Matt and Greg.'

Turning, she softly walked to the kitchen where she retrieved a crystal vase to place the rose into. Setting it on the kitchen table she nervously bit her lower lip. Her gaze shifted to the living room, thinking about Matt. Again that nagging question formed, what is he up to? Deciding best to leave him sleep, that way it'd prolong the questions, she picked up the bags and went to her studio.

The radio was turned low as she softly sang with the music. She sat in a swivel chair, staring at the images on her computer screen, studying which pictures could be deleted and which ones to keep. She jumped at the masculine voice from behind.

"I thought I heard someone."

Looking, she found him standing in the doorway. His arms were raised above, his hands rest on the top of the door frame. Her gaze flitted about his smooth chest, noting how tanned his flesh was. He wore a tired smile on his lips, lips she desired. Needing to be pressed against hers.

Hoping to get her train of thoughts shifted in another direction, she asked, "How was your day with Greg?"

Lowering his arms to shove his hands into the pockets of his jeans, he smiled. "Greg, wow." He stepped closer to sit on the edge of the desk. "He's quite a young man. We had very good, detailed, interesting, conversations today."

Her face wrinkled from the grimace, "I don't think I care to hear them either." She looked to her work, her thoughts drifting back to his lips, arms and chest as his strong male presence filled her senses. Suddenly, she noticed the trembling of her hands with the strange nervousness she felt whenever he was near. He confused her. Things were so strange, weird, like he never left. She couldn't get over how life seemed to have never changed between them except for her. She was far more aware of the powerful masculinity of his presence.

Matt grinned with her nervousness. After all of these years apart, he could still sense her moods. He reached a hand to cup her chin, forcing her to look at him. He felt her will weaken as he slowly pulled her to stand between his legs. Her eyes sparkled as he looked long and hard into them. His hand entangled through her hair, holding her head still so he could study her face. God, she's more beautiful than he ever remembered.

His anger renewed at the bruise on her precious cheek. He silently wished that Dan would dare to cross his path, again. His finger lazily trailed over her lower lip, also noticing how it trembled from his touch.

"I can't seem to stay away from you." He stated in a voice filled with wonder.

"So I've noticed."

"You know I've kissed you a few times but I think you were a bit too intoxicated to notice. So guess what?"

"What?" Stacy weakly replied, feeling her heart racing the Daytona 500.

"I'm going to kiss you now," he murmured, his hand held her cheek, feeling the softness of her flesh beneath his fingers.

"Oh really? And what makes you think I'm going to let you?" she nervously teased.

Her eager response surprised her but his touch intoxicated her to beyond extreme of just saying let's go. Somehow she managed to maintain an even breath. His thumbs were gentle as they rubbed back and forth on her lips, feeling them quiver at the caress. Her head reeled and stomach tightened at the intent, serious way studied her. Her eyes widened at his breath against her lips as he spoke.

"I just do. I can see it in your eyes but I'm not so sure what it is. You manage to keep things hidden, locked deep inside but I know it's there, just beneath the surface, aching to get out."

"What is?"

"Desire, hunger, passion, but I also see a loneliness? I don't know. But, maybe I should kiss you now." He leant closer.

"Well, maybe I won't let you."

"Who's to stop me," he whispered, slowly moving ever nearer to her face. To her tempting, slightly full lips.

Her hand slipped between them, her fingers lightly gripping onto his upper arm feeling his hand slide to her neck. "Maybe I will," she somehow managed to say through the dryness of her throat.

His lips were closer, tickling hers as he spoke. "Oh really? I don't think so. I think I won this time."

Her eyes closed when she felt him brush his lips back and forth on hers, teasing, tasting, making her more anxious for the eventful. Her hand slid to his neck urging him closer to her.

In a soft, breathless voice, she pleaded, "Matt, kiss me." A light groan slipped from her and her body relaxed to melt against his. His kiss, the gentle touch of his hand took her breath away. Matt's finger slid beneath her chin, easily tilting her head back to permit his mouth easy access to her throat. His arm enclosed about her waist easily pulling her closer to stand between his dangling legs as she pressed herself against his chest.

Leaning towards him, Stacy's arms weakly fell to her sides, resting her hands on his thighs as his persistent lips press kisses along her throat, to her ear and back to the waiting lips. Her head reeled at the luxurious feelings his touched awakened in her fatigued; combatted body.

"Oh Matt," she whispered, helplessly falling under his spell. Gasping, she suddenly felt the warmth of his hand as he slipped it beneath her shirt to her waist before lightly cupping a breast. His touch was hot through the lace of her bra. Her arms lazily wrapped around his trim waist, pulling herself ever closer to his power.

"Darling, you taste good," he murmured into her ear, wrapping her tightly in his embrace. His hand worked its magic easily unsnapping her bra, then slid to the treasure beneath, "You feel good too."

Stacy whimpered, pressing nearer, feeling her body coming to life with his attentions. She got lost with the sensuous mood, returning her passion, pressing kisses on his thick neck. Her tongue slipped from her mouth to naughtily lick at his ear, smiling at the groan emitting from him.

Easing her back a step, Matt slipped from his perch. Turning, he easily picked her up to sit her on the place he just vacated. With his eyes holding hers in a hypnotic trance, his hand slowly eased her shirt up, exposing to his hungry eyes her firm breasts. Then his mouth eagerly covered hers before slowly sliding down her throat.

Stacy's head tipped back, feeling his mouth seek the rose hardness, his finger and thumb lightly rubbed and then squeezed her other to life. She felt his hand boldly slide beneath her short skirt, higher and higher along her inner thigh until his persistent fingers slid beneath her panties, gently touching her before probing, feeling the flesh quiver around him.

What are you doing? Stacy wanted to speak but the words failed to surface. She was enjoying him, lost in his touch, his gently demanding touch. Her breathing changed to rasping gasps. She opened her legs, arched her back, pressing herself closer to his seeking hand. Her hand covered his, feeling him touch her.

Amazed with the fact that she so easily complied to his erotic wishes. A soft cry escaped from her lips as she found herself close to climaxing just from his simple caress. She pressed her hips tighter, closer to him, silently urging him on.

This was certainly the last thing on Matts mind. He wasn't meaning for things to get this far this fast but he discovered it difficult to control himself when he was near her this way. He wanted to know her all over. His slid his hand from the treasure to her thigh as he bent lower, trailing his lips down her flat stomach, wanting to taste her. Pausing, his eyes took in her diamond piercing.

That was his mistake.

When Matt stopped, Stacy gained her self-control though when she spoke, her voice was filled with breathless, passion, "Matt, what are we doing?"

He raised his head to look into her flushed features. Then watched as her hand slowly pulled her shirt down, covering herself. He saw the look of confusion in her eyes. Eyes so dark with the passionate desire he knew she felt for him.

Damn! How can she do that? How can she be in so control of herself when just seconds ago she was on the verge of total release? But, he knew she was right. Things were moving too fast even for his own liking. The hell with it. Life was too short to wait especially when the right woman was here, in his arms.

Bracing his hands on each side of her hips, he straightened his arms, raising himself to look her evenly in the eyes. His voice was husky when he spoke. "I thought I was going to make love to you."

Hearing those words coming from him in a voice filled with desire caused her heart to beat double time and her stomach tightened into nervous, anxious knots. Her confusion spread through her mind triple fold. When she spoke, it wasn't what he wanted to hear.

He knew she was lying.

"Oh, my God. I don't think I'm wanting this, not right now."

"Why not?"

She fought to rapidly get back into control of her emotions as she looked long into his confused face. "Matt I haven't seen you for so long and you're back home for two days and how many times have you seen me?"

"Two days," he easily returned.

"I've only kicked Dan out two days. I don't know what I want yet. I don't...I just don't know what to make of this. Of you."

Dan! Thoughts of jealous hate filled him. He hated that man in school always bragging about how close he was getting to making it all the way with her. That was then, this is now. Shaking those angry memories away, he pressed his lips together, hearing it in her voice the uncertainties she felt. Then he watched the passion change to a look of apprehensive; or is it fear? He must have gotten an angry look on his face as her eyes widen before her body tensed.

"What's wrong with you?" He asked her.

"You're mad."

"No, I'm not."

"Yes, you are, I see it in your eyes."

"Darling what you're seeing is desire for a beautiful woman. A desire to want to make love to a beautiful woman. I am not mad."

"Don't hit me. I'll do whatever it is..."

"Why would I hit you?" he sharply demanded. He stood to his full height while bracing his hands on his hips.

Stacy's eyes closed, mad at herself, cursing herself for her blunder. She needed to get in control of herself and try to forget those past few years with Dan. She opened her eyes seeing confusion on his face.

"Shit, did I just say that?" She angrily muttered.

He touched her bruised cheek, "Did Danny boy smack you around more than once then I take it?"

He watched her lower jaw jut out as she cast her gaze down before she answered him. Well, there was a sign he thought he completely forgotten about. It's the I can't look you in the eyes and lie thing she always did with him.

"No."

"Yeah, right," he quickly answered. When she asked if he was going to hit her, that completely destroyed the mood, hell any mood that he was in.

Straightening her shoulders, she looked him square in the face, "And, what is *that* supposed to be meaning?" she demanded, her temper flowing to the surface.

He returned a Cheshire grin. "I know you and your quirks and I have just seen one."

"You don't know me..."

"I *do* know you Stace and this nonsense about not wanting this right now, that's a bunch of bullshit too," he impatiently added, "I felt that passion in you. If anything, you're more afraid to let your wants, your needs go. You're too caught up in the thing called life."

Her mouth snapped shut as she put her hands on his chest to ease him away at his cold words. Her eyes angrily narrowed into slits as she brutally jabbed a finger into his chest with her tirade.

"I'll let you know Mr. World Traveler that I have had a tough life. I am a single parent raising a son in this often times cruel, hard world. In the beginning we have had to do without a few things but so far, we have managed quite nicely. I have to think about my son over my needs!"

Frustrated, Matt brushed her hand away. "You're only human too, Stace and humans have needs. Maybe you made a wrong decision with asshole Dan but I'm not him!"

"I didn't say that you were! I'm saying that he has been around off and on and now that I don't have him in my life, maybe I don't want another man in my life at this moment!"

A cold smile curved his lips, "Oh so that's what it is. I get it. You want to be little Miss Independent..."

"What's wrong with that?"

He slowly shook his head while raising his hands in the air, giving up. He turned to leave her sitting on the desk, I'll see you around," he called over his shoulder.

Stacy released an impatient hiss. She braced her elbow on her knee, placing her head in her hand to wearily rub at her throbbing temple. Why did men give women these headaches?

"No wait," Matt interrupted her thoughts.

She snapped her head up to see him walking back to her with a finger pointed at her. Her breath caught in her throat at the look in his bright eyes. A look of this isn't over yet until I get my final say.

"I think that you're afraid of me, maybe not me personally but what I imply to you."

Her mouth dropped open at his impertinence.

"And...just...what...could...that...be?" She slowly asked.

"Of the fact that I could bring you happiness? If I remember correctly, and I think that I do, you never cared one shit for changes in your life. You've been lonely forever yes, even with asshole Dan around, you have been lonely. Hell, I can see that in your eyes, even your actions," he knowingly stated the fact, ready for her reply.

"I am not lonely. I have Greg, remember?"

His gaze was intense, pinning her to her seat. He took slow steps to her as he nodded. His arms once again slipped around her waist, causing her to straighten to place her hands on his upper arms as he brought his face close to hers.

"Greg can't make you feel like the luscious woman that you are and asshole Dan was making you feel like a piece of meat, his property. I have partially brought that temptress vixen that I know you can be, out of her shell."

"Matt, get real. I am a mother," she began before her mouth was taken over by his in a slow, lazy kiss as his hand gently gripped the back of her neck.

She felt her resolve quickly weaken beneath his tender assault. Once again she was amazed how fast her body responded to his, wanting to feel his strength but not wanting him to know she surrendered. But it was useless. Her arms wrapped around his neck, holding him tightly to her as she fervently kissed him back.

Matt reached for her arms, struggling to remove the vise hold from his neck. Finally, he succeeded as he moved away. On his lips he wore that knowing grin as his finger traced her lips. Stacy quickly became annoyed with his sense of presumptuous, over confidant, know it all attitude with her.

"Even mothers can be temptresses. I'll see you around," he repeated this time turning with an impish smile on his face along with a chuckle on his lips.

"I hate you," she called out.

"You love it!" He replied over his shoulder.

* * *

Stacy laid buried deep beneath the covers in her warm bed. Once she finally crawled in, sleep was a long time coming. Matt's words; touches; kisses kept repeating in her head. He had her body doing things she hadn't felt in such a long, long time and she was shamefully craving more of it. He also had her so confused. Could he be right? Was she afraid to show and let out her true feelings? Even he sensed it, boldly stating she had a fear of him and true, he was the strongest presence in her heart so why did she stop him?

She worriedly bit at her lower lip as she stared to a dark ceiling, watching the slow spin from the shadow of the fan blades. A delicious shiver coursed through her as she replayed the feel of his hungry lips on her body. And then of his persistent, gentle hand very much knowing where to rub and touch brought dormant feelings back to life and he also got her so damn close to her breaking point. He definitely has matured, she thought as sleep slowly over took her to be replaced with pleasant dreams of a blue eyed man.

A patient Greg quietly stood outside of his mother's closed bedroom door. One of the rules were that he never enter without knocking first. Well, he'd been knocking for some time and she still wasn't answering.

"She must really be tired," he muttered.

He pranced back and forth wishing she would wake up. He wanted to tell her about his day with Matt and how much fun he had. Giving up, he turned to stalk downstairs to watch his show again of Blue Angel Pilots. Man, to think that he really knew one.

Stacy slowly woke to the good smelling aroma of toast and tea. Stretching, she opened her eyes to gaze at the clock. She found it already after ten in the morning. Instantly, Matt's heated kisses filled her memory. Hell, everything about Matt last night filled her memory. She rolled onto her back, taking the extra pillow with her in a hug. With a lazy grin, she crawled from the comfort of her bed to get ready for her day.

"Hey cook," she cheerfully called out when she entered the kitchen to find Greg buttering a fourth slice of toast then adding enough jelly on top for three sandwiches.

"Mom! It's about time! I've wanted to tell you about yesterday!" Greg anxiously stated as she gave him a hug.

She removed a cup to prepare tea prepared as his voice droned on.

"We had the best time. He told those three assholes from school..."

"No swearing," she interrupted, putting sugar in her glass.

"Oh yeah, anyway, he told them he was my dad and that he hoped that in the future they would conduct themselves in a gentlemanly way and stop teasing me or there would be hell to pay. Isn't that awesome?" his voice squeaked.

Stacy's brows furrowed as he rambled on.

"He bought me these really cool aviator shades. Then we went to the ball game instead of the museum. It was fun! We talked about some stuff, pilot to co-pilot stuff," he added with a devilish grin. "And then I asked if I could call him dad and he agreed. Mom, he's the best!" He finally ended, looking at her.

Stacy stared out the window. She stood as still as a statue, stunned with what she heard. Her arms were braced out to her side, her hands resting on the top of the kitchen counter. Her eyes widened and mouth slightly open as she stared at nothing out the window. Greg's excited words echoed in her mind. Those words! Those all too close to hitting home words that Matt said to his classmates that he was his dad and then later agreed that Greg could call him dad.

Could he know?   Could that be why he came back? For Greg?

Her mind reeled with all of the inclinations and she was seeing red. Slowly, methodically, her fingernails tapped the drumming rhythm on the counter.

"Mom?"

"Back up a minute Greg. What do you mean that he said he was your father?" She gently asked, turning to give him a level look as she crossed her arms in front of her.

Greg felt like a snowman in a heat wave feeling melting away to oblivion beneath her angry, heated stared. "It was nothing," he muttered.

"Gregory Cannon. It'd be in your best interest if you fess up to me. It'll be for your own good if I don't have to beat it out of you."

His eyes widened. She was kidding him. She never had to beat him. Still, he hadn't heard that tone of voice since he helped paint graffiti on the school walls last year. A minor mistake that he made to try and fit in with the wrong crowd and boy did he catch hell, a good smacking and rounding.

His fingers went to a string on the hem of his shirt as he began to twist it around. Slowly he began.

"Well, they were teasing and that's what he told them. You should've seen them stutter around."

"But why would he tell them that?" she repeated.

124

"Later when I asked, he said that every boy should have a father figure then I asked if I could call him dad and he said sure, if it was ok with me and mom, it sure is."

"Well, it isn't okay with me," she snapped, folding her arms in front of her to take on her angry stance.

"Mooom! I like Matt..."

Stacy shot him an un-withering glare. That look brought instant silence to him. He hadn't seen that look for a long, long time either.

Through clenched teeth, she spoke, "Ouuu, just wait until I see him." She vowed vengeance as she disappeared down the stairs to her studio.

The shrill ringing of the telephone broke the tension. Greg shot off to answer, thankful for the diversion from his mother's temper. "Hello?"

"Hi Greg, is your mother there?"

Greg hatefully glared to the voice on the end of the phone line. He wanted to tell him no and she never will be here again but knew how immature that sounded.

"I asked you a question!"

Greg tensed at the impatient tone. It brought back instant memories of how cruel he could be and at the few backhands he received from him, too.

"Yeah, hold on," he muttered, purposely dropping the phone onto the floor before giving it a kick against the wall.

Dan winced at the loud banging noise through his earpiece. "Brat," he hissed.

"Mom! It's Dan."

CHAPTER 12

"Dan!!!" she whispered, tensing and then automatically withdrawing into her shell. A trembling hand reached for the nearby phone. "I got it. Hang up the phone, Greg!" she called out, waiting for the extra loud click before she began. And boy did she hear it. It sounded like the receiver bounced off the wall a few times before being slammed onto the phone.   "What do you want?"

"Is that anyway to talk to your fiancée?"

"I broke that off, remember?"

"Well I didn't. Stacy, I love you and I want us to try again."

"No Dan. I will never endure what you did to me ever again."

"How can you say that? We dated through high school. When I came home; it was you I went in search of, not Sandy. We have a history."

"That isn't it."

"Well then, what the hell is it?"

Her chest rose and fell at the long, weary sigh. She rest her elbows on the desk. He didn't seem to get it. "It isn't black and gray, it's black and white. Need I tell you everything?"

"Yes. Yes, you do."

"Dan, you hit me..." she paused at the scoffing tone. "You did it to me, a lot. I tried to make excuses to myself like what did I do this time to upset you and why you were doing what you did and nothing came. I reached the end of my ropes with you and these circumstances."

After a long silence, he spoke, so soft, sincere.

"Sweetheart..."

Her eyes closed from frustration. She should just hang up but she heard the sadness in his voice but it was too late for the endearments.

"I'm sorry. I'll change."

"No. No more," she quickly answered. "Dan, to be truthful, I never truly loved you...wait, let me put it another way. I loved you but not as strong as a woman should love someone."

She knew he would become enraged at those revealing words. No doubt stunned, too. He was too proud, stubborn and arrogant to ever believe he had any kind of faults.

"I don't believe you." On hindsight, he knew that something was missing in their relationship. Finally, he understood it all and realized that whatever was missing had to be the reasons she kept dragging out their engagement. "Right. It's to whoever is the father to that damn kid of yours. That's who you love."

Her hand clenched onto the phone. "Listen to you! If you were sincere with wanting to try *and* to change that would have never come from your mouth!"

"Who was that jerk you were with the other night? And not even a day after kicking my ass out?"

"You didn't recognize him? That was Matt."

"Oh, the best friend."

She shot him an incredulous look through the phone. "Are you jealous over that still?"

"I watched how he watched you. It's the way a man looks when he's interested in a woman and sweetheart he wants you, too. I'm not about to give you up so damn easy," he voiced the threat.

Her nose wrinkled and his vehemently spoken words. Then to what he said about Matt. She never imagined that Matt truly would be interested in her but his kisses and caresses constantly remind they were now adults. Maybe he did come back for her. Her heart did an involuntary flutter with that wild thought. No, that'd be a story in a book, she silently scoffed. She shifted her mind back to her problem at hand, Dan.

"Give up because I don't want you back! I don't want any one in my life. I only want to be left alone!" She ranted, the frustration of her situation soaring through her.

"We'll see," he ended their conversation.

Stacy slowly dropped the receiver back in its place to rub a hand over her face. Dan's revealing words sent a tremor of trepidation through her. She only wanted to be left alone. Was that too much to ask? And Matt and his lustful attentions were also causing her alarm. She knew she still loved him but words were never spoken. She gave a rueful grin, actually, there was never any time to speak about anything such as feelings or emotions.

"Stacy."

She looked up as Amy entered with a huge smile across her thin lips. Her green eyes were alive with happiness as she took a seat on the edge of the desk.

"You look dreadful." She placed a friendly hand on Stacy's hunched shoulders. "What's the matter now?"

With both hands, Stacy covered her face to release a muffled, frustrated scream in them.

Amy grimaced, "Ouu, that bad?"

"It's worse than bad it's catastrophic," she muttered still hiding her face in her hands.

"It can't be that bad, can it?"

Stacy slowly raised her head to give Amy a look of total apprehension. Amy pursed her lips at that dark look.

"It's that bad. Well, tell me about it."

Stacy drew in a long breath before rattling off what all had been going on in her life since yesterday. With each sentence, Amy's mouth dropped open a little bit further. Her eyes took over a glazed look of amused disbelief.

"How can you tolerate all of this chaos in your life at once? It's a wonder you didn't pack a bag and take off for a few days to an undisclosed destination."

"Tell me. And now I have to confront Matt about this idiotic notion that Greg can call him dad! Do you believe it?" Stacy ended, her voice raising an octave higher than normal.

Amy sucked in a long breath then expelled it before slowly answering. "Well Stacy, after all, he *is* you know."

"I know, I was there," she scoffed. "But he doesn't know it. What am I going to do?"

Amy crossed her arms in front of her. Tilting her head back, she gazed at the white tiled ceiling in deep thought. She pressed her lips together and narrowed her eyes. After what seemed a long time she looked back at Stacy, "I'm staying out of this one."

"Oh well, thanks a lot dear friend of mine," Stacy added with a derisive snort.

"I know when to keep my mouth shut and this is definitely one of those times. Anyhow, I came to invite you and Greg over for a cook out this evening. Can you make it?"

"Yeah, I guess so."

"Well good. And, how about my pictures?"

"When have I had any time?"

"How about now?"

"Sure, I'll get right on it."

"You don't have to be so cynical, you know."

Stacy's features softened, "I'm sorry. You're right. The best thing to do is to not hang onto these problems until I face the idiot in person then I'll deal with it and him."

Amy's eyes widened along with an extra sweet smile before blurting out, "Did I mention the idiot will be there, too?"

* * *

Greg went to Randy and Amy's to take advantage of swimming in their pool while Stacy remained in her office, busy double checking and editing the proofs for Amy's wedding portrait. This gave her the quiet time to think and rethink what she would say to Mr. Matt Sadler as she expertly looked over the pictures. Finally, she sat back, smiling, satisfied with the outcome. Reluctantly, she went upstairs for a shower and get dressed for the party. Wearing a towel around her, she sorted through a drawer, choosing a pair of black shorts. Her hand reached for a baggie small floral shirt when her eyes fell on a strap hanging from a partially opened drawer on her dresser.

With a grin so naughty to match her mood she changed directions, reaching for the strap, pulling out a bikini top. Grinning, she slipped out of her shorts to put on a black bikini swimsuit then slipped back into the shorts, choosing to keep the top as is. She gave the bruise on her cheek a smirk as she pulled her hair into a high tail, the ends brushing her shoulder blades. Then she applied a mild amount of makeup, just enough to enhance what she had. Standing back, she eyed the finished results.

And, liked them.

Sliding her black framed sun glasses onto her face and with a nacho salad in her hands, she went to the happy gathering. Her eyes fell onto Sandy's car bringing a smirk of disgust. She should've known that she would be here, she hatefully thought. Then her eyes fell onto the Harley parked around the corner of the house. Since she didn't hear him arrive, she believed that he wasn't here yet.

His deep, rich laughter, mingled with Greg's and Ray's. Turning her head to see what they were doing, she watched them play dodge ball while in the pool. The large red and white striped ball soared through the air. As it made contact, sprays of water filtered upwards to hit Greg in the face. Steering off in the other direction, she entered the house to find Amy getting a pitcher of iced tea.

"Hi Amy," she said placing the salad in the refrigerator.

"Hello. Well? What did you get done?" Amy anxiously asked.

Stacy grinned, "I got them edited, not much touch up because of your beaming beauty and may I add they are superb. Outstanding. A masterpiece in the making. A one of a kind. You can come over tomorrow and choose the one you want enlarged for your reception."

"But could it be anything else? I can't wait. Um, I also can't miss how well Matt and Greg are getting along," Amy hinted with a grin.

"I noticed it, too," Stacy slid her glasses to the top of her head as she turned to look out the window. Then she heard it, for the first time, and it sounded nice but a mixed emotion filled her as a foreboding chill swept up her spine like the winds on the coldest winter's night howling through the bare trees.

"Dad, watch this!" Greg's excited voice called out.

She watched as Greg went to the low diving board to execute a sloppy jack knife.

"That was great but I think you'd do better on a higher board!" Matt encouraged.

Stacy bit her lower lip. Seeing them together like this is a dream come true but she had to remain angry with him. It was important if she wanted to emphasize how wrong he was. It wasn't right for him to make such a serious decision like that without letting her know. Her thoughts were so keenly focused on them that Randy's voice startled her.

"Dad?" Randy's deep voice echoed Greg's word as he entered the kitchen where Amy and Stacy stood. "Excuse me Stacy, but, have I missed something?"

Startled, she jumped. Turning, she looked into his confused face. "Believe me; I'm not very happy either. This all came about without my knowledge and he will find out how upset it has made me," she vowed.

Randy look at the dark anger on her face. "No doubt about that," he muttered, glancing out the window. "I've never seen Matt acting with any parental instinct, or heard him speak of it but he's doing it all well. He even acts like he's enjoying it."

"Oh Lord," Stacy muttered, following him outside.

They joined the others at poolside. Stacy slid her sun glasses down to cover her eyes, hopefully to cover the fact that she was glaring in Sandy's direction. Oh sure, Sandy is busy trying to get Matt to rub sun tan lotion on her back. She shoved the bottle in his hand then blatantly undid the snap at her back then half-heartedly held the front over her breasts. Smiling, she turned her back to him to wait for the touch of his hand on her back.

"Amy, how did she ever become your sister? She's such a phony," Stacy sneered, sitting in a lounge chair on the opposite side of the pool. It'd be better if she kept her distance from that schemer.

Amy refused to be sucked into Stacy's despondent mood. Instead, returned with a question. "Why don't you like my sister?" Amy gave her a direct stare, waiting for an answer.

Stacy slowly swung her head to look at Amy, flippantly replying. "I like her..."

"You're lying to me."

"All right. She's always all over him," she stopped when Amy's mouth dropped open before she began laughing. Stacy's eyes narrowed into a sharp glare as she watched Amy.

"Is that all?" Amy gasped, trying to hide her gaiety behind a hand. "You are jealous of my sister!"

"I am not and isn't that enough? She was the same back then too but with everyone."

"They dated in school!" she chuckled, loving to see her jealous. "And, we *are* supposed to be mature adults now so gets those claws back in."

"I know, I know but look at her now, falling all over him like that. He's so embarrassed."

"He's so loving it. A man likes to have a fuss made over him now and again. That's how I got Randy," she hinted with the information.

Stacy slowly slid her glasses to her forehead, giving her a level look, "And just what are you implying?"

"Show him some attention, that's all. I mean, I know that you like him, more than you let on."

If I show him any more attention, I'll be having sex with him she thought as a surprising tremor of excitement swept over her. She swore that she could, right at this moment, feel the heated touch of his hands on her and his slow kisses, everywhere. She sighed, wondering why her body said one thing but her brain screamed another.

"Besides, I'm angry with him at the moment."

They were so intense with their discussion that either didn't see Matt slowly swim towards them. He folded his arms on the edge of the pool, resting his chin on top as he looked to Stacy. Since she came outside, he kept a close watch on her, especially from the corner of his eyes as she slipped from her shorts to lay on the lounge and get some sun. Like a moth to the flame, her presence drew him nearer. Even after she had a child, her figure was still slender except for a certain maturity about her rounder hips and fuller breasts. He grinned as the sunlight glimmered from her diamond piercing. It hit him hard as he realized that no other woman stirred his blood like she did. Oh sure, a lot tried in the past. Hell, even until last week, but he couldn't forget about this special woman.

"Good afternoon, ladies."

Both turned their attention to Matt. Stacy noted the sparkle in his eyes. So did Amy who once again wore a broad smile. He has to be in love, she thought.

"Matthew," Stacy muttered through a forced smile.

His eye brows rose up with her tone. "Are you drunk? You seem to call me by my full name when you are," he teased through a smile.

With a delicate finger, she reached to her sunglasses and with a light tap, they fell over her eyes as she laid her head back.

"Or pissed," he added, giving Amy a playful wink.

"I think you'd be safer with that term," Amy chuckled.

Stacy smirked at their playful words, "Matthew, we'll discuss this later."

"Hey dad..."

The words faded in his ears as the discernable scowl formed on her face. He grinned, so that was it, Greg calling him dad. He knew that he'd definitely hear about it. It'd prove interesting and he'd be ready. He eased himself out of the water. "What son?" he replied also knowing *that* would add to her anger. He saw her head shoot up as she looked at him.

Stacy's eyes opened in time to see him push out of the pool. The lucky water ran in rivulets down his chest, stomach and legs. Her eyes widened as in one smooth move, he bent to easily scoop her into his arms.

"What are you doing?" she squealed.

She instantly felt herself being tossed in to the air. With a scream, she landed with a big splash in the water. Another loud splash followed as Matt jumped in behind. She surfaced, sputtering water out of her mouth. Her hand pushed her hair from her face and out of her eyes. Greg's gay laughter rang in the air to be joined with the others. Her hands went to her swimsuit, yanking the top, which slid upwards, back in place. She turned, watching Matt swim slow circles around her like a shark swimming for the kill.

"Ouu, you wait. You thought I was angry with you before, try totally pissed now. You're in big trouble, buster," she threatened, wiping water from her eyes.

"I can't wait," he returned, hitting his hand on the water to send sprays to her face. He laughed as she flinched.

Deciding to get this conversation done with, she ordered, "Well then follow me."

With interest, he watched her climb up the ladder to get out. Watched the water glide down her long legs as her hands roughly tug her bottoms down over her round buttocks. Like a child ready to be scolded, he silently followed. With rough yanks of her hand, she grabbed a towel, slid her feet into her flip flops to walk out the driveway towards her home.

"Must be serious," he said to Randy.

"It is," he answered giving him a salute.

* * *

Stacy vigorously rubbed her hair with a towel as she waited in the living room. With quick, angry steps, she paced, not caring that water dripped onto her carpets. She wanted to get this done with. Son! He dares to call Greg that, knowing damn well that she is already upset. When the front door closed, she spun to look into his handsome face, seeing a mixture of wonder and a playfulness still there.

"Well. What did I do to you?" He asked, keeping his alert stance in the doorway. He watched as she continued to pace, only seeing her this mad one other time and then it was over Sandy. He fought the urge to smile.

Suddenly she stopped, glaring into his amused face. Placing her hands on her hips, she began, "First thing, how dare you give yourself permission to tell Greg that it is just fine to call you dad!"

"He asked..."

"I'm not through yet!" she practically screamed.

He pursed his lips at her outburst, "Okay, sorry. Go on." He waved a hand in the air.

"It was inconsiderate of you, it was thoughtless of you, or to put it in your simple terms, it was damn wrong of you to assume that it'd be fine."

He waited a moment to be sure she was finished. "Are you calling me simple?" His eyes changed into a stormy blue with his own growing temper. She knew he was now pissed, too.

"I don't know, am I?"

"Sounds like it. This is anything but simple. Any way, you didn't see him that day and how he acted to those boys!"

"Matt, I see him every day with those boys and how he comes home extra quiet on the days those same boys have been more harassing! I see him every father's day and see that look of wonder in his eyes. I see him when he comes home from school with a note from the teacher stating it's bring your father to work week or write an essay about your father and the special things the two of you do; or write an essay about what your father does for a living. And guess what, that same teacher is dear Sandra!"

He remained quiet, his thoughts rolling.

"So I ask you one more time, how did you deem it acceptable to just come back home and simply, take over my life?"

"I told you that you didn't see him that day! Hell this is all new to me having a boy look up to me like that!" he snapped.

"Ouuu Matt!"

"He asked me if he could. The way he asked, the way he was looking at me, I couldn't tell him no. I couldn't tell him I'll have to ask permission from mommy."

"That would've been better if you had."

"Well, I think he needs a father figure around especially since this so called man that got you pregnant isn't around. And by the way, why isn't he around to help you?" There, he issued the challenge, let's see how she responds to that!

"He has other commitments! But this isn't about him, it's about you feeling like you have the okay to tell Greg what to do without consulting me first! I am his mother!"

And I'm his father! he almost shouted back. Pacing, he quickly bit the words back. He wanted her to tell him. He took in a calming breath and decided to go about things the other way. He stopped to angrily frown at her.

"There is nothing more important, no job, no commitment, nothing more important than one's child. So who is this loser?"

Stacy shot him an irritating glare before stomping past him to go up the stairs. "You don't know him," she stated.

Matt's mouth dropped open, watching her disappear upstairs, flinching when a door slammed shut. He was now at his wits end

with her. He only wanted the truth from her and even running himself into the ground wouldn't do it.

Frustrated.

Weary.

He ran a hand through his hair, looking at the stairway. Before he realized it, he spouted out the crude comment Dan had said.

"Maybe Dan's right and that you're a bit of a loose lady. Hell, you went to someone else damn fast after we made love!" He heard the door open and a gasp of rage. Before he gave her the opportunity to retort, he stormed out the front door, slamming it shut.

CHAPTER 13

"Mooom!"

Stacy looked up from the oven. She was about to put another batch of cookies in to take to her parents. Her gaze shifted to the wall clock. He was home already from school? I guess it is that time of day. "In the kitchen!" she called back.

Greg burst through the doorway, a huge smile on his face and a look of hopefulness. "Did dad call today?" His hand went for a warm chocolate chip cookie.

Her lips tightened his words. "What, no hello? Instead I get did d...dad call." Her voice faltered on the word dad.

"Hello. Well, did he?"

"No sweetheart."

"It's been two days. What did you say to him? He came back to Randy's in a bad mood."

"That's none of your concern, all right?"

"But mom, I really like him. He's the best..."

"*Greg!*" Realizing her voice came louder than intended she stopped

139

to compose herself. "Greg, please not now."

"Yeah, and you always say that too whenever I ask about him. I'm going to call Grandpa Sadler. He'll tell me!" Greg declared, spinning away to go to the telephone.

"Hold on. We're going to grandmas for supper. Maybe he'll be there, and then you can talk to him."

Those words seemed to make him happy since he came running back into the kitchen demanding to know when they would be leaving. A low rumbling noise filled the air causing further discussion to stop.

"What is that?" Stacy asked. They ran outside, looking to the skies. Four jets flew in precise formation over her home.

"Awesome!" Greg shouted, turning to watch as they did a slight turn to fly back over before disappearing into the heavens.

"Impressive," Stacy muttered.

"That was dad, I just know it!"

She'd decided to give up telling him not to call Matt, Dad. "Greg, everyone can't be him."

"But I know it. Why would they do that over our home! It never happened before!"

"All right, it was Matt," she agreed, looking to the skies. It was hard to imagine flying one of those let alone, knowing a man who did.

"Besides, they were F/18's. That's what he flies!"

"Greg, calm down," Stacy laughed at his excitement. Looking back to the skies, she realized that she felt the tremor of excitement too. It was awesome to know it was Matt flying over.

* * *

Matt landed his jet then climbed down to the waiting crew. "Good flight men," he greeted.

"What was up with that maneuver over those homes?" Mike asked.

Grinning, he answered, "That's the area where they live. I'm sure they saw us."

"Flying that low, I'm sure they saw you wave too. So your son, if he is your son, is really into planes?" Mike asked as they walked to the locker rooms to change.

"Big time. He's wonderful. Even if he isn't mine, I still love that kid," he answered, slipping from his suit.

"Now that you two met, what do you think?"

Matt and Mike's eyes met in a long stare. Both grinned before Matt said, "He's mine. No doubt about that. I just can't understand why she won't tell me."

"Maybe she isn't sure."

"That can't be either. I know she knows. Right now I have her so on edge that she doesn't know which way she's going; what she's thinking, or feeling."

Mike laughed.

* * *

Stacy finally had Greg's attention and they were about to leave the house when the phone rang. Stacy answered, her face paling with the words.

"No!"

"Yes!"

"It can't be true. Mom, you're lying, tell me that you're lying?" Stacy softly demanded into the receiver.

She slowly plopped onto the chair, numbed by the terrifying news she just received. Her eyes swept to the back yard to where Greg sat on the grass, watching the air for another fly over as he kept busy building another model of a fighter jet. He often chatted away about one day becoming a fighter pilot and now with meeting one, his interests had gone sky-high. Her eyes rolled to the heavens. Beth's voice broke into her wandering thoughts.

"I'm telling you he was here, very drunk. And you know how he gets when he's been drinking."

"Is he driving? I mean, of course he's driving. Where did he go?"

"He said he's coming to talk to you. Stacy, call the police, please."

Stacy let go a long sigh. She was hoping that she'd never have to deal with him and his moods. Lord, how she hated when Dan got this way. Since she kicked him out, he repeatedly called her but this would no doubt be the worse. They'd be repeat performances of those times when he still lived with her.

"I can handle him, mom. We'll be over."

She jumped at the screeching tires outside. After saying a quick good-bye, she hurried to the door, debating whether she should lock it but knew how futile it would be. When Dan drank, nothing stopped him. Her hand clenched onto the brass door knob. Taking in a long, shuddering breath, she bravely stepped onto the porch to face him down.

Remaining cautious, she watched as he weaved up the red brick sidewalk towards her. In his hand he carried a bouquet of flowers. It looked odd. Dan calling on her as though nothing is wrong, wanting to win her love back but he showing up sloshed to the gills. She cast a worried glance over her shoulder, hating the fact that she hadn't the time to tell Greg to hide in his room.

His voice caught her attention.

"Their she is. My lovely woman."

Stopping at the base of the steps, his body swayed as he held out the flowers to her. She remained silent, not sure what to say to him. She was tired, so tired of these confrontations. Her eyes went to the flowers then back to his face.

"Aren't you going to invite me inside?"

"No Dan."

"Hell, I'll come in anyway." He staggered up the stairs.

She backed away but his hand snaked out to grip onto her arm, turning to lead her inside. Her body tensed as a cry escaped at the tightness of his grip. Roughly, he pushed her into the living room. She spun to face him.

"What, no welcome home kiss?"

"Dan. I've already told you that we are through. Why won't you listen to reason?" She lightly rubbed the place on her arm that throbbed. Acting as though he never heard, he stepped closer.

"All I want is a kiss. I missed you sweetheart. I got you some flowers," he added, once again holding them out in hopes she would take them.

"I don't want them Dan."

His anger surfaced with her refusal. It showed in his tone and his next question as he flung the flowers through the air, at her.

She flinched as they hit her in the face, but failed to move to catch them.

"So, how is Matt doing?" He sneered, taking a seat on the couch.

"I haven't seen him."

"What's he doing back? I thought he was some sort of fly boy," he snickered.

"Randy's getting married, remember? How long have you been drinking?"

"All damn afternoon."

"Hey mom, is dad here?"

Dan swung his head to Greg, his eyes narrowing with his words. Slowly he looked back to her, "Dad? Just who the hell is he calling dad?"

"Greg, not now."

He turned, glaring at him. "Greg. Who are you calling dad?"

Greg hatefully returned that glare. He wanted to hurt him the way he always hurt his mom. Squaring his tiny shoulders, he proudly state. "Matt."

Stacy wearily closed her eyes. No, she mouthed.

Dan rose to his feet, stalking back and forth in front of her. "I've been in that brat's life forever and he has once called me dad. How the hell does Matt get off returning home and in less than a week that kid is his damn best friend?" He turned, angrily glaring at Greg.

"Go upstairs Greg, now," Stacy ordered.

"Greg, get back here boy!" He bellowed but Greg disappeared. The sound of his feet racing up the stairs then his door slamming shut filled the house. Dan turned his wrath to Stacy, noting how she stood, bravely facing him down. He needed to get her back in control. In three long strides, he was in front of her, his hands tightly gripped onto her upper arms, ignoring her wince of pain. Roughly he shook her, sending his questions to her.

"I'm warning you that you'd best tell me what the hell is going on around here! Dammit you answer before I do something," he threatened.

"Let me go! I don't have to answer to you!"

Abruptly he stopped, his mouth roughly covering hers in a drunken kiss. He pushed her against the wall, his tongue forcing it's way deep inside of her mouth. She struggled but he refused to release his hold.

Fear rose inside of her but Stacy knew she needed to keep in control of her emotions. She quickly felt herself loosing this battle as his strength easily over powered her. Becoming more determined to win, she clenched her fists, hitting him on the arms. Her stomach rolled as she gagged on the mixture of alcohol and cigarette stench coming from his breath. Her hand went to his throat, pushing on it then to his chin to try pushing it in the air.

As a last resort, she buried her teeth into his lower lip. Frustration and anger at being this helpless pushed her adrenaline level high. No, she refused to let him crush her this way. There was no way in hell she'd let him win.

The pain cut through his angry, drunken senses, then he heard her brief cry of victory when he loosened his hold. Dan took quick steps away from her as his hand went to the blood he could taste on his lip. His voice came calmer but his hands shook. He covered his face, peering through his fingers at her.

What he saw killed him inside. She wore a look on her face of fear and anger and defiance.

He slid his fingers through his long hair, "I'm sorry Stacy. Oh God, I'm sorry."

He watched as she braced herself against the wall, her arms crossed in front of her trembling body, shielding herself from any more harm. He hadn't meant to hurt her. He knew that he had to stop with the abuse if he held any hope in winning her back. But first he needed to get over this other problem he had. Greg.

With cautious eyes, she studied him, listening. She never heard him sound like that. She noticed the remorse he possibly felt and was almost taken in by his charade. Yes, a charade. It had to be that. Where did he ever show any concern for her feelings? They were rare. Even before the hitting began he was never compassionate. He always needed, craved having the upper hand in dealing with her. Gotta keep the old lady in line, he always spouted to his friends, and like a fool, she let him do it. In her own way, she had created the monster in him.

Needing to get some space between them, she took tiny, sidesteps, sliding against the wall away from him. Her eyes widened at the step he took towards her, causing her to move faster.

"Leave. Dan, leave here now." Her voice was hard, cold, as her heart froze over. Her lips pressed together, biting back any further words as he paced back and forth. His turnabout from being drunk to sober astounded her.

Dan stalled, wanting to talk to her. Hell, he needed to talk to her and try to make her listen to him. Bending, he retrieved the bouquet of flowers he threw at her to again try as he held them out to her. They were in sad shape, bent and broken. Coldly, she turned her head away. She only wished he would leave.

"Go Dan," she repeated, still looking away from him.

"We'll talk later," he softly vowed.

"Stay away from me, I mean it."

Her eyes closed as her body remained stone still, trembling inside. At the sound of the front door latching closed, she looked. On weak legs she went to the window to peer out. She remained still, alert, until he pulled away from her home. That was when she felt her strength crumble as the tears burst forth and her body shook in spasms. A cry erupted from her mouth. Slowly she fell in a trembling heap on the floor, burying her face in her hands to hopefully hide the sound.

Fearfully, Greg lay on his stomach on the floor at the top of the stairs listening, waiting, not wanting to hear the cries of pain or the sound of skin hitting skin. But they came. Tears formed in his eyes to slide down his cheeks. He glanced to the baseball bat lying next to him then back to the living room. He gripped the weapon getting ready to stand.

This time he would be ready to strike back. Stopping, he heard the door open then close. He perked up when the first cry flowed up the stairs.

"Mom?"

The sound of his sweet voice caused her more concern. Oh my God! What all did he hear? More tears erupted. She watched as Greg hurried towards her, the bat slipped from his hand, dropping with a thud onto the carpeted floor. He knelt in front of her. His hands lightly touched her arms, giving her little shakes.

"Mom? Everything will be all right."

Stacy dropped her hands to look into his face. It wasn't a face of a little boy any longer, but instead it was a face of someone who witnessed far too much in his young life.

"Greg. I'm so sorry for all of this..." her voice trailed off when the door opened.

Beth and Adam entered, alarmed when they found her on the floor. Assuming the worst, they were instantly at her side. Beth placed her hands on Stacy's face, forcing her to look into her eyes.

"Did he hit you?" Adam coldly demanded. "If he did I'm ready to search him out and lay him out cold."

"No, he only grabbed my arms this time."

"Thank God for that," Beth murmured, taking her into her arms to rock her baby.

Stacy clung to her. Soon her nerves calmed down enough to pull away. When she opened her eyes, Greg was sitting so close, intently looking into her face, watching, taking it all in. Wearily she stood. She came to a decision. Greg needed to be somewhere else just in case Dan would come back. That was when she first eyed the baseball bat lying nearby on the floor.

"What was that for?"

He shrugged his shoulders. "Just in case."

She caught on to his meaning. "Behave yourself Gregory."

"I always do!"

Stacy rolled her eyes to her parents, catching their concerned grins. With a sigh, she wrapped him in her arms, resting her cheek on the top of his head. "I know that you do," she uttered feeling so tired. A grin shaped her lips when he returned her hug.

"Someday I'll be rich and take care of you. Then we won't have to worry about Dan."

She snapped to attention, giving him a surprised look. "What?"

Greg squared his shoulders. "I hear things mom and each time he yells or hits at you, I want to do the same to him!" he angrily declared.

Again she was speechless. She could only stare at him for the first time seeing the anger in his young face. She bit her lips feeling the guilt rising.

"Oh my God, Greg I am so sorry that I put you through this shit. Maybe it'd be best if you live with grandma and grandpa until I get my life in order," she suggested to him instantly receiving a stubborn glare. Also that look indicated that he would fight her tooth and nail to stay with her.

"You mean to make sure that bastard never comes back?"

"Yes, and don't you dare give me that look. It isn't going to work."

"But mom…"

"And don't but mom me. You are going."

CHAPTER 15

The house was quiet. Too quiet. A car door closed and Stacy jumped. Gripping the bat as certain restlessness set in, she rose from her seat on the couch. Peering through the closed curtains, making sure Dan wasn't back, she double checked the window locks then the doors. As she stood near the front door, the sound of a loud bike drew near. She grew hopeful, wondering if Matt were coming to her house. Remaining watchful, she saw him along with Sandy pull into Randy's driveway. Hatefully, her eyes narrowed.

"I should've known that it wouldn't take long for her to make her move," she muttered, loathing and jealousy filling her. She stepped back when he gave her house a glance.

Disgusted, she smirked and then turned away from the view to hopefully focus on her work and try and get something done with her pictures. With a heavy heart she sat back in her chair, staring at the same portrait of a beaming, bride and groom as they stood at the altar.

"Enjoy it now, while it lasts," she muttered.

The ringing of the door chimes echoed through the house, causing her to jump. Fearing the return of Dan, she cautiously neared the top of the stairs. Peering through the curtain she grinned at Matt, standing with his hands in his back pocket. He grinned when he spied her. He showed a hand that held a bag of her favorite candy, shaking it up and down. She knew what he was doing, trying to coax her out of hiding. Temporarily forgetting her anger with him, a relieve smile spread on her lips. Opening the door, her eyes went to his hand.

"What's that?"

"I brought you a peace offering."

"M&M's. You remembered."

Her laughter came easy and he knew that he was easily winning her over. "Always. Stace, I'm sorry for what I said to you."

Her gaze went to his face, seeing sincerity. "Come in." She stepped back as he walked past, holding the bag out. When she reached for the candy, he jerked it out of her grasp.

"I wasn't done yet," he mocked the words she spoke to him.

She crossed her arms, fighting her smile.

"I've thought over what all you've said and you're one hundred percent right. I had no right to do anything where it concerned Greg until I discuss it with you. And, I will not do it again." He finished, giving her a long look. Holding the bag, he noticed that she stalled. He gave it a little shake, rattling the sweet treats inside. "Friends?"

"Friends." Her fingers brushed the brown paper as he jerked it away again. Like a little girl accidentally touching a spider web, her hand jerked away. "Matt quit teasing me."

"I have one more offer before I give these to you."

With a look of skepticism, she tilted her head to one side. "Oh? And what could that be?"

"I'd like you to accept a ride." He pointed to his bike. "Care to go?"

"What about your other sidekick?"

Oh, so she had been watching and he didn't miss the jealous tone. "Who? Sandy?"

"Who else is there?"

"I took her on a small one. She asked me but *I'm* asking you."

Amy's words repeated through her mind, 'Give him attention'. Relenting, she gave him a joyous smile. "I'd love to go."

Grinning, he gave her the candy, their fingers lightly touching, lingering before she turned to disappear, to change, wondering if he felt the jolt sparking from their touch. Soon she returned with her long hair in a braided tail. She wore a simple white tank top and faded jeans and black leather boots. His gaze slowly roamed up and down her figure.

"It'll do."

He led her to the bike. First he turned to place his helmet on her head. When he tightened the strap beneath her chin, his finger lightly touched her chin to tilt her head back so that he could look into her eyes.

He remained silent, gazing long into her dark brown depths framed in long black lashes so easily getting lost in them. They are eyes he knew he'd never forget; so revealing when she could be and so cold and hard when angered. Smiling, he slipped a pair of aviator sunglasses, he bought for her, on her face then putting his on. With a nod they were on their way to destinations unknown.

She didn't ask where. She didn't care, they were just going. She hadn't felt this carefree for such a long time. Actually, since the last time she rode with him on his trail bike did she feel like this.

Matt wore a complacent grin. So far, his plan is successfully working. He came to the quick conclusion that he needed to slow things down and get to know her all over. Obviously, she changed. She became an adult, a far too serious adult and he knew that somewhere beneath that mother exterior was that carefree girl he once knew. One way or another, he was determined to get that girl back. Twisting his wrist, he gave it the gas, getting a war hoop from her as she wrapped her arms tighter around his waist.

They drove down the highway at a fast speed the coolness of the late afternoon air feeling refreshing against their skin. Snuggling closer, Stacy rest her chin on his shoulder to watch the road in front. The feel of Matt's warm body and the way his muscles moved against her body touch exhilarated her. She still found it simply amazing that he was back, back into her life in such a peculiar way. The not having to worry about what she said or how she acted for fear of being reprimanded lifted from her shoulders and it felt so wonderful. With Matt, she could be herself. Carefree laughter floated on the wind as she sat straight, holding her arms high in the air as they continued. Matt's rich laughter filled her ears.

He glanced in the mirror, not missing the excitement on face. It felt good to know that he was the one who put that look there. "Hold on!" he yelled over his shoulder, grinning when he felt her arms return at his waist, wrapping around him. His thought strayed to another time when she clung to him, during the heat of passion. Needing to change his course of thoughts, he gunned the engine, sending them racing at a higher rate of speed. They caught up to and sped past a pick-up truck.

Greg sat in the back seat of the extended cab, his arms folded in front of him and his lower lip protruding in a pout. "I hate not being with mom." He swiped the back of his hand across his nose. "Especially knowing that she needs me."

"She'll be fine," Beth replied wishing she felt as strong about the words she spoke.

Heaving an angry sigh, he looked out the window when he heard the bike come nearer. Turning, he looked to find them ready to pass.

"Hey! It's mom and dad!" his voice rang out.

Adam's eyes widened and Beth gasped with his words, looking at one another. "Who?" Adam wondered.

"Mom and Dad on the bike. They're coming beside us!" Greg excitedly repeated, peeking his head between the seat and the window to look at them.

Stacy's hand tapped on Matt's shoulder to gain his attention then pointed to the truck. They waved then Matt gunned it to get in front of them.

Beth's eyes remained on the figures as they gradually pulled away. "Did you see the smile on that face?"

"I sure did. I believe he's good for her. Greg, who did you call dad?"

"Matt. I like him a lot and he likes mom a lot...ooopps."

Beth twisted in her seat in time to see a look of masking a mistake. "Ooopps? Greg what are you not telling us?"

"Well, I think Matt loves mom and he came home for her. Isn't that gross?"

Beth shot Adam a knowing look. Crossing her arms, she leant back in her seat, a long sigh slipping from her smiling lips. "Romantic," she said, imagining how Stacy felt when she realized the man of her dreams came after her. She had that woman's intuition going and knew where Stacy's heart truly lay. "Just like a love story."

* * *

Matt turned from the main road onto a chipped and tarred side road easily maneuvering a series of curves. Then he turned onto a dirt road through the woods as they wound through the tree cover arched across putting them in a shade line back road. Stacy kept alert, her eyes looking back and forth as she soaked in the beauty of nature. She didn't recognize it. Leaning her mouth closer to his ear, she loudly asked.

"Where are we going?"

"To a place I thought I had forgotten."

She watched over his shoulder. A tiny clearing opened in front, revealing a large pond. Tall trees grew around, shielding the edges from the sun. A myriad color of wild flowers erupted from the tall green grasses surrounding the water. They stopped, he turned off the motor.

Matt braced his feet on the ground, holding the bike up so she could get off before placing the kick-stand down. His hand reached out, fingers gently grasping onto her upper arm, stopping her, before straying to undo the strap of her helmet. He returned it to the seat then watched as she did a tiny turn, her eyes taking in the beauty of nature. Remaining silent, his vision caught the dark, discoloration. Bruises formed on her upper arms. His eyes locked onto them, swearing they darkened as he stared at them. Her voice, so soft and feminine broke his attention.

"How did you find this place?"

He shifted his gaze to find her watching him. Her natural beauty enhanced the formation of nature's beauty. The backdrop of the green watered lake with the blue evening skies reflecting on the waters and Stacy, standing with bright eyes and a look of pure awe in front of it all. Silently he cursed himself for not having a camera.

"On a fishing trip with dad, years ago. It seemed like no one else ever came when we were so I made this my own special place." He took slow steps towards her, stopping to look at the beginning sunset. Cumulous clouds tinged in pink remained motionless. The myriad shades of gold, blues and pinks blended through the clouds. "I came here a lot whenever I wanted to think."

"You never brought me here or even mentioned it."

He briefly looked onto her face before shifting his vision to the waters beyond. He thought, that's because you were what I was thinking about. Shaking away that memory, he looked at her.

"I told you, it was my special place. No one ever knew about it so, consider yourself special."

She grinned.

Holding out his hand, palm up, she trustingly slipped hers in his. His large hand easily covered hers, twining their fingers together. He led her to a large log lying near the water's edge. Sitting, he refused to release her hand. Flipping his arm up and over, he pinned her arm to the top of his thigh. He felt her hand tighten in his as she got comfortable. He glanced to her to find her looking at him.

"What's going on Matt?"

Her question was blunt, straight to the point.

"What's going on?"

"Yes, what are you doing home?"

"Randy's getting married, remember?"

"Besides that. There's something working on your brain. Something that has you so quiet. Disturbingly, thoughtfully, quiet." She paused, waiting for his reply. He shifted his gaze back to the calm waters.

"I *am* having a problem and I got a couple of months leave to help me deal with it. I'm having this certain distraction and I can't seem to concentrate on my job and I cannot afford for that to happen. Especially when I'm flying a jet. One mistake and I'm dead."

A grimace wrinkled her brow with his words. They're so final, depressed. Her hand tightened in his in a silent show of compassion.

His gaze remained on the waters. "I'm retiring this year from the Blue Angels."

"Maybe that's bothering you. You really don't want to retire."

"I have to. Age thirty-two is the oldest you can be as a Blue Angel then I go back to the Fleet. No, there's something else. Someone else."

She shifted in her seat to better stare at him. His words completely caught her attention. Someone else. Did he fall in love and need her

155

approval? She released a slight scoff with her rampant thoughts. Her approval is the last thing he needed. And the way he touched her, well, what could she say? Her eyes closely studied as he watched the sky; watched as an airliner flew over, leaving a white trail behind.

Matt became somber, casting him in a deep, quiet mood. He could feel a difference in himself. It seemed this is what he needed. To sit here, quietly with her, and watch a sunset.

"Matt? Are you okay? You're not sick or anything, are you?"

At the tender touch of her finger tracing his jaw along with the gentleness of her voice, he looked at her. The sun reflected its golden brightness in her eyes. He read concern in them. Concern for him. He grinned. With his free hand, he reached out. His knuckles lightly brushed her cheek down to her jaw feeling the satiny soft beneath his touch. His hand opened, his finger lightly tracing her lower lip before sliding to her neck.

"Do you know how beautiful you are? I mean *really* are?"

His words surprised her. Her shoulder shrugged, "I'm not sure what one would consider as beauty..."

"Well believe me. It's you," he added, drawing her hand to brush a kiss on the back then hold to his chest. "Look up the meaning of the word in a dictionary and I'd bet your name is in the description."

"Hardly," she scoffed. Her eyes narrowed. "Matt, what is going on?" she repeated. He completely baffled her.

"You're beginning to frighten me."

He looked long into her eyes deciding it was time to reveal a bit about him. "Okay. A lot has happened since I have left, but our last encounter has overwhelmed me, my mind as I played that memory over and over and I wished to hell I never had to leave. I've been in a lot of relationships over the past years, always searching but never finding. Other relationships I've been in haven't worked. They can't work. Not with a brown eyed bewitching beauty on my mind."

CHAPTER 15

Stacy relaxed her jaw and eyes widened from the profound words. Her breathing shallowed and soon she felt the slight swoon as her head began a slow spin. Matt watched her with concern, fearing she was about to pass out. He dipped his head lower to gaze into her shocked face.

"Stace?"

"Oh my God," she whispered. "This is the last thing I expected to hear especially from you."

Stacy shifted her eyes to the calm waters in front of them. What a contradiction. Nature was so still, calm and she was a smoldering, train wreck mess. Her thoughts whirled like a loose mass of leaves lifting in the air during a violent wind storm. Matt couldn't quit thinking about her? Her emotions ranged from a torrent of highs to lows. Then she felt his hand on her arm, lightly gripping.

Matt worried that he spoke to soon regarding his feelings. Hoping to get her thoughts somewhere else, he looked down to her arms, seeing the bruises. Though he had a good idea where they came from, he needed to hear her tell him. When he spoke, his voice sounded hard, more menacing than he intended.

"Did Dan do this, too?"

Glancing down, she found his fingers covering the bruises. It was the exact, identical spaces where Dan's fingers tightly held onto her. His imprint formed on her skin. She lifted her face to look into Matt's eyes and saw anger burning deep in their depths.

"Did he?" He asked.

"Today. He came over wanting me back. Words turned into action." She spoke so soft, so low and kept her gaze averted from his, shamed to be in such a situation with a man.

Matt silently vowed to seek him out and have a few words with the caring man. "I can fully understand why you don't want a man in your life now. That jerk instilled a fear and mistrust in you."

Releasing his hold on her hand, he swung his arm over her head to wrap around her shoulder. He eased her against him, smiling and feeling content when she laid her head against his shoulder.

With a slight sigh, the tension began to slip away. She laid her arm on top of his thigh, savoring this moment of quietly sitting next to this strong willed, charismatic man whom she fell in love with so many years ago as she discovered something she kept hidden deep inside. Something she swore she would keep hidden forever.

Her heart never forgot him either.

A revitalization seeped into her body, her soul. The feeling of wanting his touch as he made love to her. No!! Her mind screamed the warning. Stay away from him. He'll only break your heart all over when he leaves. Despite her raging inner battle, a smile curved her lips when she felt him press a kiss on the side of her forehead and then resting his cheek.

"How would you like to watch a practice session of the Blue Angels?" Matt asked.

"Really?"

"Yes. That's where I go every day to keep on top of things."

"Was that you today over the house?"

"Ahhh, you noticed us."

"Couldn't miss you with the noise between the jets and Greg shouting," she laughed.

"We'll get everyone together and go later this week. I need to get clearance first. Can Greg get out of school?"

"Yes. There are only a couple of weeks remaining anyway. And he'll love it."

"You mean that you're going to actually tell him? Is that a good idea? I know how excited he can get."

"I think it would do him good."

* * *

The night sky showed blinking light trails of jets mingling with the stars. Greg sat on the porch steps watching them as he anxiously waited for Matt to return. Beth and Adam quietly sat on the porch swing, each noticing Greg's anxiety. Since they spotted Matt and Stacy on the bike, he had been antsy. In the distance came a distinct sound of the bike as it soon came louder to pull into the driveway. He watched Matt get off before calling out his name.

"Dad?"

The word drew the attention of Beth and Adam. Once again they looked at one another then to Greg.

Matt's head jerked up when he heard Greg's voice. "Greg, what are you doing up?" He asked, taking long strides towards him.

Greg dashed from the porch, meeting him half way. His arms wrapped Matt's waist. Matt paused, surprised at the show of affection before embracing Greg in a long hug. This felt so damn good, too. Releasing his hold, Greg took a step away.

"I wanna know how things are going. Is mom in love with you yet?"

"Greg," he scoffed. "It's going to take a while."

"Well, how long?"

Matt chuckled at his impatient tone.

"That's something a person never knows. It just happens. Remember, it's our secret."

"Uh..."

Uh oh. He recognized that tone. "What did you do?" Matt asked, bracing his hands in his back pockets.

Greg's hands slipped into his own back pockets. "Uh, I sorta, kinda let a bit slip to Grandma and Grandpa."

"Which ones."

"Cannon."

"Greg. Even though I did reveal my feelings this evening, which seemed to scare the living sh...daylights out of her, she can't know what I'm up to."

"I'm sorry dad."

* * *

The brightness of the sun already filled a blue sky when Stacy slowly woke to the silence of her home. Her finger lightly traced the area on the corner of her lips where Matt placed the gentle good night kiss before leaving. Contentment engulfed her as she grinned. He suddenly became a gentleman. The memories of those many fervent kisses they already shared heated her body and she started to wonder why he wasn't as persistent?

Then Amy's words filtered into her groggy mind, 'Show him some attention.' Sighing, restless, she rolled onto her back, flinging an arm out to the side, imagining Matt here with her, his hand stroking her body; bringing her to life as he made passionate love to her. The emotions were strong with the desire she aroused with her erotic thoughts. A familiar tightening formed in her loins and she realized that she wanted him more than she cared to admit.

Sighing, she rolled onto her stomach, resting her chin in her hands. She wondered what it'd be like to be with Matt the man in place of the young Matt she knew. She bit her lower lip at that precious memory she held so dear.

"Oh, for crying out loud!" she squealed. "I can't believe that I'm lusting after the touch of a man I only knew one time. What has he done to me? Good Lord! He seems to have worked his way into my blood! He's constantly in my thoughts and my dreams. Even my imagination!" Looking at the clock, she decided to go to her parents' home. She sure missed hearing Greg. He always helped to keep her grounded at times.

* * *

"Mom? Dad?" Her voice called out as she entered the kitchen.

"In here," Adam replied, "Your mom and Marge have Greg with them." He answered her unspoken question.

Bending, she brushed a kiss on his rough cheek before grabbing a banana from a cut crystal bowl on the kitchen counter. Taking a quick glance out the window to the Sadler home, she found the bike in the back yard but no sight of the owner. He must still be in bed, she thought.

"Okay, he'll love that. Ya know, I think I'll go for a walk and take a few photos."

He gave her an unsure look. "Since when have you taken a walk back there?"

She grinned, "I don't know. I seem to be feeling nostalgic today. I'll be back later." Grabbing her camera, she began her journey back to

162

the past.

It was a day of reminiscence of the last time she visited. The air was warm, almost next to being humid for mid-morning. Stacy slowly strolled the remains of dirt path through the fields and woods, the path now partially overgrown with the undergrowth of the abundant green fern and may apple. She paused, the white blossom from the may apple catching her attention. The angle of the sun shining from behind, gave it an almost ethereal presence.

Kneeling, she focused her camera on the delicate white wild flower, snapping a few pictures of it. Then a grouping of morel mushrooms growing among dead leaves and red blossoms of the native wild flow, Five Stars caught her eye. Pivoting on her heels, she gave this natural art exhibition her attention.

Soon she came upon the old neighborhood swimming hole. With uncertain steps, she advanced to the large flat rock where branches hung over now shading part of it. Stopping in the center, she gazed at its smooth surface, remembering the last time she was here and what happened. A chill fingered down her spine at that heated memory.

Funny how time changes but places don't, well, at least some places don't. Why had she never come back after Matt left? She didn't necessarily change, she just became a mother and got a bit busy for doing things like this.

Her gaze fell on the smooth, mirror surface of the clear water. Low branches hanging over the embankment reflected on the water giving the area a near secluded appearance. With the heat of the day making her body hotter, the water sure looked inviting. Well, what's stopping her now? Nothing, that's what. Casting a mischievous gaze back and forth and down the path the led to the woods, she heard nothing.

Surely, people didn't use this any longer. There weren't tell-tale signs of teens using the place as a party area. No empty beer cans; condoms or cigarette butts anyplace.

She stripped her shorts from her hips to drop them on the rock.

Then removed her camera from her neck to set on top before covering it with her tank top to protect it from the heat of the sun. Next she removed her shoes and underwear. Slowly, she progressed down the short dirt path to the cold water. Testing it with a foot first, she jumped at the spring mountain coldness.

"Just do it," she said before taking sure steps into the clear stream, dunking beneath the surface to get her body used to it.

* * *

Matt woke from a restful sleep. Remaining quiet, he lay in bed reliving last night with Stace. He grinned at the memory of her freedom from being a mom. If even for a little while, she enjoyed herself. Yeah, he decided, that's what she needed more of, the feeling of being uninhibited. After dressing, he went to get a cup of coffee. Peering out the window, he was pleased to see Stacy's Jeep parked in her parent's driveway. Changing his course, he went outside. Adam had his truck parked in front of hers, washing it. He smiled as Matt come closer.

"Hi Matt, what can I do you for?" Adam asked, holding the hose in the air in light mist to enjoy the water hitting him.

"Hello, Mr. Cannon. I'm in search of your daughter. Is she nearby?" Matt blinked as some of the water hit him on the face.

"I think she went for a walk. Maybe twenty minutes or so now."

"Which way?"

Adam aimed the spraying nozzle in the direction behind the house. "I do believe that way."

"Thanks."

Matt followed the trail he knew by heart. Hell, he and Randy were the ones who put the trail there in the first place so many years ago with their bikes. Ducking the low hanging branches, he walked through the waist tall weeds. Pausing, his gaze hungrily fell on the feminine, bare back. Daily, he fought the desire but found her constantly in his thoughts. Now watching her in her natural beauty only managed to add fuel to the fire.

Stacy stood in a shallow part, the water reaching just above her hips before bending to glide into the deep end beneath the water then resurfacing a good fifteen feet away. She wore a relaxed smile on her lips. Her hand swiped the excess water from her eyes. She always hated that, he remembered. Removing his shirt, he walked onto the rock watching as she swam, the underbrush reaching over the water helping to keep her out of his hungry sight. That was when his eyes fell on the strap peeking from beneath her discarded shirt.

Bending, he reached out his arm, his hand picking up the camera. Sitting down, he focused on her naked body, the water softly diffusing the flesh to his eyes. He snapped a couple of pictures then waited as she resurfaced and with his dumb luck, with her back to him. She reached her arms out to her sides, lightly skimming her hands on the top of the water before scooping handfuls to let run down her chest. Matt wished she faced him as he patiently, quietly waited with the lens pointed in her direction. With his patience thin, he pursed his lips.

He whistled.

CHAPTER 16

There it came again, a whistling bird chirp she never heard before. Stacy's brows furrowed. Ignoring it, she heard it again. Suspicious, she raised her arms in front of her, crossing them at the wrists. Slowly her head turned as she looked over her shoulder.

Smiling, he pressed the button, getting a few shots of her looking at him as she slightly turned body, her arms up covering her breasts, her beautiful face looking over her shoulder. Then another as her mouth dropped open, shocked to see him there.

"These are mine," he called out, chuckling at her stunned silence still taking pictures.

"Uh, uh...no, they aren't!" she finally squealed, managing to find her voice.

"Yes, they are and you are going to develop them for me," he knowingly added.

"No I won't."

"Then you won't get your camera back will you?" he teased while placing the camera down. In one fluent movement he stood, easily sliding his shirt upwards, stripping from his chest, up and over his head. Then his hands went to the snap of his jeans, removing them.

Her eyes widened, a gasp of alarm escaping from her stunned

lips. Finally, she demanded, her voice quivering. "Now what are you doing?"

"I'm going to take a swim. It's a hot day today."

Before she could protest, he was already stripped down, diving into the deeper end. Stacy remained motionless, her shocked eyes widened at his very taut, masculine physique before he disappeared beneath the water. A tremor of unexplained excitement swept over her, sending the hairs on her arms to stand on end.

"Did *he* ever mature. I am in deep shit trouble," she nervously muttered, surprised at the how her body reacted when she witnessed him in all his glory. Hot, wanton thoughts of undeniable pleasure filled her senses of wanting to do anything, *anything* with him. Frozen to the spot, she kept looking around the water to see his form. Gasping, she finally felt his warm hands on her legs as they glide up her hips to her waist as he emerged behind. Just as quickly, his hand reached to her head to easily dunk her beneath.

She sprang up, sputtering and wiping the water from her eyes before giving him an angry glare. She lowered herself, the water lapping against her shoulder, hoping she was shielding her nakedness from him. Playfully, Matt's hand repeatedly smacked the water, sending sprays towards her face. He watched as she flinched with each time the water hit her.

"Do you still hate that?" he laughed.

"Yes, now quit it!" she squealed. "Ouch."

He stopped as her hand went to her eye. "What's wrong?"

"There's something in my eye, thank you very much," she complained, rapidly blinking in hopes of dislodging the foreign object.

"Here, let me take a look."

She felt his gentle hands on each side of her face, easing her higher from her coverage to tilt her head back so that he could see. His thumb gently tugged the lower part of her eye down to hopefully find what was inside.

Stacy kept her arms in front trying in vain to conceal her bared breasts but the warmth of his stomach and chest so close to her had a definite titillating effect on her. Try as she might, those damn nervous shudders persisted to course through her. Why did he make her act like a school girl? She hadn't willingly been with a man for a long time. The encounters with Dan was usually from force resulting in receiving bruises, somewhere.

Shaking those disturbing memories away, her gaze focused onto Matt's handsome features as he so intently studied her eye. Her gaze strayed to his kissable lips pressed in a firm line as he continued searching. She wanted to feel those lips on hers and anyplace else he wanted to put them. At the heated thought, she noticed her breathing coming shorter. Nervously, her teeth played with her lower lip, praying he didn't notice her slight discomfort. Matt shook his head.

"I don't see anything," he muttered as his eyes roamed onto her face seeing the unhidden desire as she looked at him.

He knew that look and felt the want, the need too. For twelve long agonizing years, he felt it and fought it. Today, he wasn't going to and hoped he read the same want, desire in her eyes. Releasing a long breath, his head dipped down. His mouth took possession of her very tempting, parted lips. His arms slipped beneath the water to pull her tighter into his embrace, delighting when he felt her arms slide around his waist, pressing her full breasts against him.

His mouth moved from hers, sliding to her curve of her neck as her head fell back luxuriating in the strong emotions bursting forth. He heard her soft moan of pleasure before his mouth again captured hers, slanting to slide his tongue into the heat. He pulled slightly away to gaze into her dark eyes.

"God, your body is so smooth, you feel good."

"I'm wet..."

He grinned at the naughty inclination, "Ouuu," he whispered, his hands sliding where they willed to her hips then buttocks to ease her against him.

"I...I mean, from the water," she stammered with a blush, feeling his hardness press into her stomach.

"Oh it isn't because you want me?" he teased with his lopsided grin, his blue eyes holding a naughty stare.

Stacy paused in her reply. Her gaze held a hunger she felt. Yes! Yes, she wanted him! Why did she always stop herself? Deep down she knew why. Things would change. Their friendship would be jeopardized once they'd be together. She felt the heat of his hand stroking her back to squeezing her buttocks arousing her senses. She released a long breath at the need coursing through her.

Damn the possible jeopardizing!

Feeling the passionate, deep, desirous, rising inside, she whispered. "Oh Matt, I do want you."

That's all he needed to hear. His hand caught her wet hair. His lips covered hers in a sensuous kiss. He walked her backwards through the water to the grassy embankment, briefly breaking contact to lay her down. He followed, his elbows holding him up as his body lay off to the side as a leg lay between hers. Instantly his lips met hers, his kiss becoming intent with the need of have her.

Stacy returned his kiss with unbridled hunger, savoring the touch of his hot flesh on hers, of his tantalizing kisses. Kisses that made her shudder, silently begging for more. She felt his mouth slide from hers, nibbling on her throat before trailing kisses to her chest. She felt his hot mouth cover her flesh, trailing a path to her breasts. His teeth lightly nibbled, tugging her nipples to hardness before gently suckling causing her to moan with pleasure.

Her hands lightly lay on his shoulders, feeling him slide further down her quivering body, kissing her stomach. His teeth lightly tugged on her diamond navel piercing then moved further until he found what he was in search for. His hands held her legs open, kissing her before licking at her inner depths. His deep moan of longing filled her ears as a whimper of fulfillment slipped from her.

Her legs sensuously slid over his broad shoulders, her toes pressing into his back as he made slow love to her. She felt his hand slide from her inner thigh to her opening, rubbing then lightly probing as his tongue glide along. Every soft touch, gentle caress brought her soul back to life. Her breathing now came labored, her fingers slid through his short hair, elevating her hips, pressing herself down, wanting the release she so craved. His mouth remained on her, giving her pleasure.

Her body was on the verge of losing control. Her back arched and she was so close to going over that wonderful sensation of total release.

Then he stopped.

Startled, her eyes shot open to see him moving to hover above her, moving to lay between her legs, bracing his hands on each side of her shoulders. He looked into her face. "You are a beautiful woman."

"You mean that you stopped to tell me that?" She panted, her grip tightening on his upper arms with hopes of urging him down on her hot, starved body. Her eyes boldly held his, watching the smile play on his lips.

"An impatient, beautiful woman," he added as he slowly entered her aroused, waiting body. "Ohhhh yeaaah," his groan escaped.

Slowly he moved, her body moving with him. He felt her legs slide up his waist, taking all of him into her hungry core. Her fingernails raked across his shoulders, the gentle pain causing a guttural moan from his throat. Her body pressed towards him. Laying his length on her, his mouth covered hers in a deep kiss.

Stacy broke the contact, her lips trailed slow hungry kisses down his throat; to his ear lobes. Her tongue traced their outline. She couldn't get enough of his touch, taste. She heard the sharp intake of his breath. Her eyes opened when she felt his weight leave her. He straightened his arms to gaze into her face and she saw a look of possibly love?

He wanted to watch her face; watch how she looked during love making. Her lower lip being held by her white teeth. She kept an even pace with him as he took her along on the ride. A cry of pleasure escaped from his mouth as he thrust deeply into her, spiraling out of control to finally meet with a forceful commanding wave after magnificent wave. Her hands clutched at his shoulders, keeping the rhythm, wilding moving until both lay numbed, sated with the delicious conclusion each strived for.

Bending his arms, his lips meld with hers in a lazy, kiss. Taking comfort in the feel of her hands lightly roaming over his chest, to his shoulders to languish down his arms. He moved away to pull her against him, for the first time in forever feeling the sense of completion, contentment, hell, so peaceful. His eyes remained closed, resting his chin on the top of her head. Their breathing slowed to normal as they lay in the afterglow. He never felt so calm, so relaxed after making love with a woman. Not like this. A slow smile formed as he felt kisses on his chest and neck then her hand lightly lying where her lips were.

Stacy curled her tired body against his. She could not believe that she and Matt made wondrous, exciting love. He was definitely more experienced in the art of love making too. She had only been with two others and they always managed to leave her with a feeling of needing more, missing something. With Matt, she felt near exhaustion, satisfied.

Very satisfied.

His hand cupped her chin to ease her face upwards. Opening her eyes, she found his blue eyes looking, studying her; seeing a strange light in them as if he searched for something.

Matt remained silent as he studied her flushed features, he knew that he helplessly fell deeper in love today. He wanted to shout it to the world. He wanted to jump up and down for joy, take her into his arms and never let go. God, he wanted to tell her but knew that he couldn't. He shouldn't, not yet. That may cause her to once again become the distant woman and possibly make her pull away and he knew he could bear such a significant loss as that. He felt the need to apologize for his haste in their union. He wanted to wait for a better place, not here on the rock. He shifted his body onto his side to look her in the eyes.

"I'm sorry Stace."

Her body tensed. Her gaze froze, locking onto his lips, watching those words trail into the breeze, sending her back to twelve years ago when they finished and he said the same damn thing. It could only mean one thing; he was leaving again! The ache suddenly filled her chest. Pressing her lips together to still them, she put the wall up. Hell no, she would not cry! Not this time.

"No," she issued the lone word. She didn't want to believe that it was happening all over.

"Huh?"

She didn't want to be hurt again and damn if she would let it happen. This time she'd hurt him. Her words came cold, cruel, "Was it a mistake this time, too?"

"What?"

She roughly pulled from the haven of his arms, standing to rush to where their clothes lay. Her voice was sharp with her anger. "I said, was it a mistake this time too?"

CHAPTER 17

Matt felt confused as he looked at her with disbelief. Just what the hell is she speaking about? He only said he was sorry. Why would that piss her off? For the life of him, women were nothing but a total mystery and sometimes he wondered why he even bothered.

"What are you talking about?" He remained alert, watching, waiting. Then it came. The thing that men couldn't seem to endure that a woman did. The sound came again. His eyes briefly closed with remorse when he heard the first sniffle. He silently watched her struggle fighting those damn tears. With quick movements she yanked her underclothes on and then her shorts and top before turning to watch as he stood to walk to her.

"Stace."

Her eyes slowly roamed the length of him then closing when she noticed his eyes darkened to a stormy blue.

"What the hell are you talking about?" He repeated. "What you said sure isn't making much sense."

"Put some clothes on, Matthew," she spat.

He rolled his eyes to the heavens. Matthew. Now he knew for certain that she is pissed about something. Bending, he retrieved his underclothes and jeans as she turned away.

She kept her back to him, her arms folded and fingers angrily tapping as she listened to him getting dressed. The light touch of his hand on her arm sent a jolting fire through her veins as he eased her around to face him. She stubbornly pressed her mouth in a firm line. She crossed her arms tighter in front of her, a toe patiently tapped as she waited for an explanation.

His voice was gruff with his impatient anger. "Was it the term mistake? Is that what set you off?"

"Perhaps," she remarked with a dainty shrug of her shoulder.

Bingo, he realized.

"No. It wasn't a mistake this time or the last time."

His confessed words slightly surprised her but she wasn't about to let him see it. She folded her arms tighter against her as she tipped her chin upwards a bit more.

"Twelve years ago when I used the term mistake it was because after I, we made love, I didn't want to leave. I just had to." The annoying tapping came to a fast stop. Her mouth slightly dropped open with his words.

"Oh..."

"And it was a mistake this time because, you said that you didn't want a man in your life right now. That part is the mistake, for you anyway. For me, it wasn't. I'm just sorry that I didn't, couldn't wait until you want someone..."

He stopped at a slight grin on her lips. Deciding to strike when her emotions were soft, he began rattling off apologies for anything and everything that he did. Gesturing to the air, he began.

"I'm sorry that I didn't keep in contact with you. I'm sorry that I can't forget about you. I'm sorry for never coming back home. I'm just sorry Stace that I wasn't here for you when you needed me."

Stacy couldn't help but smile. He was being so apologetic for making her feel like she was a woman; like she was wanted, needed by someone besides her son. Needed by a man. Sure, he didn't know it but that's how he made her feel. But on the flip side, his words also confused her.

"Is that why you were being, let's see, what word am I thinking? Um. Chivalrous? Gallant, patient, courteous, giving."

Relaxing with her change of mood, his hands slid to his back pockets. "Well, if that's what you care to name it then yes, suppose I was."

She stepped closer in front of him. Her hand lightly touched his bare chest. Standing on tip toe to press a kiss on his cheek, he bent to receive it.

"Thank you Matt," she whispered, taking the step away.

"Thank God we're back to Matt. You're very welcome." Bending he picked up the remainder of his clothes and her camera. Holding his hand out, palm up, she easily placed hers there. He pulled her nearer as they slowly walked the trail. Back to the present. Back to reality. He held her camera in the air, to remind her. "Remember, you have to develop these for me."

She heaved a steady sigh, "All right."

* * *

Greg impatiently sat on the top step of back porch, watching the field for their appearance. He bit at his lower lip from anticipation, worry about what could be happening. When he found out where they were, he wanted to go search but Adam kept stopping him. Gasping, he perked up seeing them walking towards the house. A huge smile crossed his face as he noticed them walking hand in hand. Hopefully things were going their way and she was falling in love with him. How cool would that be, he wondered. Standing, he jumped the four steps to the grass and then took off at a run to join them.

Stacy stepped away from Matt, reaching out an arm to Greg as he turned to stand between them to walk along.

That evening, Stacy worked in her studio while Greg went to Randy's to swim. She had just gotten Amy's portraits back from the developer, framed them and was admiring her work when she spied the camera she used today. Instant memory flooded her of what exactly could be on that card. With a nervous grin, she picked it up and decided to see what was on it and get them developed for him.

She placed the card into the reader, waiting for the program to open on her computer. Her hands paused on the button, thinking about today and everything that transpired between them. What had she been thinking? Definitely not with her brain. But yes, with her body. When he touched her, oh Lord the way he touched her, looked at her in the manner that he did, well, she fell apart. Oh well. It was done with. She and Matt made great, satisfying love under the blue skies and she wasn't regretting it.

Grinning, she watched for the pictures to download. Once again her hands paused, as it slowly dawned on her. The truth was, she never even thought about it but there was no protection worn. Her eyes narrowed at the implication. Could it happen twice? Put it back in your mind. Softly she exhaled as the images appeared, one by one on the screen as she relived today's events. A grimace of disbelief formed on her face as she waited.

"Oh my..." she whispered. "How long had he been watching me? Fifty-seven shots?"

She sat back, eyeing the photographs shown to her as a slide show. Her gaze scanned them as she looked very, very inviting for any man whose testosterone level was kicking in high gear, and his definitely was. She gasped at the sudden knocking on her door.

"Stacy, are you in there?"

Dan? Damn, I thought I locked my door. What does he want?

"Yes. Just a moment. I'll be right up," she called out, grabbing onto the constant companion baseball bat before taking the stairs.

Dan watched as the door opened a bit then she managed to slide through before closing it behind. Stacy sniffed the air and smelled no alcohol coming from him and that surprised her. Her voice remained cold.

"What do you need Dan?" she repeated, hiding the bat behind her in one hand.

"Is that anyway to speak to the man who loves you more than life itself?"

She shot him a get real look. "For a man who loves me so damn much, he sure knows how to put bruises on my body," she declared.

The words hit him hard. Before he could speak, she began.

"Dan it's come to this. I am done. I refuse to play games. If you don't quit harassing me like this, I'm going to get a PFA order against you."

He straightened at her verbal slap on the face. "I'm sorry for being such a horses' ass about this, but it's been bothering me for my whole life but I need to know one thing. Who is Greg's father? Is it me? We were together yet you won't tell anyone."

Stacy ran an impatient hand through her hair as she bit her lips together.

"I mean, he looks like me, then again, he doesn't."

"Dan. If he were yours. I would tell you."

He began pacing. "You know this is what's been my trouble. You wanted to wait for marriage before we had sex but some ass nails you and gets you pregnant and you never marry him. This guy who, may I add, remains anonymous is running around, never paying child support. You expect me to pay for things for Greg..."

"I've never expected anything from you. I have never asked anything from you either!" She snapped. "You know what, just leave me the hell alone! Please! That's all I want from you more than anything in the world!" She demanded, turning to slam the door shut on his face.

* * *

Sandy opened her front door, surprised to find Dan standing there. Years ago he had made it perfectly clear that he wanted nothing to do with her, ever! And she obliged him, wanting to keep the voices of the people from talking any more than they had. Still, the speculations flew around the small community, very strong, especially when both she and Stacy become pregnant close to the same time and both were seen in the company of Dan Black.

Curiously, she eyed him. Despite thinking about how attractive he looked wearing a tight shirt and jeans over his hard body, she still remained wary of his serious demeanor. He stood on her doorway acting as if it was natural he were always here, calling on her. Truth be known, he rarely spoke, especially since the birth of Ray and that had been twelve years ago. It had been a mistake, a huge mistake.

She bit at her lower lip before speaking in a voice as cold and distant as her eyes, "What do you want?"

He chuckled with sarcasm, "Seems to be the normal question of the night. Can I come in?" Relenting, she stepped aside, permitting him entrance. He wrapped her in his arms, pressing a soft kiss on her cheek then muttered, "I want you to tell Mr. Matthew Sadler that Ray is his son."

"But he isn't and you know that," she responded, leaning her torso back.

"Come on, do it for me," he seductively urged, taking her deeper in his arms.

Knowing what he was up to, Sandy pulled from his inviting embrace. Her eyes shot murderous daggers into his. "No. I won't. Ray is not his, you know it and I know it and Matt would know it."

"I don't give a shit. I want you to tell him that."

"Why?" She stubbornly stated the one word, her hands bracing on her hips as the tender moment slipped away.

"I got my reasons."

"What would that gain me? He knows that we didn't do anything before he broke it off with me."

She flinched as Dan's large hand slapped onto the kitchen table. "Didn't that son of a bitch hurt you when he broke it?"

"Yes. But I got over it. Unlike someone else," she insinuated, giving him an even glare.

Taking a step back he asked, "What?"

"When you and Stacy broke up, you have done nothing but to let your anger fester over all of these years. I don't understand why you remain so passive about her but you need to move on and let her alone forget whatever it is that she did that has pissed you off so badly; get rid of the anger that you harbor."

Dan's eyes narrowed into an intent glare. "Just do this."

She crossed her arms while fearlessly demanding, "Why? Why should I help you to get a woman back who doesn't care if you breath?" She simply asked, then it slowly dawned on her. The possible reason Dan was such an angry man. "It's Matt isn't it." She stated with an understanding nod.

"What?"

"For crying out loud! Now I remember. Matt and you never got along and the main reason was because he and Stacy were best friends."

"You are way off target lady," he growled, taking a long drink of his beer.

Her gaze turned thoughtful. "Oh no. I don't think that I am. You need to begin over and to forget about her. The best way is to find someone else to love you."

She remained silent, hoping he would catch her meaning. She always loved him. Yes, despite his temper, she adored Dan Black, praying that one day he would open his eyes and see which woman was really good for him and it wasn't Stacy Cannon.

With an angry hiss, he stomped away, slamming the door behind, to leave her alone in her apartment. With a nervous clenching and unclenching of her hands, she watched out the window as he got into his truck, even more curious with his words.

CHAPTER 18

"It's here! It's here!" Greg happily called out.

"I know. We all know thank you, Greg," Stacy answered.

The day finally arrived to watch the practice of the Blue Angels. Stacy was so relieved that the day was here since she made the mistake of telling Greg about Matt's offer and four days later, she was a total basket case with his demands to know when, where, what time, when were we leaving and the list went on. Each time Greg asked her about it, she realized that Matt was right. She should have remained silent on the whole ordeal until they were parked and sitting in their lawn chairs.

It was early afternoon when the family arrived at the air strip and placed their chairs along the edge of an airport field. Everyone chattered at the same time, anxiously waiting for the pre-show to begin. Greg pranced up and down the fence line, straining to see Matt. His fingers tightly gripped onto the metal fence and eyes grew luminous as he recognized the crew members dressed in flight suits.

"Awesome," he spoke, his words gaining the others attentions.

Stacy had her camera ready, already taking a few shots of the blue jets tipped in bright yellow sitting on the grounds. Each had a number painted in yellow on the tail. They were so impressive and to think these men flying them fought in war battles to protect and serve our country. A tremor of excitement nervousness swept over her at the realization of

Matt being one of those men.

"There's Dad!" Greg squealed, his finger pointing in the direction.

The others looked in the direction he pointed. Stacy took a picture of Sam Sadler standing, his chest puffing out with the pride he felt. Then, she looked at Matt and felt herself swell with pride. He looked magnificent in his flight suit.

The sixteen men from the team stood around, talking among themselves. She zoomed the lens, getting quite a few good candid shots. They seemed to be so at ease as they laughed with one another while casually holding their bright yellow helmets in their hands by the straps or tucked beneath their arms.

Then all snapped to attention as an older man joined them. After executing crisp salutes, they began talking. She watched as Matt pointed in their direction, the older man turning to look. Shortly after, they climbed into the cockpits to fire up the huge, metal beasts causing Greg to begin jumping up and down, his cheering voice getting lost in the wind.

"Greg, wait until they take off!" Sam laughed at the over anxious boy.

The show began as they taxied in formation to the beginning of the strip. Then in a rush of high powered jets and low rumble, they took off, zooming straight up, high into the air. Soon the precise flying techniques were displayed from the blue devil dive where long lines of white smoke trailed behind to the grouping, appearing to be soaring hundreds of miles through the sky but only inches apart. Suddenly the lead broke left as the others maneuvered to the right all doing spirals.

The flights demonstrated was so graceful and aerobatic that it was hard to imagine anyone maneuvering the tight formations at such a high rate of speed and not have a collision. Stacy gasped when two jets soared towards one another then they flipped over, just missing to spiral away. The one was Matt.

"Oh my God," she muttered with disbelief, her hand going to her chest hoping to quell the rapid beating.

Amy leant towards Stacy, not missing how intent she was watching. "Excuse me; are you my best friend, Stacy Cannon?"

Stacy snapped her head to the left, looking into her amused face. "What?"

"I was wondering what you did to my friend Stacy. She has been sad and moody lately but you seem to be bubbling with laughter and enjoying life."

"Oh come on Ame."

"I think that my friend, Stacy, has fallen head over heels or should I say has her head in the clouds in love."

Stacy grinned, her eyes going back to the jets. "After all of these years the love I felt then is still there. I have always loved him," she softly confessed.

Amy released a loud shout. "I knew it!"

Her voice caused the others to briefly look their way. Amy waved back, her gesture gaining looks of uncertainty.

"Ou look! The four plane diamond 360!" Greg shouted, his arm stretching out as a finger pointed to the heavens.

After the practice, Matt showed them around the jets. Greg slowly walked around the F/A 18 Hornets, his luminous eyes taking everything in. The name on Matt's caught his attention. He smiled, liking it. Captain Matt 'Phantom' Sadler.

"Mike, this is Stacy and Greg Cannon. Stace, this is Mike. We've been through it all together," Matt introduced.

"So, you're the mystery lady," Mike said, reaching out to take her hand in his one hand, covering hers with his other. "It's an honor to finally meet you, ma'am." He smiled with a nod then released her.

"Huh? Mystery? I mean, it's nice to meet the men that Matt works with."

"May I add you're more lovely than your pictures."

"Oh thank you, I think," she curiously answered.

"And this is Greg. Greg meet Captain Mike. My co-conspirator." Matt shifted Greg closer to get Mike's attention from Stacy who was shooting him confused looks. He grinned at her receiving one back.

"Awesome to meet you! Dad, why do they call you Phantom?"

Mike looked at Greg then to Matt. His one eyebrow shot upwards at the word. Dad? He mouthed, getting a smile and a brief nod from Matt.

"Well now, let me tell you a story, *son*," Mike intervened, his arm draping over Greg's shoulder. "Your dad here has flown in many missions. Somehow, he always manages to sneak in beneath any radar detection, called the Sneak Pass. That way he'd get in, do his duty, and get out. A lot like a phantom. Hit and run and never be seen but the after effects were entirely, eerily real."

"Really?" Stacy asked, her wide eyes looking at Matt. She found herself caught up in the story too.

Matt pressed his lips together, only nodding.

"Really," Mike answered with a nod.

"Awesome," Greg muttered, giving Matt a new look.

"How many hours do you now have?" Adam asked.

"I have over thirty-two hundred hours logged in, sir."

"That's quite impressive," Adam stated, giving him a brisk salute.

Greg climbed the metal ladder to sit in the cockpit and mugged a grin for Stacy's camera. Then she got one with Matt standing beneath his name and Greg still seated in the jet.

"Hey, let's get a picture of the family. Matt, Stacy and Greg," Mike suggested, receiving a level look from Matt.

Matt strolled past him, "You're pushing it," he muttered before posing, placing his arm around her waist and a hand on Greg's shoulder.

"Aw. That looks real homey," Mike teased while pushing the button on the camera.

"Hello." A masculine voice spoke behind them.

Mike spun to see Admiral Baker strolling towards them. Matt stood taller, now worrying about what *he* would let slip.

"Good afternoon, Sir," Matt and Mike said in unison.

"At ease. So, these are your parents, Captain?" He asked Matt, his gaze roaming over the group.

"Yes sir, Sam and Marge Sadler; my brother Randy and fiancée Amy and friends, Adam and Beth Cannon. This is Stacy and her son, Greg," Matt proudly offered, his eyes closely watching the Chief, waiting for his response yet dreading what it would be.

Chief Baker gazed long at Greg then looked to Matt. The corners of his eyes crinkled as he grinned and nod. Then showed his smiled and nodded to Stacy. "Wonderful to meet the lady who has Captain Sadler's best interest."

"An honor Chief Baker to meet such brave men."

"Well thank you. We do it for our country. Yes sir..." He loudly began looking back at Greg.

Matt squinted with dread. He didn't miss that long scrutiny between Greg and himself. He prayed it wouldn't come out of his mouth. A huge breathing sigh escaped from him as he continued speaking.

"...we are proud of Captain Sadler and we're going to miss his flying expertise when he retires."

"We're proud of him too," Sam stated, giving Matt a loving smile.

Chief Baker returned his attentions to Greg. "So I hear you like airplanes."

Greg stood straight, doing his best to imitate Matt and Mike. "Yes sir, I do, sir."

He smiled. "That's good news. We can use another Phantom like your dad here. You know, a chip off the old block."

Matt pressed his lips together, mildly grimacing at that tiny slip. It wasn't official yet. She still hadn't told him if Greg was his son but hell, everyone else was saying it. He risked a glance to Stacy, noticing her brows furrowed, obviously from the comment. When she looked his way, he quickly shifted his gaze to the Chief and Greg.

Stacy wondered what was going on. It seemed like a lot of people were in on a private joke. Even Mike was pressing his lips in a struggle to keep from laughing out. To keep any comments from blurting out, she bit at the inside of her lip. She turned to Greg, noting how correctly he was acting around such highbrow people. But then, anyone in a military suit was highbrow to him. Deciding to push the odd spoken words to the back of her mind for now, she smiled at Greg with pride.

"Yes sir, sir," Greg answered with a lopsided grin.

"If his mom doesn't mind, why don't take Greg for a ride."

Stacy balked as Greg spun around, grasping her hands in his, "Please mom, say yes. Please."

"He's in good hands. You know that," Matt added. "Just because it scares the shit out of you, well."

Nodding her head, she relented, receiving a cheer from Greg.

"Let's get you suited up," Matt added, laying his arm across Greg's shoulder while pressing a quick kiss on her lips before ushering him away.

"What am I thinking?" she muttered suddenly noticing how mature Greg acted. After the ride and maneuvers that Matt and the others did, she knew he'd be in high heaven. Then the words and chuckles from Mike and Chief Baker stuck with her as she again wondered what exactly was going on between them all.

Cheers and applause erupted as they landed and finally Greg ran towards them, excited to tell them about his newest experience. Stacy watched Matt as he emerged from the hanger, changed out of his flight suit. He looked so natural in this setting with the men and their planes and she wondered again how he never forgot about her.

"Hey Greg, you're a natural. Not one hurl happened!" He laughed.

"You know it. Mom, I want to be a pilot!" Greg happily added.

"I think there's still time to discuss that. We better get moving. We have an hour drive home," Matt hinted, his hand going for Stacy's. He grinned when she took it but noticed that she wasn't holding as tight. Automatically, a warning light went on in his head. It's going to be a long ride, he sourly thought.

"It was a pleasure meeting everyone," Chief Baker said, as he and Mike watched them walk away. Matt's hand was in Stacy's and his arm around Greg's shoulder. He certainly didn't miss how much calmer, more attentive Matt was. "Well, what do *you* think, Captain Darcy?"

"I think it's a go, Sir."

"Yes. So do I."

Stacy let him take her hand, their fingers twining together as they led the way. Greg's excited chatter filled the air as he talked about the demonstration. In his arms he carried a wide assortment of memorabilia and souvenirs of the show. He expertly repeated the many maneuvers and what all they were named.

"I love how happy this made him," Matt said.

Stacy nodded, still wondering just what the hell was going on.

"He's going to be one tough boy to get to bed tonight," she muttered, wearily rubbing her free hand over her face. She decided to let her wandering thoughts rest for now and try to decipher the events later.

"Maybe he'll wind down during the drive home."

"If we're lucky."

And it worked. Greg's high powered adrenaline finally lowered to a simmer as he studied one of the many books given to him with the autographs of the pilots he met today and also of all of the paraphernalia and souvenirs. Once they returned home, he hurried to his room to arrange everything in a new order.

Stacy went to the kitchen, getting them a soda to drink. Her mind drifted to their observance of the flights. She still could not believe all of those dangerous maneuvers done with such precision and what excited her was that Matt was there, handling the jet with such expertise and he was a Commander of those men. His job is severely dangerous and he loved doing it, which was obvious to all who knew him but yet to her he was Matt Sadler.

As her wandering thoughts traveled to their childhood, she soon realized this kind of excitement was something he always craved. Whether it was from the first ramp he built, when he turned ten, so that he could jump his bike over to taking the skateboard through tight maneuvers. He just craved the speed and the raw edge excitement it always gave to him.

She cast her eyes to the doorway towards the living room where he waited. Her arms trembled at the uncontrolled shiver of excitement coursing through her. This man was an enigma to her. The child, the teenager, she knew but the man remained to baffle her quite a bit. Something was going on with him. Something big and it had to be the reason for his return, and she was beginning to believe that it isn't Randy getting married. Oh no, something vital was happening in Matt's life and he wasn't willing to discuss it.

Matt sat on the plush couch in the living room but before he sat down, he saw a row of photo albums on a shelf. Plucking one, he sat to begin leafing through. A serene smile formed. Recent photographs of Stacy were inside. A few were quite seductive with her poses and skimpy clothes and a few others were more motherly. Obviously self-portraits.

They were all simply beautiful, then, so was the subject. Closing the book, he surveyed the room, taking in the book case a bottom shelf contained CD's. Curiously he went to them, his gaze going to the first one. It was simply labeled Greg. Grinning, he removed it to pop into the player. Pushing play, he sat back to watch.

It showed Stacy in her last month of pregnancy. His face softened as he watched her trying to move her rounded, tank sized body around.

"She was huge," he muttered, his grin changing to a smile, liking how she looked. The film cut away to the hospital as she lay in the labor room. Strands of her hair stuck to her neck from her sweat, her tiny body exhausted between labor pains.

"Smile honey," a man's voice sounded.

"Dad, don't. You are not going to film this. I don't know why we ever got you that thing. You've turned into a documentary freeeeak!"

"Ouuuu," Matt grimaced when her voice changed to a loud, few higher octaves at the labor pain cutting through her. He put his hand to his mouth, feeling the pain with her. His breath caught when the next shot was of her in the birthing room, listening to the commands from her doctor.

"What are you watching?"

Matt jumped. He was so engrossed that he never heard her come into the room. He gave her a sheepish look. "I think it's the birth of Greg..." he trailed off at her astonished look.

Quickly she placed their cups on coasters on the coffee table then pushed the stop button on the control. Looking at him, she answered, "Yes, that's what it is."

He noticed the mixture of shocked and determined look.

"Looks like you had a rough time," he stated.

She took a seat next to him. Shifting her hips, she got comfortable.

"Well, it's frightening when you're only eighteen and having a child. How am I going to take care of this baby? I will not give him up and all the rest that went along with it at the time. You know, everyone knew what was best for you except yourself. And not to mention 25 hours of labor. I sure proved them wrong."

"Can I watch it?"

"No!" She squealed, surprised with his request and believing she saw a sad look enter his eyes. "Do you really want to?"

"Yes."

Without a word, she handed him the remote control, watching him as he watched her give birth. There were a few moments when she had to refrain from laughing at his painful, sickening expressions. His eyes were half closed and his mouth dropped open. A few times his eyes went completely closed until he heard the cries of a new born baby. His eyes remained glued to the child, his son, he thought, as they laid him on her stomach.

He watched the tears of happiness slide down her cheeks.

He watched as she placed loving kisses on the top of his head covered with dark hair.

He watched as she became a mother; and he was off flying freaking planes.

He felt a change in him a sudden new maturity as he watched the birth of Greg, his son. He placed himself at her bedside, holding her hand as she pushed the bundle from God out of the womb. Releasing a breath of frustration, wishing beyond anything that he could take back these years and be here for her.

Slowly he turned to look into her beautiful face, loving how her eyes darkened, and that half smile curling the ends of her kissable lips. Her hair, so much longer now, drifted about her shoulders in waves. Without a word, he reached out, his hand cupping her neck, easing her towards him. With his other hand he swiped away his unshed tears and was taken off guard at his reaction. Her eyes closed when he brought his lips to hers to place a gentle, slow kiss there.

Keeping his hand on her neck, he slightly moved away to gaze with longing into her eyes. His heart already filled with love but now filled with pride at this beautiful, headstrong woman sitting next to him. This woman who gave him a son but was too damn stubborn to tell him.

"You're remarkable."

"For what? Having a child?"

"For raising such a fine son on your own."

Hearing his father's voice, Matt turned his head back to the television.

"There now. He needs to have these around, none of that girly, sissy stuff. Got that, Stacy?"

"Got that Mr...."

"Now, what did I say?"

"Dad," she answered, rolling her eyes as she watched him hang a mobile of airplanes above Greg's crib.

"That makes me Grandpa Sadler to this little one."

"I wouldn't want it any other way, dad."

Again, Matt looked at her with a look of amazed respect on his face. He pushed the button off. The desire grew. He wanted to be near her, to kiss her, to hold her and to let her know she isn't alone any more.

Stacy sensed his mood. Her hand gently touched the side of his face, surprised to feel a tear on his cheek. "Matt?" she asked, looking deeper into his bright eyes, seeing them glisten. "What's wrong?"

He released a long sigh. His gaze held hers in an embrace. "Oh man. I am so much in love with you."

"Yeesssss!" Greg's shrieking voice echoed down the stairs.

Matt grinned, his eyes never leaving her stunned face. "Greg, get your ass in bed, now!" he ordered.

"Yes dad!"

Speechless, Stacy could only stare at him; too numb to think or speak. Oh come on! She didn't hear right, did she? Her breathing came in fast gasps and her head reeled like a plane swirling through the air. She prayed to God she heard him correct. No one else on earth mattered except being near him. Feeling his touch and rich voice which seem to constantly invade her rampant thoughts. Matt lightly rubbed a finger along her jaw, catching her attention.

"Where can we go to talk without the mighty Eagle Ears listening?"

Desperately trying to swallow, she suddenly wished she had her glass of pop to help with her dry throat. "M-m-m-my st-studio?" With a nod, she slowly stood, her legs feeling like cooked noodles. Her shoulders rose and fell at the long breath as she made her legs work to lead the way.

A grin played on Matt's lips. He liked her reaction and then Greg, that rascal, yelling out like that. He thought about the tape again, wishing he knew. But at least one secret is out. His feelings were revealed and there'd be no stopping him.

CHAPTER 19

Stacy slowly walked down the steps to her studio, very much aware of the testosterone surging in the man walking behind. Each silent, apparently lost in their own thoughts. She turned to face him, catching a glimpse of his grin on those very kissable lips. She wished he would quit being so damn irresistibly good looking but it was something he did naturally. With a trembling hand, she reached, touching a finger to her lips, thinking. Tapping a manicured nail against her lower lip, she spoke.

"You mentioned something about me being a distraction to you," she began.

"Yes, I did..."

Lowering her hand, she gazed into his eyes, not believing how straight forward he was, too. That's a quality she loved in a man, the honest to goodness truth. And yet, she could not believe what all he was saying to her.

She had to ask, "But to love me? You really do love me?" Her eyes narrowed with the disbelief she felt as she whispered the last two words.

"Yes, I do and you knew that when I left here."

"But I assumed it'd be a passing feeling, a phase. One between kids, young adults that would fade once we were apart." While glancing to the floor, she wiped a trembling hand lightly across her brow.

"Love is not a feeling that leaves, especially when it's so strong like mine is for you." He stepped nearer, cupping her face in both of his hands. He forced her head back looking long into her glistening eyes. His thumbs rubbed across her cheeks, drying her tears. "You have no idea do you? How much I love and have loved you since we were kids."

Stacy went numb. Not just her thoughts but her entire body went numb. She found this all so unbelievable! She studied his very handsome face. "No..." Then she saw it, too. Saw what she'd been seeing since school but now stronger and never realized what that look was. But it was there all along! The look of love! The familiar look he had for her was in his eyes. "Oh, Matt..." was all she managed to get out before his lips claimed hers in a gentle kiss, one that soon turned into the all- consuming desire.

"You are what I need," he murmured, his lips a whisper from hers, stoking the coals lying deep inside of him. Quickly, the flames of passion ignited, burning, rising to a full blown need to make her his. To feel her beneath him, hot flesh against hot flesh, letting him love her the way he hungered.

His mouth on hers, refused to release his hold. With a deep desirous passion that matched his, she pressed herself against him, feeling the heat, the need from his body. A cry slipped from her lips when she felt his hands freely roam down her back, gripping onto her buttocks, gently easing her closer. Feeling his hardness press against her stomach.

His hand caught her hair, sliding his fingers through. Pulling away from her enticing lips, he spoke, "For all of these years when I thought of someone holding you in his arms and doing the things that lovers do, it drove me insane! I stopped writing thinking that the man who fathered Greg wouldn't appreciate another man writing to his woman. I know I sure as hell wouldn't like it."

There. He said it. He opened the door for her to easily tell him the truth. *Come on Stace! Tell me!* He looked deep into her eyes, silently pleading but she said nothing, except for the other words he longed to hear.

Stacy's fingers played along the vein of his neck, sliding to his strong chin. She looked into his eyes, straying to his mouth then back. "Oh God. I never told you how I felt because of the desire you had to see the world."

"What?"

"Why do you suppose I was so upset when I found out you were leaving? I realized then as now that I love you too, Matt."

A broad smile shaped his lips. He never imagined, never dreamed, never in a million years thought about that. As teenagers, she always denied his feeling, stating that too good of friend's bullshit.

"Think of all these years we have wasted," he murmured before pressing a slow kiss on her lips then pulling away. He looked long into her dark eyes. "I think we need to get ourselves better acquainted." He kissed her again then pulled away, his lips barely touching hers. "Starting now."

"But Greg..."

"Better be asleep."

With her hand in his, he led her up the two flight of stairs towards her bedroom. They stopped in front of Greg's room. Peering in, they saw him laying fast asleep in the glow of the television. Matt looked at her, a devilish smile forming on his lips as she now brazenly moved, tugging him behind her.

With their eyes locked together, Matt quietly closed the door behind them, then drew her into his embrace. The kiss was untamed with a wild hunger unleashed in both of them. Matt gripped her in his arms, his hands freely roaming over her slender figure, getting to know every crevice and curve. His touching eliciting cries of pleasure from her.

His lips left her parted mouth to nibble to her slender throat. Her head tipped to the side, giving him better access to her throat as a low, sensuous moan of pleasure slipped from her. Matt's body reacted with rapid longing, the sound sending his emotions into overdrive with an impassioned need to have her. Quickly, his mouth reclaimed hers.

Stacy returned his hard kisses. Missing him, needing him like she needed none other. Her hands slid to the waist of his jeans, undoing his belt then the snap. With quick moves, she tugged his shirt free then worked at the buttons. Frustrated, wanting to see him; caress him; kiss him; she gave a rough tug sending the remaining buttons flying through the air.

Matt stepped back, surprised by her urgency.

"Stace..." he said with a surprised grin.

In a voice raspy with desire, she whispered, "I'm sorry Matt. I can't seem to control myself. I need you."

Soon she felt her clothes sliding away from her emblazoned body until she stood in front of him. The moon cast its iridescent glow through the bedroom and helped her see the slow way his intense eyes traveled over her. Stepping nearer, his arm tenderly wrapped about her waist, the other her shoulder, before his mouth again captured hers. Bending, he picked her up in his arms to gently lay her in the middle of her bed.

Stacy patiently watched him finish undressing then join her. The bed sagged as he lay down. Eagerly she wrapped him in her arms, pulling him to her, needing to touch him; to feel him against her. She lay back letting him do as he will, blossoming beneath his loving caresses and now patient hand. Her body squirmed as his mouth and tongue traced wild, erotic patterns on her skin.

Matt's hand slid down her long leg as he sensuously licked his path to her hips, turning her onto her stomach to press ardent kisses on her firm buttocks then led to the tantalizing feminine indent up the middle of her back.

Stacy rose to her elbows, pressing her shoulders against him, loving the feel of his heated skin along her length. Gasps of pleasure slipped from her parted lips. Her tongue flicked out, wetting them as she felt him press against her; felt his firm hand on her; urging her; showing her; rising on her knees, as he slowly entered her from behind. A low moan of surprised pleasure escaped from her as she arched her back.

Matt eased her hips up, his hand firmly gripped onto her waist as he slowly entered her receiving a gasping moan from each of them. Slowly he moved, holding her against him. His loving hands slid along her back, to her shoulders to entangle in the silky waves of her hair to ease her head up. Twisting the softness into his palm, he pulled further until her head was back, he moved forward, reaching to kiss her parted lips. Releasing his hold on her hair, his body covered her as his hands braced on each side of hers on the mattress.

Stacy was taken by surprise by this position as she enjoyed it. Enjoyed the commanding power he held over her submissive form in this way. He shifted and she felt his hands tightly grip around her waist, encouraging her to meet his deeper thrusts. With a soft cry her back arched.

Slowly he moved, feeling her buttocks against him until he wanted to look into her face. He wanted to see the look of pure rapture of this moment as he made love to her. Withdrawing, a cry escaped from her.

"I'm not hurting you, am I?" he whispered against the moist skin on her sweating back, tasting the salt of her. His mouth began its tantalizing trail up her spine as she lay on her stomach, feeling his aroused body lightly brush against her.

"Noooo," she purred, lavishing in the feel of his lips on her shoulder, slowly urging, easing her onto her back.

His knees eased her legs opened as he positioned himself. "Good, because I never want to do that."

Burying his face in the tender arch of her throat. His teeth lightly nibbled at the delicate skin on her neck to her ear. He tenderly cradled her head in his arms as he once again claimed her body.

Stacy welcomed his weight. She opened and welcomed his hardness as he slowly slid into her hot body, willing him to begin where he left off with this sweet torture. Her hands lovingly slipped around his biceps, feeling the power, the strength they retained as he held his torso from her so that he could watch her face, watch as her features softened and showed the love she kept hidden all of these years.

His moves were faster, giving and taking the sweet nectar she offered him. Feeling her fingernails claw at his shoulders, clinging to him, pulling him to her. Feeling her sensuously move along with the ride. Together they reached for, strived for that undulating peak of pulsating power that rocked their bodies until finally they lay spent in each other's arms.

With a final deep thrust, Matt fell to his elbows, remaining in her, feeling her take him all, feeling her press soft loving kisses across his chest and neck. Feeling her hands knead into his back to hold him to her until she finally looked into his eyes and smiled such a smile of serene happiness. Slowly he moved away, gathering her into his embrace, his hand hungrily roamed over her curves while his other turned her head to face him.

"Stace, you are magnificent," he uttered, kissing her forehead. His eyes closed as sleep quickly fell over him.

Stacy smiled into the darkness of the room, her eyes going to the full moon that floated in the blackness of the night sky outside the window. It seemed to be smiling back at her.

"So are you," she whispered, snuggling her tired body as close to him as she could before she fell into a deep sleep.

* * *

Matt woke to the singing of the early birds, perched in the trees outside the windows. Slowly his eyes fluttered open, looking around to get his bearings. Smiling, he remembered he was with Stace. Glancing to his stomach, he found her feminine arm draped across his chest, her hand reaching, resting on his cheek. Her head lay on his shoulder, a shoulder that tingled with numbness from remaining in one position all night.

Flexing his fingers, he could feel the blood begin to circulate as shooting daggers formed when feeling began to return to his limbs. He grimaced at the pain as he slowly tried to remove her human pillow from beneath her head. The abrupt knock came from the closed bedroom door. He looked at it then to them, finding the sheets tangled about their legs. Tugging, he pulled the sheets to cover them.

Stacy felt the blankets move beneath her. Slowly she woke to find herself held in Matt's arms. Smiling, she tilted her head back to gaze into his very handsome face. She reached up, touching the shadow of a beard on his chin as he released a yawn, looking to see her watching him.

"Good morning."

"Good morning to you too," he answered, his knuckles lightly brushing her cheek, feeling the smoothness. "There's someone knocking on your bedroom door."

"Greg. He knows the rules. He can't come in until I permit it."

"Good rule."

"So he stands there, knocking, until I finally allow it."

Matt laughed, becoming serious with her next question.

"So, where do we go from here?"

His hand cupped that precious face of hers. It was filled with love and concern. "All I know is that we won't be separated...again."

Smiling, she rolled away, taking the top blanket with her to wrap around her nakedness. Giving him a bashful look over her shoulder, she disappeared into the master bath.

The knock lightly sounded again. Matt rose, slipping into his underclothes and jeans. He zipped them. "Come in."

Greg opened the door, slowly peering around to find Matt standing next to his mom's bed. Then to the very disheveled sheets. That could only mean one thing, he realized, remembering the many stories going around school about sex.

"Good morning," Matt said. "Do you need something?"

Greg turned his head, looking at the master bath when he heard the water from the shower spraying. He gave Matt a lopsided grin, "Does she love you too?"

With a grin, Matt answered. "Yes."

The black truck parked in the shadows of the trees down the street. Dan's eyes hatefully narrowed as he watched the Harley drove away from her home. Having Stacy in his life seemed to have come an obsession with him and he wasn't about to lose her to a fly boy. His eyes shifted back to her house, his house, and by God, he would live there again.

CHAPTER 20

Sam looked up as the back door opened, watching with amusement as Matt entered. His eyes coolly went to the round, wooden wall clock then back to him that hung over the sink, then back to him. He's been gone for over twenty-four hours. Well, he figured that could be good. He also couldn't miss the huge smile on his still unshaven face. Sipping at his cup of coffee, he remained silent, deciding to wait this one out.

Matt pulled a chair to take a seat opposite him at the kitchen table. Silently he poured himself a glass of orange juice and buttered a bagel for himself but his eyes kept going to his father's face. He was waiting.

With a suggestive grin, the elder Sadler raised an eyebrow as he returned his cup to the table. "Are you hungry son?"

"Yes. I've been busy..." he trailed off.

Matt looked back at his father, waiting for the normal ten questions so he could tell him the news but Sam stayed quiet.

Sam slowly nodded as he calmly reached for a bagel to slowly spread with butter. His eyes crinkled at the edges from his smile, he then ever so slowly brought the bagel to his mouth, taking a long bite.

"All right! You forced the news out of me!" Matt loudly said, "I love Stace and she loves me!"

"No kidding?" Sam returned in a muffled voice.

"You knew?"

"By the way you've been chasing her skirts, hell yes."

"Was I that obvious?"

"Son, we could tell. Congratulations. We all like her, hell love her."

"Thanks."

"Problem though."

"What's that?"

"Mom is already out ordering the wedding invitations." He released a joyful guffaw at the stricken look crossing Matt's face. "Just joking."

Matt relaxed, "I know. But I'm thinking that it wouldn't be such an awful idea."

"That's good news too."

"But, I *am* having a problem."

Sam look up from the morning paper into Matt's worried eyes. "Uh oh, trouble in paradise already? What's wrong?"

Matt pressed his lips together, wondering how to say the words. Wearily, he rubbed his hand across his chin, feeling the roughness from the stubble. "Well, I'm pretty damn positive that Greg is my son."

Matt jumped as coffee spewed forward from his father's mouth then the hacking cough as he almost choked. Springing up, he hurried to his side, giving light taps on his back.

"Are you all right? I didn't mean to shock you like that. I believed that you had an idea of your own."

Sam stood, his fist lightly tapping at his chest while trying to catch his breath. Finally, he returned to a semblance of normalcy, and able to give Matt an incredulous look.

"No! Are you sure?"

Matt removed his wallet, showing him the picture his mom had sent to him. "Look at him dad. Look at him close and hard."

Sam took the wallet.

"Can you see any resemblance?"

Sam nodded, "Well, when you look at him like this and how he's looking, yes, I suppose I do."

The silence went on for what seemed like hours. Matt stared at the picture and then at his father.

"That's me, dad."

"What?"

"That's me at the same age," he flipped the plastic over. "That is Greg."

Sam sat down, stunned, his eyes going back and forth between the two pictures. "Dear God but yes. I see it."

"Mother played a dirty trick and sent me both of them but didn't write anything on the back, year; age, nothing. When I called to ask she began giggling. When I asked what was so funny, she confessed what she did. She noticed it way before anyone did. I've been studying these two pictures ever since."

Sam's brows drew in. Perplexed, he added, "Lesson one with women. They're experts for sniffing out and sorting through anything that we're not supposed to catch on to and they will let us know in their own mean way."

"Dad," Matt scoffed.

"Oh you mark my words, son. You and Randy have a lot to learn on the whims and emotions that they go through. Get them mad and they'll let you know. It might not be at that precise moment but, they *will* let you know."

"Well, Greg isn't my problem. I can't seem to get her to tell me. That's what I want more than anything..."

"Besides her."

"Definitely. But, I want for her to confess it to me. I want her to be the one to say that I am Greg's father. I want her to willingly confess it to me. I don't want to be the one to say, Oh, by the way, am I the one who got you pregnant? That is so cold."

Quietly Sam stared at his youngest, seeing the frustrating clenching and unclenching of his jaw. He could see the anger flowing through him of the woman he fell in love with not telling him the truth and knew from personal experience of himself and dealing with Randy and Matt at how angry the Sadler men can be with not told the truth.

* * *

Amy lightly knocked before entering Stacy's house. Soft music drifted from the basement studio. She hurried down the stairs to the room, anxious to see the finished picture she picked. She remembered when she first laid her eyes on them, wondering how on earth she would ever choose between all. Stacy helped to choose by picking out four and she chose well.

Amy came to a fast stop, her gaze falling on her portraits, each done in twenty-four by thirty-six frames of dark cherry.

Stacy stood back, watching, waiting for her reaction. When nothing came, she decided to help her along, "Well? What do you think?"

Amy approached, her eyes flitting to each one. When she stopped in front of them, her smile widened with pleasure. Her favorite was of her standing with her back facing the camera but her waist was partially turned to reveal her profile as she looked ahead and in the corner was a smaller image, resembling a spirit, of her standing the same way but looking at her flowers.

Her gaze shifted to Stacy, still patiently waiting for the reaction. Her mouth dropped open but words failed her as she gathered Stacy in an embrace.

"I take it that you like them?" Stacy teased, returning her a hug.

Pulling apart, Amy's eyes again went to her portraits, "That's an understatement. They're all so beautiful," she softly breathed as she once again went to them.

"I'm glad that you do. They'll look lovely in the lobby of the reception area. And behind the cake and the bridal table." She laughed as she went back to her file room to remove more pictures.

Amy followed, curiously catching how fast her hands moved as she seemed to be trying to hide a stack of something.

"Hey, what's that?" Amy asked.

"Nothing. Never mind. They're just mess ups," Stacy quickly answered, piling more photos on top.

"I find that hard to believe. Come on. Let me be the judge of that."

"No really Ame. They're nothing. Come on, I want to show you something."

Amy waited for Stacy to walk past before diving her hands beneath the pile to search what she kept hidden. After a quick sort through her eyes found the ones she guessed were being hidden. She said a silent wow as she looked at pictures of Stacy standing in water with her bare back facing the camera. There were a couple of those, then she was turned, her eyes looking luminous at whoever was pushing the button. A few of those too and others.

"*Stacy Cannon!*" Amy's voice loudly sounded a couple of octaves higher than normal. "*What are these for?*"

"What are what for?" Stacy called back, hoping to lure Amy away from her file room.

Amy approached with her arm outstretched. In her grip were the pictures. "These! What are these for?"

"Damn." Stacy's gaze locked onto those pictures then she looked into Amy's amused expression.

Amy fought the snicker about to burst forth. Quickly, she pressed her trembling lips together, hopefully to quell any desire for her laughter. Her gaze slowly slid down then back up Stacy's trim figure then back to the pictures. She would have never guessed this of her dear, straight-laced friend. Finally she spoke, trying so hard to speak in a most serious tone of voice.

"Well? Is there something that you're not telling me? Are you a closet porn model or something?"

Deciding to patiently wait and hopefully Amy would get her gaiety out of her system, Stacy shrugged.

"Care to confess something to me?" Amy tried coercing.

"Such as?"

"Ou, you little vixen."

Stacy grabbed them from Amy's hand. Rushing past, she snapped in a tone full of irritation with being the cause of anyone's humor. "There is nothing to confess," she rapidly slid them into a manila envelope, jammed them into the top drawer of her desk, shoving it closed with a loud slam.

"Well differently. Who took them. That's what I want to know."

Stacy's lips pressed into a stubborn, straight line. Well, she hadn't really had the chance to speak with Amy for a few days and she did have a lot to tell. Releasing a sigh, she began, "Matt took them..."

"No way!"

"Now, I didn't know that he was there. I was swimming. He snuck up on me and grabbed my camera and then took these without my knowledge until it was too late," she rapidly defended herself.

"And may I add, that he caught a good side of you," she giggled, arching an eyebrow.

"How are the wedding plans going?" Stacy conveniently changed the subject.

CHAPTER 21

Traffic was light as Dan drove past a local Sheetz. He still fumed over the conversation he and Sandy had.

"Just who the hell does she think she is refusing to help me?" he snapped as a smile shaped his lips, recalling her spunk when she stood up to him. That's a first time she ever did that and he liked it. Sandy was good in bed and rarely said no or backed down but this evening she was different. She stood her ground and spoke her mind.

"Maybe she's right. Maybe it'd be best for all involved if I'd move on and forget about Stacy."

His chest puffed up then relaxed when he released a long breath. Admitting this fault was a bit eye opening then his gaze fell onto the Harley at the gas pump then to the man putting fuel into it. He did a quick U-turn to pull in behind. Slowly, he eased forward until his bumper tapped the back of the bike, the revelation forgotten about.

Matt stared at the numbers blinking in the digital window of the pump. He was so lost in another world, thinking about Stacy and wondered at her refusal to admit anything about Greg. Christ, more than once he started the conversation, hoping and praying that she'd pick up where he was going with it. But hell, she remained persistent and each time smoothly change the subject. Then his thoughts roamed completely in another direction, thinking about her welcoming arms as she held him to her.

He grinned, his thoughts went on Stace and amazement overwhelmed him and the peacefulness he felt just thinking about her. The memory of her soft skin beneath his touch and her feminine moans of desire filled him. Her sultry voice and broad smile encased him. He found to his pleasure that she bewitched him, to cast a spell over him and his emotions. She's everything. She's the tempting lady, the playful woman, a mother, his lover. When his bike jumped his thoughts broke. He snapped his head to cast an angry glare to the driver behind him.

"Hey idiot! Didn't you see me standing here?" he loudly asked, then a sly grin shaped his lips when he recognized the man in the truck.

Dan.

Just the man he wanted to see and it was appearing Dan wanted to see him, too. Oh yeah. He wanted quite a few words with the gentleman. Still glaring at Dan, Matt finished then quickly returned the nozzle to the pump and closed the cap on the tank as Dan emerged from his truck to walk closer.

Matt fought the scoff threatening to slip when Dan tried to appear menacing with his puffed out chest and his arms slightly held out to his sides. It was obvious to him that Dan didn't realize who he was dealing with. He'd been taught a lot in the Navy, including the art of self-defense, and that was something he was itching to use.

Dan's gaze coldly stared Matt down. He eluded an air of confidence, boldly swaggering towards the fly boy. His glare never left Matt's alert gaze. He proceeded to take the few steps around him. To any by-standers, he appeared to be a vulture circling in on his prey as he kept watching him, sizing him up. Dan stopped a couple of feet away from Matt before speaking.

"Why the hell won't you get your ass back to wherever you came from?"

"This is where I'm from or have you forgotten?"

"You know damn well what I mean, *fly boy*," he sneered. "You need to keep away from Stacy too."

"Sorry man. I can't do that."

"I'm warning you to stay the hell away from her and from *our* son!" He added, seeing the slight narrowing of Matt's eyes.

Matt silently studied the bastard who so easily declared the parentage of Greg. Could he be mistaken thinking that he was Greg's father? Maybe Greg *is* Dan's. No. Impossible. Greg looked way too much like him to be considered Dan's. But her lack of agreement didn't help as the doubts filling his mind were beginning to nag him. Dan had blue eyes too and Stacy had the dark brown hair. No he remained firm. He needed to go with his first, basic instinct. Greg is his and I'll be damn if I let any asshole bastard tell me other ways!

"He isn't your son," Matt declared, his chin lifting a notch boldly staring into Dan's hateful, smug face.

"The hell he isn't. We were together the week after you left. She got pregnant and we were happy until you came back..."

"You're lying. She kicked your ass out."

"We're only doing a trial. She wants me back. She calls me, begging and pleading for me to come back home."

"You're lying Dan," Matt repeated. "How *can* you love her? Shit, you like to use her as your own private punching bag!" Matt's arms rose to his sides, "Besides, she doesn't love you. She loves me," he added pointing his fingers to his chest before lowering them.

Dan's eyes narrowed. Reaching out, his thick hand gave Matt's shoulder a light tap. "You're a no good, lying sack of shit," he growled.

Matt looked to his shoulder then to the offending hand. His eyes rolled upwards to look at Dan's smirk. "You don't ever touch me like that again, or else..."

Remaining silent, Dan boldly repeated the gesture, a smug leer forming on his lips.

Knowing that Dan would take the challenge, Matt narrowed his eyes, loving it. This confrontation was a long time coming and he wanted nothing better to do than to get it started and ended.

He spoke, his tone mocking. "Do you want to know what I just cannot tolerate? I can't tolerate when a man beats on a woman. That only proves that he's nothing better than the regurgitation from an owl after he finishes with his meal and that's exactly what you're going to look like when I'm through with you, you fucking son of a bitch." Matt's threatened.

He slid his gaze to Dan's hands, finding them clenching and unclenching, a good indication of what would happen next. The punch. With his training he stood on the defense, patiently waiting for the attack sure to come.

Dan's taut body flinched.

Matt grinned.

Dan moved, swinging a closed fist towards Matt's jaw. Matt remained firmly planted where he stood, leaning his torso back, feeling the breeze as the punch barely missed him. He straightened, wearing a teasing smile on his lips.

"What's wrong Dan? Can't you hit me?"

Angry, Dan's lips pressed together as he executed another swing, and again Matt swayed away but then retaliated with an upper right hook, connecting with Dan's jaw. The blow stunned him as he staggered back a few steps. He gave his head a few shakes to clear the impact as he touched a finger to the split on his lip and the blood seeping from it.

"Not a woman, right?" Matt mocked.

Seething with renewed rage at being made the fool, Dan's mouth opened as a loud yell filled the air. He lunged. Wrapping his arms around Matt's waist, he dug in his feet, pushing Matt hard against the grill of his truck. Matt's arms wrapped around the shoulders, going backwards with his attacker. A rush of breath left Matt as the impact caused the wind to be forced from his lungs. Soon, the pair was on the ground, rolling around in a clinch.

The attendant's eyes widened he looked out to see the men rolling on the ground in a tight clinch. "Oh shit," he muttered, picking up the phone.

* * *

On the seventh ring, Randy picked up the telephone. "Yeah!" he shouted, hoping that whoever would still be on the line. He had been helping Amy and Stacy with some decorations while waiting for Matt so that the four of them could go out to supper.

"Thank God you're home," Matt anxiously stated.

"Why?" Randy asked, his eyes narrowing, not sure he heard him correctly. His gaze traveled to Amy and Stacy. The tone of his voice instantly stopped them from going over the to do list for the wedding. "You're where?"

"In jail."

"Christ Matt, how did you get there?"

"How do you think? A patrol car," his voice was very heavy with sarcasm. "What's with the questions? Are you turning into dad?"

Randy's lips pursed. He's definitely not in the best of moods and he really couldn't blame him one bit. He stalled before answering, "This isn't like you. What happened? What did you do?"

"Dan picked a fight."

"With fists?"

Stacy gasped with his words. Amy placed a hand of comfort on her shoulder as they listened to this one sided conversation and it didn't sound very well.

"How else is there to fight?"

"Whoa. Must have been one hell of a scuffle. What did he do? What happened?"

"Just come down and bail me out. I'll explain the details to you later."

"Did you get hurt?"

"Just a bruised cheek."

* * *

Matt sat on a wooden bench, his back braced against the cold, tile walls the color of drab, boring white. He stretched his legs in front of him and ankles crossed. For what seemed like the hundredth time, his eyes focused on a ragged crack following the trail to the opposite wall. "Christ, I can probably trace that crack by heart," he muttered.

The voice echoed through the corridors. Through the bars, Dan's angry voice yelled out more insults to him. Matt smirked. He's been doing that off and on during their incarceration. Lucky for Dan they put him in a separate cell. Personally, Matt thought, he was far from being done with any dealings concerning him.

Matt flexed the fingers of his right hand, listening to them crack as he worked the bones. Tomorrow he'd feel the effects that the hard punches on Dan's face would cause but for now, he had to remain silently satisfied with the messy outcome he caused.

Sighing, his eyes went back to the crack to once again follow its trail. His thoughts were troubled. Troubled from the words Dan so convincingly stated when he declared that Greg was his son.

"Can't be," he muttered, uncrossing his ankles to switch the top to the bottom. Being with Greg felt so right. So natural; feeling a close kinship connection and comforting when Greg called him dad. "This can't be," he repeated, praying that Dan was cruelly playing a game by tossing a bluff his way with the hopes that he'd give up and leave. A cold smirk curved his lips.

"Yeah. That has to be it. But when I get my ass out of here, I'm going to confront her. I'm going to make her talk about Greg," he spoke the vow, looking up when more curses from Dan flew to him. He grinned. "Yeah, keep it up Dan and you'll be held longer."

"Sadler. Your bail has been paid."

Matt looked up into the stern face of the short, overweight officer wearing a dark blue uniform who unlocked his door. Standing, he gave him a nod, following another officer through a door towards his freedom.

"Thanks," he uttered as he walked passed him then the holding cell where Dan stood, his arms loosely dangling between the bars. Matt cast a cold glance his way.

"This ain't over yet," Dan hissed.

"I'm counting the minutes."

"Hey, you're not out of here yet," the officer warned.

Remaining silent, Matt followed. He entered the front office, his gaze falling on Randy's face, seeing amusement written all over it. Amy and Stacy stood nearby. He couldn't miss the concerned looks each of them wore.

"What's she doing here?" he asked Randy.

"She was with us when you called. She followed, wanting to be sure you were all right. Are you?" Randy asked, noting the tense way he carried himself and the tightness of his mouth, a trait he recognized of controlling his anger.

"Yeah, I guess so."

Stacy slowly walked to Matt, watching as he retrieved his personal affects. When he stuffed his wallet into his back pocket, she finally spoke. "Matt, what happened?" She reached a hand to tenderly touch she bruise forming on his cheek.

With an impatient gesture, Matt jerked his head away from her touch. His time in the holding cell gave him the chance to think and boy did he ever. He was ready to take the bull by the horns and get to the bottom of the only question he was dying to know the answer. He also didn't want Stacy to touch him. He knew that he couldn't trust his own feelings. He knew that with one touch of her soft hand his anger would dissipate and he'd want to take her into his arms and hold her.

Stacy watched as he finally turned to face her, his eyes an angry, dark blue with an intent stare. His voice came low, demanding.

"We need to have a talk."

Stacy slowly dropped her arm. At the tone and glare, an uncertain chill swept up her spine, standing her hair on edge.

"Okay..."

"Now. Let's go. Randy, take my bike." Turning, he led the way out of the police station, leaving her standing next to the quiet Randy and Amy.

Looking at them, she sighed then looked back to Matt's retreating back. "I guess we're going to talk. I wonder what it could be about?"

Randy wrapped an arm around her shoulders. "I don't know but good luck. He's really pissed. He didn't tell me what the fight was about."

"Fight?" She echoed, recalling the words she overheard when Randy spoke with him.

"Yeah, he and Dan. I guess Dan's still inside."

"Oh God," she whispered, knowing that if Dan was involved as well meant it couldn't be good. Exhaling a long breath, she swallowed.

Matt stood next to her Jeep, patiently waiting. Remaining silent, he reached a hand out for her keys, then held the passenger door open for her. Silently she took her seat as he closed the door.

Curiously watching, she waited as he crawled behind the wheel, then waited for him to take her to where ever. Starting the engine, he shoved the gear shift into first and gassed the engine harder than necessary, jerking them away. A nervous shudder claimed her body, sending it into an uncontrollable spasm wondering what caused him to be pissed at her this time. She learnt quickly that Dan was one to fly off the handle at any given time over any given thing but Matt hadn't, until now. She cast a wary glance at him. That bruise on his face proved to her that fists had flown during an argument, and that argument was no doubt over her.

Biting at her lower lip, she looked ahead. The silence was a very tense nerve racking silence. So deathly that it made her want to jump from the moving vehicle and escape the tomb like confines. Anytime she opened her mouth to ask him a question, either his hand shot in the air to silence her or he would give her such an angry glare that she quickly swallowed any and all speech. And if he was too angry to speak, she knew that it had to be something major. Releasing a long sigh, she sat back in her seat.

Matt drove them to his favorite place by the lake. He slammed on the brakes, sliding the Jeep to a stop, sending swirling dust into the night air.

With her hands braced on the dash board, Stacy shot him a disbelieving expression. Oh Lord, she couldn't miss seeing that jaw clench and unclench as he stared at the glared at the shimmering reflection of the moon on the wavering water in front of them. Taking a nervous swallow, she began, "Matt, are you going to tell me what this is all about?"

He shut down the engine. With a smug grin, he opened his door to get out. Stubbornly she got out too, to follow, wishing that he would say something, anything to get it started and over with. She leaned against her vehicle, watching his long, abrupt strides as he paced his anger out. He kept shooting her silent, thoughtful glances.

Matt studied her and with the help of the full moon, he couldn't miss the foreboding, fearful dread look on her face. Good, that meant she would easily listen instead of being argumentative.

He kept restlessly pacing in front of the deathly silent Stacy trying to keep his temper in some form of control. He'd never been so angry before in his life! Angry! Hell that isn't the correct term. Try totally, mind boggling, over the edge fucking furious. Heaving a long sigh, he spun on his heels marching back and forth. Each time he passed Stacy, he cast an angry glare to her. A grimace scowled her pretty face.

His voice was loud, demanding when he spoke. The tone causing her to jump. "It's one word. It's Greg."

"What about Greg?" she warily asked.

She stood with her arms crossed in front of her as she leant her buttocks on the fender. Her alert eyes remained glued to his angry stalking, watching as he spun around to walk back past. Greg? Did he know that Greg was his son? That could be why he's acting so angry. She wondered who the hell told him her secret. If Amy did, she is dead meat, she angrily vowed.

Matt stopped, bracing his hands on his hips as he angrily glared at her beautiful, stubborn face. It was a face he knew very well and couldn't miss the tightly pressed lips. This time when he spoke, his voice came sharper than normal.

"Stace, is Greg my son?"

He never flinched at the surprised gasp.

Oh my God! She thought it may be his problem but to hear the words took her off guard. How should she answer? Their future was still in a chaotic mess. True they admitted their love for one another but never really discussed what they were going to do? She believed that he'd leave her here when he returned to the service.   Her lips trembled and a scowl creased on her forehead. She swung her hands up to cover her face as her shoulders rose and lowered from a long breath.

Matt remained silent, watching the telltale signs and that was answer enough but he longed to hear her speak those words to him! Why won't she say anything?

The crunching of metal close to her startled her. A scream of alarm filled the night air, interrupting the sounds of frogs. Jumping, her hands snapped down, watching his fist crash down again and again onto the hood of her Jeep, placing a dent in the middle.

"Matt! Stop it!" she cried out, her flailing hands trying to grasp onto his arm to stop his attack.

Angrily, he shrugged her off of him as he stalked away.

"Jesus Christ!" he loudly swore, tilting his head back to look into the sky at the millions of twinkling stars.   He looked back at her as she remained standing against her vehicle, her arms crossed as she hugged herself.

Her eyes followed him, remaining on guard, watching as he glared at her, patiently waiting for her to speak. The time had come and there was no way else to tell him than direct.

"God, this isn't how I wanted to let you know," her gaze went to his face as he stared at her. Moonlight reflected from the unshed tears in her eyes. Then a tear slowly slid from the corner, down her rounded cheek. When she spoke, her voice was low. "Yes Matt. Greg is your son," she meekly confessed.

"Oh really? How can you be sure? I was told something else. Weren't you with Dan that same week?" He angrily demanded.

She inhaled before slowly releasing it. What now? The truth. Her face grimaced with that awful memory. She had gone to Dan with the foolish notion that once she was with another that the heated passion stirred by Matt would leave. But it didn't. He was nothing at all like Matt. His caresses were rougher and he was fast, wanting to get to the core of the sex without any pleasantries. Her eyes remained fixed on him. She hated this conversation. Hated where it was leading.

"Yes. I was," she whispered.

"So how can you be certain?"

"Just one look at Greg should be enough."

He silently agreed but he still would rather know for sure. That way Dan couldn't ever come back causing them problems. Matt felt his world reeling about him like a jet spiraling out of control.

He took in a long breath then slowly expelled it. He had a son! He's a father and never knew it! "Thanks to mom, she told me you had a son and then later, as he grew and with the aid of pictures she sent I noticed who Greg looks like. The realization of I could have a son occupied my thoughts daily to the point of an obsession of needing to, wanting to know the truth. It took over my life to the point to cause me to be inconsistent on my job," he rattled off.

But now, being here and hearing the words made such a different impact. He prayed that his anger would be held in check. But when Dan's taunting words flooded his thoughts, those jealous emotions burst open like a volcano in full eruption.

His arm shot into the air. *"Why in God's name didn't you tell me!?"* he demanded, bracing his hands to his waist. *"Stace why!?"* His gaze remained locked on her, as his hands shoved deep into his pockets, not trusting himself or what he would hit next.

The silence went on for what seem an eternity. The sounds of the night filled the air. Crickets chirped and the bull frogs joined in the chorus. In three long strides, he stood in front of her. His hands tightly gripped onto her upper arms, giving her light shakes. "Don't you think that a man has a right to know whether he fathers a child?"

A startled squeal escaped from her as her eyes closed, tensed with his attack, waiting for the slaps like Dan did.

"What do you have to say?" His voice now came not as loud as he got himself in a bit of control.

When none of the hits came, she slightly relaxed, opening her eyes to look into the face of an upset, distraught, pissed off man who was demanding answers.

Her voice was light, on the verge of crying. "You had a dream," she finally answered.

"What kind of cock and bull answer is that?" He snapped, releasing his grip to place his hands on his hips.

With a deep swallow, she squared her shoulders as her voice came stronger. "You had a dream and I couldn't write you to make you come back! You wanted to see the world!"

He shot her a scathing look of disbelief. "Oh, for Christ's sake!" He moved away, bending to pick up a rock to angrily throw into the lake, easily doing ten skips before plunging into the darkness of the water.

She watched his agitated movements. Taking a step after him, she answered.

"Matt, I couldn't take that away from you!"

He spun to face her, the disbelief still on his features.

"So instead, you seem to think it important to keep the fact that I have a son away from me! Flesh and blood! *My flesh and blood*! You seem to think that I wouldn't care, is that it? Well, here is the big surprise, darling, I would have wanted to spend time with my family!"

"Do you mean to tell me that at the age of nineteen or twenty you would've rather stayed at home with a dead end job you didn't care for rather than become a pilot?"

Turning his complete attention to her, his heated, intense gaze pinned her to the ground. With slow breathes, he believed that he had his anger in some form of mild control. He stepped closer, stopping mere inches from her as the angry tirade began.

"I thought you knew *me*, Stace. I've always been a man responsible for my actions! I would have been here for you. Or better yet, I would have come back and taken the both of you with me. And, to think what all I have missed with him! *I'll never get that back! I'll never get that chance again!*" Tears of frustration formed in his eyes. With a helpless, disgusted wave of his hand, he turned to walk away from her stunned face.

Walked away into the night.

Stacy turned, watching as he left her alone. Her head slowly shook, surprised; stunned; shocked with his confession. Dear God, was she ever wrong!

"I'm sorry! I didn't know what to do!" she frantically screamed out, her voice fading into the night air. *"Oh God! I'm sorry!"* She realized how lame those words sounded with the pain she unknowingly inflicted on his heart.

"Yeah, right!" He replied over his shoulder.

She couldn't leave him walk away like this. Emotions were to taught, high strung to just let things hang like this. Desperate, she took a step after him.

"Oh my God! Matt where are you going?" she frantically called to his retreating back.

A hand briefly waved into the air. He remained silent as he walked away, his body disappearing into the night.

"Matt?"

Upset, confused, she ran her fingers through her hair as she weakly fell to the ground. She pulled her legs upwards, wrapping her arms around her knees as she hid her face in her folded arms.

3CHAPTER 22

Stacy didn't know how she made it home. After the demanding difficult task of telling herself to quit the constant onslaught of tears, she finally succeeded with getting composed enough to drive. She drove up and down roads, her head twisting from side to side, hoping to see Matt walking along the highway but he seemed to have vanished into thin air. She even stopped at neighboring bars, going inside to search for him. Looking at the dash to the clock, she found it to be after three in the morning and decided that he didn't want to be found.

It was after four when she wearily crawled into bed but sleep was sporadic as she kept reliving their intense argument and remembering the true anger she witnessed. Releasing a weary sigh, she lay awake, listening to the sounds of the tiny neighborhood. Next door, Mr. Smith backed his car from the garage to go to work at the local factory. Then a huge truck stopped outside, the tell-tale beeping sound filled the air as it backed up soon followed by the clanging of the garbage cans as they were emptied.

Her breath caught and heart skipped a beat when she swore she heard the sound of his Harley coming nearer but was quickly disappointed when it was only a beater truck from one of the neighborhood boys who didn't believe in exhaust pipes. Frustrated and weary, she rolled over burrowing herself beneath the covers, wanting nothing more than to die.

The shrill ringing of the telephone on the nearby night stand shattered the blessed sleep that finally fell over her. She woke with a startled gasp, her eyes instantly going to the alarm clock.

After one!

"Shit," she muttered, tossing the blankets aside to sit on the edge of the mattress as she reached out to answer the noisy thing. "Hello," her voice was a breathless whisper as she struggled to gain her wits.

"Stacy?" Amy asked, concerned. When she watched Stacy leave last night with Matt, she had been itching to call to find out what all had happened.

"Yeah."

"It didn't sound like you. Are you still sleeping?"

"Yeah. I didn't get to sleep until, well, I honestly don't know. I do know that I watched the sun rise." A loud yawn erupted as if to show she spoke the truth.

"Is, uh, is Matt with you? I mean, I can call back if this is an inopportune time."

Stacy used the palm of a hand to quickly swipe at her tired eyes. Her voice quivered as she spoke. "No. I don't know where he is. After we argued he took off, walking. I tried to find him but he wasn't anyplace."

With a helpless feeling, Amy's eyes rolled to the ceiling. Christ, she hated doing this. She heard the pain in Stacy's voice and wanted to come clean.

"Oh. I haven't seen or heard from him either," she slowly replied as she sat nose to nose with Matt, noticing bloodshot eyes, anxiously staring back. Her eyes moved to Randy who placed a steaming cup of coffee on the table in front of Matt.

During the early morning hours Matt arrived to their house, pounding on the back door. Randy opened the door to find him very distraught. Matt stated that he and Stacy had an argument that he needed someone to talk to.

Amy paused to make sure that she wasn't needed. Turning, she went back to bed but Randy remained awake to talk things out and to hopefully get something figured out to help with this argument.

Later that morning, when she finally came out of the bedroom, Matt pounced on her, worried about Stacy. He asked her, well more like told her to call and find out any news, *and* he made Amy promise not to tell her that he was here.

A wry grin formed on his lips when Amy nodded her head in confirmation that Stacy was at least home. It was the toughest thing he ever had to do when he walked away from her last night.

He easily stepped into the nearby woodlands, watching her in the moonlight, his heart breaking more. When she plaintively called his name out to the night, he remained silent. He was too angry with the situation to want to speak with her or to anyone until the long walk to Randy's house helped him to cool down.

Being the best older brother a guy could ever have, Randy patiently sat, forcing his eyes opened and holding his face up with a cheek in his hand, listening to the frantic ramblings. Randy offered his suggestions and made a few good points. But Matt wanted Stace to tell him, to offer the information that Greg is his son. He didn't want to have to fish around. And now with Dan also saying he is Greg's father well, it didn't help with the situation. Amy's voice brought his tired mind from wandering any further.

"I was wondering if you'd be able to help me today with the finishing touches to the decorations for the hall?"

"Oh sure. I definitely need the distraction. I'll be over in an hour."

"Good. See ya later," she softly hung the phone up. Her eyes went to Matt's noticing how anxious he watched her. "She's home but doesn't sound very well."

Matt nodded as he reached for his cup to bring to his lips. "That's good. At least I know she made it home," with a tired sigh, he buried his face in his hands.

"Do you want to hang around and talk with her?" Randy asked.

"No. Take me home."

"Matt, you two need to sit down."

"There's something I didn't tell you about last night. I asked her if Greg is my son and she said yes."

Randy's mouth dropped open. "Serious?"

"Yeah and she was also with Dan after. I was her first but Dan said Greg is his. I say Greg is mine, Stace says he is mine too. But damn it, Dan put those damn seeds of doubts in my mind causing me to now believe otherwise. Dan and I both have blue eyes. Stacy and I have the dark hair, not Dan."

"But Matt, Greg has your same interests in airplanes. He has your cute, crooked little grin. You both walk with your hands in your back pockets," Amy added receiving impatient looks from both of them. "Just offering more details," she added with a shrug. "I'll leave you two alone."

"Yeah. Why don't you do that," Randy suggested.

With a sniff, she gathered the wedding items in her arms.

They waited until Amy disappeared into the living room before continuing with their discussion. Randy looked to his little brother, "So, why are you so damn pissed?"

"Because she didn't tell me about Greg. I had to ask."

"That's it?"

"No. When I had no doubts, I would have gladly taken the information in any way. Now, I'm so damn frustrated with the notion that I *don't* know if he's mine and I want nothing more than to be his father, biological."

"What if you aren't? Would that change how you feel for Greg? He's quite a boy."

Matt grinned. "No. I love that kid."

Randy gave him a long look, impressed with his words. "And what about Stacy? Would the fact that Greg isn't your son change your feelings for her?"

Matt pressed his lips together before answering, "Hell no."

A huge smile crossed Randy's face. "Whoa Matt. That's nice to hear come out of you. Stacy needs you and you need her. Go talk to her."

Matt released a weary sigh. Deep down, he knew that Randy was right and that he needed to get his ass out of his chair, swallow his anger and march across the road and talk to her without the temper flaring. He glanced to his watch.

"I know that I do but now is definitely not the right time. I'm still too damn angry to be able to sit down and have a sensible conversation with her. I need to cool down and get some sleep first. Let's get home."

"You're gonna let a little thing like your temper get in the way of true love?" Randy teased, hoping to get a smile but instead got a very serious response.

"Yeah. At the moment, distance is the best thing I could do. I have so much turmoil right now on my mind that I'd do more harm than good."

"I still think that you should..."

The low rumble from outside caused the both to glance out the window in time to see Dan's truck pull into Stacy's driveway. Matt rose from his seat, instantly alarmed should Dan be in an angered, get even mood and possibly do some harm to her.

Randy reached a hand out to grip onto Matt's tensed forearm.

"Now, sit down. We can't have you going off like that and get your ass back in jail."

"I can't wait to see if he'll hit her again either."

"Just hold on. Stacy is surely smart enough to meet with him on the front porch instead of permitting him inside."

Slowly Matt relented his attack stance and did as Randy suggested. But his eyes were burnt onto the peaceful house

across the road. They watched as Dan knocked on the front door, then Stacy step onto the porch gripping a baseball bat, closing the door behind.

* * *

When the persistent knocking echoed through her home, Stacy hurried as fast as she could, hoping and praying that Matt came to his senses and wanted to talk with her. She yanked open the door, shocked to find Dan standing in front of her. She was ready to slam the door in his face until she got a good look at how messed up it was. She fought the grimace at his very badly battered face. His one eye was almost swollen shut, his nose had a bandage across it and his lip had a nasty split on it.

Her eyes widened at the dark bruises on his cheek and the swollen shut, black eye. Grabbing the baseball bat, she stepped onto the porch. "Oh Dan..."

He only nodded.

"Is that what Matt did to you?"

"Yes he did."

"Well, you deserved it and if you're looking for him, he isn't here. I haven't seen him since last night."

Dan slid his hands deep into his pant pockets. "Actually, it's you I've come to see."

Instantly, she took the defensive with him. "I've told you over and over that I don't love you and I want you to just leave me and Greg alone..."

Dan shook his head. "No. Stacy that isn't it."

Her eyes narrowed, not sure what he meant. "What are you speaking about?"

"Let's just say that my eyes have been opened, at least until this one swelled shut," he said with a laugh while pointing to it.

She gave him an unsure look. Dan Black was making a joke about himself *and* laughing about it? There's something very, very rotten in Denmark.

He reached for her hand, feeling the tension in her arm as she fought to relax beneath his touch. "It's okay."

She eased her hand from his light grip. She sensed a change in him but she didn't know for what, the better? Or possibly it could be for the worse and if it was that, she was in a lot of trouble.

"Sweetheart..."

"Dan. We've been all over this."

He nodded and raised a hand in the air to silence her, seeing the flinch on her face and her gripping the bat tighter. Quickly, he lowered it.

"Would you be quiet and let me speak my piece? And put that bat down."

"Well, okay," she was hesitant with him.

"I've been a stupid, asinine fool. I should have never done the things that I've done to you and I am so, so very, sorry. Stacy, I'm letting you go. I don't deserve you. Hell, I haven't deserved you for a long time."

Once again, her eyes narrowed. "Dan. What kind of medication did they give to you for the beating?"

He let out a wry laugh with her words. "A strong dose of humble pie. I have been humbled by Matt Sadler. That guy is nuts about you and obviously, you are him. You have been for a hell of a long time. When I realized it, I went off the deep edge and again, I am so damn sorry."

"Are you serious?"

"Yes," a look of sadness crossed his face. "Stacy, I don't quite know how to tell you this one. Well," he faltered, kicking a foot against the floor. "Actually, I've been cheating on you."

"You've been doing what?"

"I've been cheating on you and that also made me realize that, hell, if I really loved you as much as I proposed that I did, I wouldn't be doing this."

"Oh."

"And she had a child who is mine and I'm going to make it right with her and get to know him better. And I'd also be very grateful if you would keep this as our little secret. She'll want to tell the family herself before word gets out."

Stacy's jaw fell open at the shocking words. "Wow," she softly spoke. "Can I ask who she is?"

He grinned then grimaced through the split in his lip. "It's Sandy."

"Ray is your son?" She could not believe that one.

"Don't look so damn shocked. Yes, he's mine. Um, with the return of Matt and how he acted with Greg, well, it didn't take a fool to see who fathered him. This has all opened my eyes."

Stacy could not believe what this as one more time, her mouth dropped open, "Are you serious?" She asked, her voice carrying an octave or two higher.

"I told you yes."

She shook her head with disbelief.

"Are you all right?"

"Yeah, just surprised, that's all," she muttered.

"I have one final request."

"What is that?"

"All I would like is a last kiss."

Fear swept over her, filling her with caution, "Oh, I don't think so," she began protesting.

He smiled, knowing that she would react that way and could he blame her? "Please. I'm not going to hurt you ever again. Just a last kiss and I'll be off. If I wanted to hurt you, I would have by now," he reminded.

"Well."

"I'm sorry Stacy," he whispered before his lips lightly, Brushed her cheek in a very platonic, friendly kiss.

CHAPTER 23

The erupted oath was vile, his angry voice filled the room as Matt bolted out of his chair. Randy followed, his hands gripping onto Matt's arms to get a jump start at holding him back. He too witnessed the odd scene. His concerned gaze remained on Matt.

With his eyes glued to the couple, Matt angrily shrugged him off. His clenched hands flew to the window to press on the warm glass. With narrowed eyes, he leant as close as the glass would allow. He stared, dumbfounded at the hated sight across the road. He could not, in a million years, believe what he just witnessed. Stace permitted that jackass to give her a kiss! A sure sign that she was enjoying that damn, jackass's attention!

"Do you believe this?" Matt growled.

"Don't go jumping to conclusions..."

"Oh hell. I don't have the need to jump. Just one look at that and it tells all!"

"Slow down. Matt, something isn't clear. Look, she has a bat in her hand. Why would she have that if she was taking him back."

"Come on Randy! It's *damn* clear. Look! Just look at them! Actions speak louder than words ever can! She obviously has made her choice and it isn't me."

Weary, Matt plopped onto his chair. Tilting his head back he released an angry groan. The truth hit him like the proverbial sledge hammer in his heart. He was being made the scapegoat. What a damn fool! Now it's clear to him. "She'd been playing him along to get Dan so jealous that he'd go back, hell, possibly even change."

"Do you hear yourself? I've been around them way longer than you. She hasn't been happy for quite some time," Randy explained.

"It's true, Matt. She hasn't ever truly loved him. He was someone she settled for," Amy added.

Randy's eyes remained on Stacy and Dan. He didn't miss the aloofness in these so called, love birds, as Matt hinted to them. He slowly shook his head refusing to believing it. He remained silent, watching Dan leave Stacy alone on the porch. He gave her a wave before driving away. Not the usual peeling out to lay any black-marks, just sensible driving.

"He just left and it wasn't any love shown," Randy added. He looked at Matt seeing hurt and anger in his eyes and on his expression.

"Get me the hell out of here, would you?" Matt demanded, standing so fast from his seat that the chair fell onto the floor, crashing loud as it hit the vinyl flooring.

"Amy, I'm taking Matt home!" His hand cupping her face as he leant in to press a kiss on her parted lips. "It doesn't look good. We just watched Dan and Stacy kiss," he whispered as he left for the garage.

"I saw it too and it wasn't a serious kiss," Amy explained.

* * *

Amy sat in the middle of the living room floor amongst the rolls of mauve ribbons, piles of white lace and bags of candles and holders. She waited for Stacy for some major help. Her eyes repeatedly roamed over the mass quantity of confusion while her hands picked up one stack to place on the opposite side of her then returning it back. Concentration was difficult. Her mind felt as chaotic as the jumbling mess around her with all she needed to do yet. Her eyes went to the door when it opened.

"It's about time," she complained with a whining moan while helplessly tossing lace around. Stacy giggled at the mess surrounding her.

"You're in pretty bad shape," she stood shaking her head as she braced her hands on her hips looking at the frilling chaos of lace and ribbons.

"No kidding, Einstein," Amy grumbled. "Sometimes I wonder what I ever thought with wanting to make tiny bows to match the bows on the pews to place on the tiny, five-inch-high, white wrought iron candle holders?"

"It's all in display and is simple. You wanted to use as centerpieces on the tables at the reception as a match of the church. Piece of cake."

Stacy plopped next to her, sitting crossed legged. With a smug smile, she gingerly picked up a holder giving it a quick look over before holding it for Amy's inspection. Her hands went to the ribbon then to the candle and holder. Expertly, she twisted this, turned that, tied a knot, added lace, twisted some more as she began with the decorating then held it in her hand for Amy to inspect.

Amy's lips twisted into a smirk. Eying the finished product she then looked to Stacy, surprised to find a grin instead of tears.

"It's perfect," came the dry response. "Like anything else your talented little hands touch."

At the sarcastic tone, Stacy's smile left to be replaced with a friendly smirk of her own. "Who pissed in your precious bowl of cornflakes?"

A sick grin formed on Amy's lips. With a weary, long sigh, she shook her head, her blonde hair bouncing with the gesture.

"No one. I think that I got me the pre wedding day jitters. That's all."

"Well, calm down. That wedding day is still a week away..."

"Correction, less than a week away."

"All right, it's six days. We got plenty of time to get this mess organized," Stacy added, her eyes sweeping over the mess mentioned. "I think."

"Good. That's what I needed to hear."

"Good. Glad I could be of some assistance. I hope."

Even though it sounded nervous, Amy surprisingly let out a laugh, then asked, "Have you seen Matt?"

A grief stricken look washed over Stacy's face. She shook her head. "No. Not even a call from him. And I even called his place and he hasn't been home yet."

"Perhaps when he cools down, then he'll call."

"I hope so. I'm so afraid that I've lost him a second time. Amy, I don't know what to do."

"Look, Miss Little Happy Homemaker. It's obvious how much you love him."

"It shows?" Stacy asked, her eyes going to Amy's all too knowing look.

Amy fought her grin while she gave her head a quick nod. "Believe me, it does. You are so deeply in love with him. Don't give up. Keep calling the guy. He's just pissed and like all men, he hates when he's proven wrong."

Stacy turned back to the piles of lace and ribbon, lightly tossing them up in the air. "But, I don't think he was wrong. This time it's entirely my fault. I was wrong. I should've told him about Greg as soon as I was told the news."

"Oh, so that's what happened, not you and Dan together."

Stacy shot her a level look, "Oh hell no. Never again. By the way was it you who squealed to him?"

"No! Whenever I'm told to keep a secret, I keep a secret. No way, it wasn't me."

"Well, okay," Stacy answered while giving her a leery look.

"Then, why were you kissing Dan this morning on your porch?" Amy questioned her voice fading at the look of disgust.

"He begged for forgiveness and vowed to never bother me ever again and wanted a good bye kiss. You saw that?"

"Yep. Sure did. So did Randy and Matt."

"Whoa. What are you saying?"

"That when I called you he was watching me. I'm sorry for not telling you but he made me promise."

Oh, so he wanted her to worry about him? Stacy remained silent. The sad part was that his little plan worked. She sat up all night long worrying and crying about him. Amy was talking, adding how angry he became and his further reaction to it. A wicked smile formed on her lips when Amy repeated how upset he had become, and demanded that he be taken home.

Stacy was tickled with that information and she believed that as God's way of getting back with him for making her worry if he was hit by a car or still out there, somewhere, walking around. As she realized that Matt was home and Greg was next door with her parents, she believed that she better high tail it home too, just in case.

"Shit's about to get deep, Amy."

* * *

Greg waited on the front steps of his grandparent's porch when Randy's truck pulled in to drop off Matt. Both men got out. Greg's face lit up when he spied Matt. With the energy of an eagle flying after its prey, Greg jumped from his seat to run to him.

"Dad! Dad, where've you been?" Greg's anxiously called out.

Randy grinned, slowly getting used to Matt being called dad by Greg and it showed on Matt's face the love he felt for the boy. Randy turned to get the motorcycle out of the truck bed, still watching Matt.

A warm grin curved Matt's lips, surprising Randy at the instant change in him. Remaining silent, Randy watched Matt hold his arms out as Greg ran to him. He was, for the first time, looking and making comparisons between the pair. Greg *did* look like him, a lot. He wondered why he never noticed the resemblance before.

Soon, Greg felt strong arms around his shoulder, holding him close in an embrace. Then, surprising him even more, felt Matt's lips press a loving kiss on the top of his head.

"I'm sorry that I haven't been around much lately," Matt muttered, slightly releasing his hold so that he could look into Greg's innocent, face. His hand cupped Greg's chin as he studied his eyes.

"Where have you been?" Greg repeated.

"I've been pre occupied lately with some problems..."

"Hey, where did you get the black and blue cheek?"

Hearing a chuckle, Matt glanced at Randy in time to see him press his lips together. He was enjoying watching his little brother play dad and yea, it was surprising him at how naturally well he was doing it.

Matt released Greg's chin. "I was in a fist fight," he truthfully stated, raising his eyebrows when Greg's eyes widened.

"Awesome. Who with?"

Matt faltered with a reply, wondering if he should tell him or let Stace tell him. Hell, it's obvious that she's going back to that jackass.

"It was with Dan," Randy spoke for him.

Greg's eyes widened more, "Whoa. For real?" He was loving the fact that that bastard finally met his match.

Matt shot Randy a thank you glare over Greg's head. Looking back to Greg, "Yes, for real."

"Awesome. I wish I could've seen that one. It would've been so totally cool to watch you beat the living shit out of him."

"Young man. What did I tell you about that? Don't swear." Matt smoothly reminded.

Greg clenched his teeth together as he rolled his eyes at the light scolding. "Sorry."

Randy's chuckle erupted into a full blown boisterous laughter. Finally, he got into a semblance of control of his emotions, Randy added, "He sure did too."

"That's enough, Randall," Matt stated rolling his eyes down to Greg's over anxious face then back.

"Oh yeah. Never mind."

"Matt. Is that you? Where have you been? We've been worried about you!" Marge scolded as she and Sam emerged from their home.

As they walked nearer, a gasp of alarm escaped from her.

"Not again," she scolded. Her eyes instantly picked up on the bruise and the rough way he looked with his chin stubble; blood shot eyes and the rumpled clothes he wore.

"What happened son?" Sam asked, leaning closer to take stock at the injury as Marge's motherly hand reached up to lightly rub the bruise.

Matt grimaced, moving his head higher. "Do you have to?"

"Does it hurt?" She wondered, remaining steadfastly stubborn to touch it.

He relented, grimacing. "Maybe a little. I'm sorry I snapped mom."

"Yeah mom. He's been a like a bear with a burr in his ass since I bailed him out of jail last night," Randy kindly offered the information as Matt turned to give him another threatening glare.

Her hand slightly paused in the air close to his eye. "You were in jail?" She loudly demanded.

"Awesome!" Greg excitedly added.

"Thanks Randy."

"Anytime. What's a brother for?"

"Oh I don't know, maybe to beat up on, too?"

With a look of mocked fear, Randy raised his hands in front of him. Marge once again tried to touch the injury.

"Okay you two," Sam threatened, giving his sons that fatherly tone along with the familiar warning glare. As the pair quit with their nit picking, he asked Matt, "What did you do?"

"He beat Dan up!" Greg rapidly replied, his face still holding that amazed look.

Matt briefly closed his eyes in the grimace of disgust as Greg thought that was the most amazing thing ever accomplished by a person.

"What was it about?" Sam asked as Marge still lightly fingered the bruise.

"I really can't talk about it right at the moment," Matt growled, his hand lightly wrapping around his mother's wrist to hopefully stop her nursing administrations.

Sam looked at Randy who discreetly pointed a finger to Greg then rubbed his hand through his hair as he hoped to hide the gesture. Understanding immediately filled him. Sam turned his attentions to the boy. He couldn't miss the admiration Greg held for Matt. The bonding flowed naturally between the pair and he hoped to God that things would work out with Matt and Stacy.

"Greg. I hate to do this to you buddy but, could you please leave so that I can have a serious, father to son conversation with Matt?"

Greg's eyes slowly went from Matt to Sam then back again. Then it dawned on him. They really wanted rid of him.

"I want to hear about it. I know you guys won't talk about the incident until my precious, little ears are far away. I want to hear what happened and how bad Dan looks!" He turned to look at, his matching gaze looking upwards into his eyes. He was searching. Searching for hope that he would relent and say it was all right to stay but that didn't happen. "Aw come on."

"Go ahead. We'll talk later," Matt gently urged, his hand again cupping Greg's chin.

Greg slowly grinned at this strange man who came into his life sending his mom and him into a whirlwind of emotions, and whom he held a deep devotion and adoration for. Greg believed he noticed a searching in Matt's eyes as he studied him. Greg felt warm, loved when he felt Matt's strong arms wrap around him to embrace him close to him.

He just has to be mine, Matt thought. "Remember that I love you," Matt whispered, feeling Greg's arms wrap around his waist.

"You're not leaving, are you?" Greg demanded, his eyes blinking back tears. He stepped from Matt's now loosen grip.

"Not yet. Now, get going. I'll talk with you later."

With a nod, Greg slowly turned back to his grandparents' home.

With sadness, Matt watched him leave. "He's definitely mine," he softly spoke his earlier thoughts.

Randy stood next to Matt. Both watched the extra slow steps Greg took, his heart going out for the little guy. "Hmm. I know. How about a DNA test?" Randy suggested, seeing the thoughtful expression crossing Matt's face.

"DNA?" Matt echoed.

"Sure. If things happened as you said, then, I believe that would be the best thing, or a blood test."

"What's going on? What's this all about?" Marge asked, urging them into the house.

Each took a seat on the living room furniture as Matt related the events that sent him and Dan to jail, Sam and Marge kept giving one another quick glances. Then, when he added that Dan claims Greg as his son, Matt's jaw clenched as did his fists. He wanted nothing better to do than beat the shit out of him again.

"I don't think that you need one of those DNA tests. Hell, one look at the little man and he's you all over," Sam consoled.

Marge nodded. "I agree. Matt, stop fretting over it. Greg is your son. We all know it. I feel it in my heart. When he's here there is so much of your actions, your movements in him that I swear you're back as a child."

"I only wish that I knew for sure. Stacy did confirm and deep in my heart I know he's mine but when Dan said he was with her that same week," he muttered before he excused himself for a shower and to get some much needed sleep.

Waiting until he heard the water from the shower, Randy explained the other situations that transpired, bringing this all to a head last night.

Matt paused outside the bathroom door, quiet, thoughtful, as Randy's voice filtered up the stairs.

DNA? Would Stace agree with such a test? He released a drawn out sigh. One look at Greg showed the close resemblance but he still wanted to be certain. He needed that beyond anything. Even though he loved Greg, he wanted that closure.

CHAPTER 24

The extra quietness of the house was relaxing, peaceful and managed to drive him further over the edge. A few times the ringing of the telephone woke him and the light whispering of his mother's voice perked him up.

Maybe it was Stace!

Then, when he heard the soft sound of the phone being hung up, it'd send him crashing down to earth with hopelessness. Tossing and turning, Matt slept five rough hours before deciding to give it up and get the hell out of bed. His turbulent rambling thoughts kept him on edge, frustrating him more than not getting that much needed sleep.

Inhaling a deep breath, he rose to only slip into a pair of jeans before padding, bare-feet, down the carpeted steps. He begrudgingly walked past his parents who remained silent as he went outside to the front porch.

Marge and Sam were upset at the story Randy related and what all happened. It seemed as though things were going well between the young couple and now to hear about the explosive argument. When they discovered the cause of the confrontation, it was just as upsetting. And then to hear that Dan and Stacy were spotted, by Matt and Randy, sharing a kiss! That would definitely send a man to wanting to do battle. Their concerned gaze went back to one another. Sam covered Marge's hand with his in a silent hopefulness that they would work things out but they didn't miss that the protrusion of his jaw.

The screen door slammed shut when Matt went outside, shoving his hands into the pockets. His searching eyes went to Adam and Beth's porch, seeking and finding his son. Somehow, he already knew that Greg would there, watching and waiting for him. A soft grin formed on his lips as Greg didn't let him down. Greg remained silently watching him as he sat on the nearby steps on the porch. A white plate that at one time held a sandwich and an empty glass of pop rest next to him.

"Have you been there all day?" Matt called out, his voice sounding raspy from the struggles of sleep.

Greg straightened in his seat, "Yes dad."

With a chuckle, he waved his hand, motioning for Greg to come on over to join him on the wooden glider. In a flash, that Matt swore could have broken the sound barrier, Greg was seated across him on a matching ladder back rocking chair.

Matt waited for Greg to get comfortable before speaking, "I can tell that you're upset about something. So, what's on your mind?"

"Well...mom won't give me an answer," Greg stated, giving Matt a long look.

Matt's eyebrows rose at that intent expression. "And, what is your question? Maybe I can help."

"What happened?"

"Say what?"

"Why are you and mom not speaking? I thought that you loved her."

"Greg, I do love her."

Greg gave a relieved look with Matt's confession. "Then what's going on?" He asked in a voice next to crying.

Matt debated whether he should or shouldn't mention that he may be his father. Hell, he sure knew that Stace would be totally pissed off if he did say anything without her consent. But, hell, what would she care? Wasn't she going back with Dan?

He bit at his lower lip. Bull! He is Greg's father and he has a right to talk with him on any damn subject he desired.

Greg's voice interrupted his rambling thoughts.

"Did you really beat the crap out of Dan?"

"Yes I did. He deserved it, not only for what he was saying but for any pain he inflicted on your mom and you in the past. I was just giving him his just desserts."

"I'll bet he got a sweet tooth now!" Greg gleefully stated as he laughed.

"A good one." Matt became serious, wondering how he should begin. He decided to come to the point. "Greg, have you ever wondered about who your father is?"

At the serious sound of his voice, Greg listened then nodded. "Uh huh. I wonder a lot. Especially lately when the kids at school call me bastard and stuff. And I know what that means."

Matt's lips straightened in a grim line as he nodded he leant forward, bracing his elbows on his knees, clasping his hands. His eyes looked closely at Greg. He wondered exactly how to broach the subject but it seemed that Greg was unknowingly helping him with that problem.

"I asked mom if Dan was and she came back with a fast no, he isn't," Greg muttered, mocking the way Matt sat.

Matt grinned, noticing how Greg always did things as he did. Before he realized it, he blurted out, "Would you like me to be your father, Greg?"

"That would be awesome," Greg breathed, his eyes wide with hope believing that maybe Matt was going to ask his mom to marry him. "Why?"

"What is going on?"

Both jumped at the very loud, familiar shrieking voice very close to them. When they looked, their gaze fell on Stacy, who stalked closer to the steps. Each caught the angry, shocked expression she wore.

"Uh oh," Greg whispered, recognizing that look. "This isn't looking very good."

"You sure got that one right," Matt echoed, also knowing what it meant.

Stacy took fast steps up the sidewalk to the back porch. She pulled into the driveway when she spied Greg hurrying across the yard to, where she guessed, Matt also was. Was she ever glad that she decided to follow. She had a very good idea what the topic of conversation was which they were having and just where it was headed. And, when she heard that question coming from Matt, well, that set her temper over the edge!

Matt quickly stood as she came nearer. He shoved his hands deep into his back pockets. He sure didn't miss the blackness of her dark brown eyes. He had been lucky to only have the opportunity to see that look and what it could produce a few other times in the past.

Stacy was right with her assumption. Matt was so close to telling the hugest secret kept from a child. Stacy slowed her steps, strolling around them like a commander of an army barracks giving his squad the once over. Her eyes flitting back and forth between the pair; she wasn't missing the definite guilty look on Matt's face as he cautiously watched her. She stopped, raising a hand to the side, palm up, flicking her fingers.

"Well? Aren't you going to answer me?"

Matt and Greg exchanged quick glances before looking back to her.

"She's talking to you," Greg offered, taking a cautious step away from them.

"Gee, thanks for the tip," Matt muttered, bravely turning his complete attention to her and found himself balking at the disagreeable expression she shot at him.

Fiery dark eyes shot death killing sparks of anger at him. Her cheeks were flushed and dear God, she looked so damn good in the heat of rage. Her long hair was loose, in luxurious waves that he longed to get lost in. He wanted to reach out and take her into a gentle embrace and apologize until he couldn't apologize any longer. But in reality, that was never going to happen. Not when she is so pissed off.

Stacy crossed her arms in front of her chest, her sandaled foot patiently tapped on the wooden floor. Her eyes remained glued to Matt's unsure face, not missing the quick anxious swallows as he no doubt thought about what to say. She hadn't seen him like this since he explained to her that he was going away to join the Navy.

"I'm waiting."

"I know. I'm not sure whether I can say this in front of Greg," Matt confessed.

"You were certainly saying it rather fine a moment ago to him," she huffed as a smirk curved her lips.

His eyes bored into her as he released a long hiss, "You are not making this easy."

"Because it isn't easy and you of all people should know that!" She turned to Greg. "Greg, leave us alone, please."

"Aw mom..."

"Didn't I say please?"

"Yesss."

"I'll talk to you later, Greg," Matt said.

"Okay," Greg quickly answered before turning to rush away from the angry tension. "Good luck," he shot over his shoulder as he jumped down the steps.

Matt didn't miss the tightening of her precious face when Greg quickly and without argument, did as he said. He raised both arms, his hands forming the shape of guns, pointing them in her direction.

"Give it to me with both barrels."

Frustration set in. She swiped a hand through her hair before bracing her hands on her hips, her gaze falling back on Matt. "I am trying so damn hard to keep my sanity with you but I'm losing control!"

"What are you talking about?"

"I'm losing control in keeping my temper and losing that hold I have on Greg. Just look at him! Whenever I suggest or tell him to do anything, I get nothing but arguments. That didn't happen until you came into our lives! Before he met you he was a sweet little boy who listened to his mother!"

"Stace, don't be ridiculous."

"*I am not being ridiculous!*" She screamed out while turning her back to him. Yes, she was and she damn well knew it, she reprimanded herself.

Matt stared at her very straight, very rigid back. He didn't like to talk to her this way but he had no other choice in the matter.

"What is your problem? Is it because I may pose as a threat to you?"

She spun around to face him, tears of frustration filled her eyes and slowly rolled down her cheeks, causing a sigh to escape from him.

"He's my son," she whispered.

"He's mine too and I think he needs to know who I am. Hell, he should know. Don't you agree?"

This was all so foreign for her. All his life, she was the one who had been here for him. She was the one who protected him and now, and now Matt was back and he wanted to be here for Greg. And true, he had that right. She realized that she hadn't been fair to Matt. Not at all. From the very beginning, she knew that as soon as she knew about the pregnancy, she should have told. She released a long sigh, her hand rubbing along the sides of her temples at the painful throbbing from within.

Matt reached out, gently cupping her stubborn chin in his hand to force her to look at him. He held her vision with his. His gaze was soft, searching as he spoke.

"You of all people should know that I would never do anything that would harm you or him. I would fight to my dying breath to defend anyone or anything that would dare harm those who I love."

She looked into his eyes and saw the sincerity of his words echoing in his expression. "Then, why were you so angry with finding out the truth last night?"

"Christ, I can be so damn stupid at times," he muttered, his hand moving to rub his chin.

"And, when did you have to tell me that bit of news?"

Despite his frustrated anger, her response got a grin from him as he gave her a quick glance. Though it was brief, it was a grin.

"Okay. I was angry because I had to ask you about Greg. You didn't offer to tell me any damn thing about him for his entire life!" He said, catching how his voice was raising as his anger was once again enflamed. "And my parents, Randy. They have a grandchild, nephew and they didn't know."

"He is here with them anytime he wanted."

"I am not done talking."

Stacy crossed her arms. Her head stubbornly tipped to the side to pin him to the ground with an angry glare. At the moment, she didn't, not for one moment, care for his tone of voice and so she decided to let him fume a bit longer.

Slightly sticking her nose into the air, she muttered, "I'm done listening and here," she added, smacking his chest with the yellow envelope. "These are yours. Now, excuse me," she turned to walk away from him and his attitude.

His hand caught the envelope, the other shot out, gripping onto her upper arm. "We aren't finished with this yet. Where the hell are you going?"

Her gaze coolly roamed to his hand then back to his face. Slowly he released his hold as she turned to face him. "Whenever you can decide to speak to me with a civil tongue and not out of anger, perhaps then I will find it necessary to have the time to listen to whatever it is you have to say. Until then, I don't give one iota."

With those words, she turned to angrily stomp down the steps and back to her parent's house, her anger showing in the extra loud stomping of her steps on the sidewalk.

Matt took a tentative step towards her, already knowing that it would be useless. Raising his arms out to the side, he called out, "Stace, darling, I'm sorry!" But she kept walking away, stepping over the row of purple Impatience that lined the yard before making her way across the paved driveway. He lowered his arms, adding, "I love you!"

She turned in her tracks, but kept walking backwards. "Talk to me whenever you can without shouting."

With that, she gave him the sweetest most innocent, alluring grin that a woman could ever muster. Her hand went to the phone in her pocket. As she turned away, he heard her voice, "Hi Dan..." before going inside of her parent's home.

His eyes dangerously narrowed. "That jackass," he vowed, his attention going to the envelope. Curiously he opened it, removing 8x10's of her. The pictures he took of her at the swimming hole. He leafed through them loving all of them. "I guess she can't be too pissed at me."

* * *

As the door closed, Stacy laid her phone on the kitchen table. Beth shared a cup of coffee with Adam. Both curiously watched out the window at the pair and to what she was doing. Beth too heard her say hello to Dan but now she just laid the phone down.

"Don't you have a phone call?" Beth wondered, her brows furrowed with curiosity as her eyes rolled to her husband who was taking this all in.

Stacy looked to her mom where an innocent grin formed on her lips. "No. I don't."

"Then," Beth began, pointing to the telephone. "Then, why did you answer it?"

"Oh, that. To make Matt Sadler even more jealous than he really is. It's good for him," she quickly added when her mother's mouth opened to ask another question as she took a seat opposite her father, who up until now had remained blessedly silent.

"Why is lying good for him?" Adam wondered, his alert eyes glued to Stacy as he waited for an answer.

"Dad. Just because he is a man, that makes him deserve a little fabrication now and again."

Adam's one eyebrow rose upwards with her words.

"Yes. It keeps you men on your toes," Beth added with a naughty smile.

"Exactly," Stacy added with a knowing nod.

"I'm not liking this conversation at all. I'm learning far too much about how you ladies really think and it's frightening me a bit," Adam muttered, his eyes flitting back and forth between his angelic wife and innocent looking daughter. Wow, looks could really be deceiving in this case.

When Greg heard his mom's voice, he slowly entered the kitchen to lean on the table next to where she was seated.

"Mom? Why are you and dad fighting?" Greg innocently asked.

Beth and Adam gave one another a curious glance, then Beth's memory float back to the day Matt left. She recalled how upset Stacy acted and the way she had avoided any and all contact of her family. All along she thought that it could be the truth and now she knew that it was. With a smug grin, she sat back in her chair, crossing her arms in front of her as she gave Stacy a new look. She was amazed at the secret she managed to keep for that long.

"Ou. I'm proud of you, young lady," Beth murmured.

Stacy snapped her head up to look at her mother. Her brows furrowed with her words. "What about?"

"For what I had always believed happened so long ago," she added, her head slightly nodding to Greg who was now looking at her with a, grandma you are nuts, look.

"Mom...I couldn't tell anyone..."

"And why couldn't you?"

"It's somewhat complicated..."

"I have time. Maybe you should have confessed this to me then and together, we could have figured out a way to change things."

Stacy gave Greg a quick look then quickly answered, "He had a dream to see the world."

"Oh Stacy Cannon. I don't think that you really knew him as well as you always let on!" Beth scolded.

"What do you mean?"

"I think he would've faced things the way a man would. I think that he would've been here at your side if only he knew, married you and taken you with him."

"I have to agree with your mom, sweetheart. You should have come to us," Adam added.

"What are they talking about, mom?"

Stacy wrapped her arm around his shoulder to press him against her in a loving hug.

"Life," she whispered.

CHAPTER 25

Matt sat at a lone, corner table in the darkness of the bar. The atmosphere matched his mood, dark, depressing. He felt used, abused, dejected, played with, toyed with, hell you name it and he felt it. By the tips of his fingers, he lightly held the neck of his drink, idly rolling the bottle back and forth, watching the trail of water forming on the table from the condensation.

This was only his ninth one but then who was counting. Certainly not him! His gaze kept flitting to his brother and his four groomsmen as they sat at another table, helping him to enjoy the last night of his freedom. Though he was the best man, he had opted to sit alone and Randy understood why.

The rehearsal had gone off rather well. It was going to be a beautiful wedding and Randy was lucky that he found someone as lovely and understanding as Amy. They truly loved one another and this evening it showed. The emotions were stronger. The tears seemed to flow easily down everyone's cheeks as the sermon was practiced.

His worried thoughts went back to his own problem. He didn't understand what actually went wrong. In a nutshell, he confessed his love to Stacy and she repeated those same words. Then they spent a magical night in each other's arms. Sure, the argument followed and he had the pleasure of watching her give jackass Dan a kiss and a hug.

Then, they had another argument and he still hadn't the chance to speak with her, well, he tried but she walked away.

He could not believe, would not believe that she was willingly going back to that jackass! Christ, the few weeks he was home; he first hand witnessed how much she feared the guy. What could he be holding over her head to make her agree to such a thing? Loud, jubilant laughter came from behind him. He glanced up as the owner of the voice strolled past. Dan! He was busy talking on the phone as he walked past to take a seat at the bar.

"She's sending me so many damn mixed messages," he talked to the bottle.

"Yeah, she's agreed to come back to me," Dan said, with laughter. "And her son, correction, *my* son has accepted me too. Isn't that great news?"

No! Can't be true! It just can't be true!

Not caring for what he heard, Matt sat up, taking on a threatening stance, the glare was strong as he stared at Dan's back. He needed to have a few words with the jackass. He needed to find out a few things and to get this ended here and now. With long strides, he stalked to where Dan sat.

Matt stepped beside him, casually resting his elbow on the bar next to Dan's drink. He remained silent, his unwavering gaze focused on the man's arrogant face. Matt cleared his throat. Then waited. When Dan failed to acknowledge him, he repeated it, only louder.

This time Dan looked up. With a confident smirk on his lips, he spoke to the phone, "I gotta go. Sadler's here."

His wary gaze never left Matt's unapproachable, penetrating glare. He wondered what the hell he was so damn pissed off about? The man should be one of the happiest men around, well, next to himself of course. He was definitely the happiest man in the world. Turning his attentions to Matt, who still silently glared at him, he again wondered just what his problem could be? Surely he and Stacy spoke since he went to her to make amends. Didn't they?

"Hey Matt," Dan cautiously began since Matt still hadn't said anything. "What's going on?"

"I guess that you and Stace have patched things up..."

"What?"

"And you're getting back together."

Slowly Dan shook his head, the wonder of Matt's words showing on his face. "No, we're not getting back together."

Matt turned his head to the side, wondering what kind of game was being played on him. He sat on the next stool, leaning his elbow on the bar to place his cheek in his hand as he gave Dan another long look. "You're not? Are you sure?"

"Oh yeah. We're not, hell I don't love her. Me and Sandy are going to work on our life. She has my son."

"But...I saw you two kissing on her porch and she looked so damn happy."

Quickly, it dawned on Dan what Matt witnessed. They're parting kiss. A huge grin crossed his lips. "Oh that! I was giving her a good bye kiss. I realize that I don't love her, really hadn't since I've been cheating on her. A real man doesn't claim his love for one woman then screws around with another. Man, that ain't love."

"Then, why were you so persistent with wanting to stay with her?"

"I'm not so sure myself. But I figure it must have something to do with male pride. My pride. That's a major issue to admit to, infidelity. I knew she wasn't the sort of woman to do that to a man but when I was doing it to her well, it hurt so damn much that I actually hated myself and what I was doing. Through my anger at myself I lashed out at her and Christ, it was so damn wrong of me."

Matt listened with acute interest to the man's words and his heart near to burst with hope. His spirits lifted to new heights.

"Well, I'm glad that you've seen the wrong in what you were doing. Women don't deserve to be hit on like that..."

"Especially if you love them. How a man does that, I can understand why, jealousy is the main issue but it's wrong. I've been going to counseling and it's helped me a lot."

"That's great man."

"Hey, can I buy you a drink?"

Matt waved him off as he walked away.

"Good luck and take good care of the boy of yours," Dan called out.

His boy. Those were the best words he heard in a long time. "Thanks."

It was after one in the morning when Matt walked his bike into her driveway. His blurred vision looked at her dark house. Somewhere in the distance, a group of dogs barked back and forth to one another telling their day's stories. The sound of someone burning off some tires echoed into the late night air along with the chorus of spring peepers.

Matt dropped his bike onto the lawn. Those many drinks were finally beginning to affect him as he slightly staggered towards the side of the house to her bedroom window. Bending, which was his mistake since the alcohol went straight to his head, making him dizzy, he picked up a handful of pebbles.

Standing, he swayed then staggered, his head began swirling. Releasing a long breath, he let them loose into the air. His aim was true as they pelted against the glass. With a groan his hand went to his forehead, rubbing where the tingling hammering sounded.

"Staaa-ceee!"

Ignoring the raging dizziness, he bent to retrieve another handful to weld in the same direction but this time the force of his throw caused him to spin and fall onto the ground. He landed with a heavy thud on his derriere. Looking at the dark window, he released a helpless sigh.

"Stace! Are you in there?" He loudly called out from his prone position before lying flat on his back.

Stacy woke with a startled gasp. She was in a deep sleep when the sound of clattering against the glass woke her. Her gaze fell to the window wondering what on earth that could have been. Sliding deeper beneath the sheets, she released a sigh of contentment. The sound of a man's desperate voice loudly calling out her name caused her to sit upright. Then the sound of more pebbles hitting at her glass and another call from below set her springing from her bed.

Sliding up the window, she peered out, failing to see anyone. As her eyes adjusted to the darkness of night, she turned her head, looking to the driveway and saw nothing then looking below she saw the chrome of his Harley gleaming from a dim light of a lamp post from a neighboring house. A man, who she knew would be Matt, lie on the ground, his arms stretched out to his sides as he called out her name.

"Stace. Are you in there?"

Fighting the grin, she heaved a sigh. On fast feet, she hurried down the stairs and outside to the front porch. Taking a few steps towards the bike, her voice softly called out.

"Matt?"

"I hear the voice of an angel," his voice slurred.

Taking a few steps through the grass, she came upon the shadow of his figure, still laying on his back with the palm of his hands pressed to his forehead. With a sniff, the aroma of beer filled her senses. He's been drinking, she thought.

Sighing, she dropped to her knees. She reached a hand to his to lightly tug them from his face. She could barely make out his features in the pale moonlight but she did see his teeth flashing white with his smile.

"Not only the voice, but the face of an angel too," he muttered, his hand snaking out to grip onto the back of her neck, gently urging her down to him. Quickly, affectively, his lips captured hers with a slow, long, tantalizing kiss. Easily, his tongue pushed past her lips to dance with hers.

Stacy tried resisting but was overwhelmed with the heated power of the need emanating from him, completely engulfing her. With the persistent tugging of the strong arm of his wrapped around her waist, her arms weakened and let her body melt onto his, taking in his strength as her kiss deepened on his. Easing away, she gazed into his face.

"Matt, why are you drinking?"

His hand slid to cup her cheek, his thumb lightly skimming over her lips as she spoke. He pressed his lips together, not really wanting to divulge his weakness.

"I was thirsty," he answered with a playful grin. "Oh, I love those pictures of you. Damn fine photographer."

"You took them," she reminded.

"Yep, damn fine photographer."

"You must have been really thirsty," she pressed, giving his shoulder a light shake. "Okay, what were you drinking?"

"Beer...and whiskey shots."

She pulled herself up, sitting crossed legged next to his body. The heat coming from him was so overwhelming! Both naturally and sexually!

"Why?" She persisted, her hand now gently being held in his as he kept it on his chest to keep her close by.

He gazed at her with that crooked grin. Knowing talk would be useless, she breathed an impatient sigh. Standing, gently pulled him along with her.

"Let's get you inside."

The moment that Matt stood, his body began to sway. She wrapped his arm over her shoulder, her arm wrapping around his waist, hoping that she could give him some sort of support.

"What's wrong with you?"

"I was fine until I bent over for those damn stones. The alcohol must have gone to my head. Christ, is it spinning," he groaned, his free hand rubbing his forehead as she led him to the porch.

"Could have been the whiskey..."

"It *was* the whiskey," he added, heavily taking a seat on the top step to brace his elbows on his knees as he held his head in his hands.

Stacy stood two steps down in front of him. She grinned knowing that he wasn't feeling the best, but he was just so damn cute being miserable. Slowly, she reached her hands out to brace the back of his head as he silently suffered.

"I need to get some coffee in you..."

"What I need is water and plenty of it," he muttered as his hands moved to wrap invitingly around her waist, feeling the silky soft material of her night dress beneath his touch.

Stacy gasped from the heated effect his simple touch had on her. Soon, she felt herself being urged closer towards him as he embraced her. His face was partially hidden against her stomach. A long sigh of contentment escaped from him when he felt her arms tightening about his shoulders as she held him tighter to her. She felt the slow movement of his head then the definite heat of his breath as his mouth sought out and began nibbling on a breast. And damn, didn't her body respond to him.

Fight the feeling Miss Stacy!

"Matt, you still haven't told me why you are drinking? This isn't at all like you," her voice was soft, breathless as his teeth tugged at her through the material.

"I'm having some pretty wild thoughts at the moment," he whispered before seeking her out with more intensity, ignoring her question.

It was undeniable. She wanted him too but not when there were issues hanging between them. After all, she was still certainly, angry with him for leaving her like that and causing her to worry about him. With all the strength she could muster to fight his torturous lovemaking, she straightened her arms, pushing herself away from that heat seeking mouth.

"Matthew Gregory Sadler!"

Matt very much enjoyed the feel of her curves beneath his hands. They were curves that he wanted to desperately get lost in and believed that he was about to pull her down and take her right here on the front lawn. Wouldn't the neighbors love that? Suddenly, he jumped at the intensity of her voice when she practically yelled his name. Tilting his head back, he looked into her face seeing a determination on it. Even in the shadows he could see that stubborn look.

"What darling?"

Stacy released a sigh, "Why are you drinking?" She once again asked, her voice whining with his tenacity to keep changing the subject. She watched as he rubbed a hand across his forehead, wincing at the obvious spinning that was once again happening. "Let's get that water in you, then you can tell me, all right?"

He nodded, permitting her to grip onto his hand to lead him inside. The light brought the kitchen to a warm, welcoming glow as he took a seat at the round table next to ceiling to floor window. He watched her pour a tall glass of water before bringing it to him. His eyes were still focused on her as she took a seat opposite him, leaning an elbow on the table to rest her chin in the palm of her hand.

She waited for his answer. He just knew it. That look of no nonsense, tell me now, was on her face. Prolonging his response, he reached to pick the cold glass in his hand before chugging the liquid down.

"More," he said, handing the glass to her.

A smirk formed on her lips and eyes narrowed at his request. Remaining silent, she did as he asked. Returning, she once again took her pose, staring him down. Waiting. As he drank, she spoke, "Matt. You have to be in a wedding today and you are going to look like crap unless you get some sleep."

"I'll be fine."

"The photos won't be," she reminded with a knowing grin. "So, before you even consider getting any sleep...talk, now."

Her eyes remained glued to his very handsome face as his emotions surfaced. She read, hurt, anger, betrayal in his eyes. Betrayal? Why would he be thinking like that?

Matt tented his fingers, staring down at them. He began, "Well. I saw you kissing Dan and you were having quite a happy look on your face. I thought that you were going back to that jackass."

Fighting the grin, "When?" She asked, already knowing that he saw them.

"You two were standing on the front porch."

"You're jealous?"

Looking up, "Damn right!" He growled, glaring at the giggle he heard coming from her. "He told me that Greg was his, not mine. His words planted seeds of doubt..."

"Oh Matt! One look at him and you should be able to tell who his father is!"

"I know, but when he spoke with such assuredness, I wasn't as certain. Randy mentioned DNA test..."

"If that's what you want to clear your thoughts."

Matt saw the truth in her eyes and knew that she would do anything that he wanted. He grinned, "No. That won't be necessary. Greg is mine."

"Then the phone call you answered, well I thought for damn sure that you were going back..." He stopped at her sultry laughter. "What is so damn funny?" He muttered, his eyes boring onto that beautiful face. Oh sure, she was having a field day with his emotions.

When Stacy finally sobered, she answered, "I didn't have a phone call that day. I just pretended that I did."

"What the hell for?"

"To get even with you for leaving me alone after that argument. You so pissed me off. I was worried about you!"

Matt's mouth dropped open. "Uh oh. You one of those women who likes to get revenge?"

"Yes. Isn't that fantastic?"

Matt stared at her as she gave him the most innocent look she could. "Well, it appears that I'm going to have to mind my manners around you," he muttered once again getting a rich laugh from her. His next words sobered her. "Okay, let's talk about Greg."

"What about Greg?"

Matt didn't miss the defensive, protective shield she placed up to protect her child. He had the gut feeling that she would be that kind of parent and he was ready for it.

"Well, I believe that he needs to know who I am, as his father. Not just as the best friend from his mother's past." Stacy looked back at Matt with relief and amazement but not surprised to hear he finally wants this. At her silence, he continued. "It's what my goal has been since I've returned."

"You don't know how relieved I am to hear those words come from you."

"You are?"

"Yes."

"I needed to discover where I really stood in your life and I think that I do."

A delicious tingle swept over her at the words he spoke and the intensity of his stare.

"When should we tell him, how?"

He reached out to tenderly brush his knuckles against her soft cheek then slid to the nape of her graceful neck.

"Tomorrow but tonight, I need to be with you," he stated, pulling her towards him as his lips captured hers in a long, gratifying kiss. Slowly they pulled apart, gazing long into each other's eyes. Stacy stood to walk out the kitchen. Pausing on the stairs, she listened as his chair slid across the floor before he followed.

CHAPTER 26

It was mid-morning during a beautiful bright, sunny day when he woke after a sensuous night spent in the arms of this woman whom he fell deeply in love with. Matt lay on his side, his arm bent as he braced his head in his hand. He remained silent, lovingly watching as Stacy peacefully slept in the afterglow of their ardent night of passion. His gaze roamed to and stuck to those lips, recalling the way she used them last night. He swore that this time, she wore him out.

She lay on her side, her hands laying beneath her cheek. A stray lock of hair fell across her face, shielding it from his view. Reaching a finger, he gently slid it to her shoulder. His gaze went back to her pursed lips causing his heated thoughts to wander back to how she controlled him with those babies.

"Unbelievable," he whispered with a light shake of his head.

Tenderly, his hand roamed down her slender body, hidden from his view by the pink floral sheets when the sudden knocking on the bedroom door startled him. Tilting his head, he looked at it then back to Stacy, now beginning to stir from the noise.

"Mom! Are you up yet?" Greg loudly asked.

"Well, if you aren't that should do it," Matt softly muttered getting a tired smile from her.

Her eyes fluttered open to look onto his handsome face as he lay his head next to hers on the pillow.

"Good morning darling," Matt spoke, touching his lips on the tip of her nose.

"Good morning," she lazily answered before rolling onto her back. Her arms went above her head as she stretched her love sated body.

"Randy is on the phone!" Greg loudly called through the door. "He wants to know if dad is here since his bike is in the drive way! Is he?"

"Yes he is!" Matt answered, holding a mock sound of impatience from the questions. His response caused laughter to slip from her.

A huge smile broke forth on Greg's lips. That could only mean that they made up. "Yes," he whispered, raising a clenched fist into the air to give a victory pump of his arm.

"Give us a moment, would you Greg?" Stacy finally said. Matt's hand lovingly cupped her cheek as he gazed long into her face. She believed that he was acting mighty peculiar this morning.

"You're beautiful, Stace."

That statement surprised her as she kept watching him, sensing a sudden change in him.

"I'm sure I am..."

"You are with your hair messed like that. The way your eyes softly look at me. Those lips holding a slight grin with what I say," he teased. "Along with a look of contentment on your face."

"You put it there darling," she whispered.

A grin softened her expression as she rolled onto her side to face him, an arm wrapping around his waist to give him a hug. Her chest rose and fell from the sigh escaping her when she felt his arm wrap around her to hold her tightly against him, feeling the heat of his flesh join with hers. He feels so good, she realized, savoring this moment.

"I'm frightened," she whispered in his ear. "I don't need to be because he simply adores you but I don't know how to begin telling him."

Matt released his grip to look at her face. He knew what she was talking about. Their impending meeting with Greg. How does one broach such a subject like this to a boy?

"We'll do just fine. Trust me," he murmured before brushing his lips on hers. His grip relaxed as she pulled away.

"You can pick up this phone," she added standing with her back to his greedy eyes.

She raised her arms above her head to give her back a good stretch, the movement causing her breasts to thrust out before she walked towards the bathroom. His gaze was trained on her perfect curves, noticing that this time, the modesty wasn't around since she failed to grab a bed sheet to drag along with her.

Bracing up on his arms to gain a better view of the sway of her hips, he repeated, "Unbelievable."

Reaching for the telephone, he sat up to rest his back against the headboard, the place where he was held blessed captive last night as he sat up and she straddled his thighs to make love to him. "Greg hang up the phone," he said waiting for the click. "Good morning."

"There you are! Mom has been going ballistic when you didn't come home last night. She called me, hell she even called the jail just to see whether you were hauled back there," Randy laughed.

Matt's rich laughter joined him, "I was being held captive in the arms of a beautiful woman last night."

Randy's brows rose upwards, "Ou little brother. You have it bad."

"You know it. So, what's happening? Anything I should know about?"

"Ha ha. It's called a wedding. I'll be expecting you at the church on time."

"If I can get out of this bed, no problem," Matt teased, his laughter erupting with Randy's mild oath.

* * *

Greg sat on the rocker on the front porch, holding a model plant as he stared at the Harley laying in the yard. When the front door opened, he turned his head to see his mother emerging. Her hair was wet, the dried ends lifting as she moved. She looked comfortable in her shorts and baggie T-Shirt but on her face was an expression of uneasiness, which quickly alarmed him.

Standing, he asked, "What's the matter?"

"Nothing's wrong sweetie. Why do ask?" She wondered, taking a seat next to him.

Greg gave her a long look. It was still in her eyes, that look of concern. "Well. You look kinda worried about something. Are things with Dad going good?"

She grinned at his grammar.

"Going well. Yes, they are. Um, we need to have a discussion with you when he gets down here."

"Oh, what about?"

Matt's voice interrupted their little talk, "About me."

Stacy and Greg turned in their seats as Matt walked towards them. His shirt was worn open, fluttering with each step he took, exposing that flat, hard stomach. He didn't miss where her eyes strayed to before resting on his eyes.

He pulled a wicker chair with him, the legs dragging on the floor to set in front of Greg and Stacy. Taking the seat, he cleared his throat, looking Greg in the eyes.

"What's this about?" Greg wondered, becoming nervous from the vibrations he felt from their own nerves.

Stacy slowly began. "It's about me and Matt..."

Sitting forwards in his seat, he retaliated. "Are you two getting married?"

"No," Stacy quickly answered.

"Oh," Greg muttered sitting back as he folded his arms across his stomach. He didn't miss the grin crossing Matt's lips.

"Actually Greg, this is about two people who were best friends in school. They fell in love but didn't know it until later..."

"Much later," Stacy squeezed in.

Matt shot her a look, "Not much. He knew it then but she was a stubborn sass queen."

"Who are you calling a sass queen?"

A smooth grin formed on Matt's lips before he replied, "Who would you think?"

Greg's head pivoted back and forth to look at them as they took their turn talking. He grinned. Man, were they behaving childlike. "Do I need to separate you two?" Greg asked, quickly gaining their attention.

They looked at Greg as he watched them, seeming so wizened for a boy of twelve.

"Okay, Greg," Stacy began. Her hands reached out to lightly grip his hands. "A few weeks ago, you asked me who your father was. Do you remember?"

"Sure do. That was after you keel hauled Dan."

"You keel hauled Dan?" Matt asked.

"Sort of," Stacy answered with a shrug.

"Man, she gave it to him good!" Greg stated as Matt released a long whistle of amazement.

Stacy shook her head, "That's not what I'm speaking about."

Seeing her frustration, Greg said, "Yes mom. Then I asked who my real father was."

Breathing a sigh of relief, she said, "Yes. I think that you should be told. It's time that you should be told."

Greg sat at the edge of his chair. This is what he's been wanting for a couple of years but she always denied telling him. He wondered what could have changed her mind?

Stacy faltered at the over anxious look on his face. Would he be disappointed when he was told the truth? Casting a quick glance to Matt, she was reassured that he would not be. She tried, a few times, to speak. Her mouth opened then closed and repeat, but the words seemed to catch in her throat.

Matt watched, sitting on pins and needles with anticipation of the truth be known by that one person who mainly mattered in this relationship.

Their son.

"Greg, this is so hard..."

"Why? Is he some sort of gangster or something?"

Finally, tired of waiting, Matt cleared his throat before beginning. "Greg."

Greg looked at him.

"It's me. I'm your father."

His reaction was strong. Stunned. Silent as he slowly turned his head back and forth between them. His brows furrowed and mouth dropped open, appearing to be in shock. He crossed his arms sitting back in his chair. Greg was indeed, shocked but not with disappointment. They were words he had so often dreamed of hearing. And, to top it all off, he heard them from his father! The main man! The king of all men!

Since he met Matt, he wanted nothing else, had been hoping he remained in his life. Even after Matt left, he hoped Matt would keep calling. But to know that now there was a stronger bond, an everlasting tie between them was the best! Tears filled his eyes, causing the blueness to glisten like icicles.

Stunned, he could only shake his head, then, "Nuh uh," he announced, now looking to his mom.

"Uh huh."

His gaze shifted to Matt who was wearing a broad smile. "For real? You're my father? For real?" He questioned.

Matt nodded, watching those blue eyes, so much like his own, fill with tears. "Hey, son. Are you all right with this?" Matt asked, the worry in his voice was heavy.

With a nod, Greg slowly stood going to Matt's arms, feeling them wrap around to hold him tight. Greg's little body shook from his tears. Stacy reached her hand out, cupping his head as he turned it to look at her.

"I love my family. I'm finally home," Matt stated holding them tighter.

"Thanks mom. This is the best," he blurted.

"I know it is," she whispered gaining Matt's arm to slip from Greg and pull her with them.

* * *

"Oh Amy," Stacy's voice held that awed tone while she entered the dressing room of the church. "Everything is just beautiful."

Amy stood next to Sandy by the full length mirror, each observing their own reflections for any imperfections. With a forced smile, she turned to greet her. "I'm wishing we just ran off now. This stress is going to kill me."

"Don't I know it," Sandy added with a knowing nod of her head.

Stacy gave Amy a brief hug, being careful to keep from smudging her make up. "It isn't too late. I'm sure that I can get Randy into the limo and he can just whisk you two to your honey moon now, where you can get married once you get there," she laughed receiving a wry grin from her.

"You should have suggested that a year ago when we began planning this."

"Relax Amy. It'll all be lovely. You're more beautiful now than when we did your portraits."

"Must be the heighten glow from fear," Amy muttered.

Stacy burst out laughing from her wry humor, actually seeing the truth in her eyes. "Hey, for the record, I just finished with Randy and Matt and Randy was trembling all over," she laughed, "Matt had to help him maneuver with the poses I was having them do."

And it was true, Randy had been having an extremely hard time concentrating. But then, so was she. Matt kept giving her some pretty strange signals the rest of the day. After telling Greg about him, he seemed to become very quiet, withdrawn, as he obviously had something important on his mind.

Amy weakly smiled as she fought to control the tears from her very emotional day. Stacy wrapped her in her arms, giving a hug of reassurance.

"It'll be all right. You are beautiful, the groom is a bundle of nerves, anxious to get married, the cake has arrived and is in place, the guests are out there waiting to see the bride's arrival, the portraits are at the hall and look lovely..."

A knock on the door stopped her. Slowly it opened, Amy's father entered with a huge grin. He gave each of his daughters a brief kiss on the cheeks, then, "Are you ready angel?" he asked Amy, calling her his pet name.

Amy took in a long, relaxing breath. She squared her shoulders, behaving in the manner of facing down the enemy on a battlefield. With a look of sheer determination on her face, she replied in a clear voice, "More than you could ever imagine."

"Good," he answered, holding his elbow out to wait for her to slip her hand in, "Let's do it."

The church was filled to capacity as the wedding flowed smoothly. Sniffles and the blowing of noses were echoing throughout the church. Amy had everything beautifully decorated but Stacy couldn't take her eyes from the striking figure Matt cut dressed in his matching black tuxedo. She pursed her lips, realizing that, oh yes, there was definitely something about a man when he was dressed like this making him exceptionally attractive.

Needing to shake these tumultuous thoughts from her wandering mind, she worked diligently throughout the ceremony, remaining as best as she could to be as inconspicuous. To her dismay, her lens kept picking up those intense looks in Matt's eyes. The one moment, she even witnessed a wink and a grin being aimed at her and she knew that she felt her face blush.

Silently waiting, she listened as the preacher declared that he may now kiss his bride. Through the slightly blurred vision from her tears, Stacy snapped off a series of the precious one in a lifetime photo. Then the preacher loudly announced to the family and friends, the new Mr. and Mrs. Randall Sadler. Applause filled the church before the traditional march sounded, sending the newly happy couple careening down the aisle and out the doors.

"Isn't she a beautiful bride?" Beth asked Stacy as she and her father strolled past her. Adam had his hand resting on Greg's shoulder, leading him forward.

"Yes, she sure is," Stacy replied, giving Greg a grin. They still hadn't formally told anyone yet that Matt was his father, just a few had guessed. They didn't feel it right to take away from Randy and Amy's day so they decided to wait until later.

At least she was until while taking the family portraits at the altar. That was when things began to fall apart. Even though it was minuscule, things began to fall. Stacy just got the pictures of grandparents taken and was getting the parents and siblings. Oh sure, things were going smooth.

Randy and Amy stood in their appointed spots. Stacy placed Marge and Sam next to them and Matt next to Randy. Then Matt spoke.

"I want my son in it too, darling."

Stacy felt her mouth go dry as all eyes turned from Matt to her. She pressed her lips together, giving him a, what are you doing look.

Matt easily read it, ignored it and repeated. "I want my son in it darling. Didn't you hear me?"

"Yes..."

"Are you insinuating what we already know?" Marge asked, her eyes going to Stacy and seeing her pale. Sure, she already knew the truth but was taken off guard by Matt's very vocal, very demanding suggestion.

Matt's deep voice rumbled, breaking anyone else's thoughts. "I'm only speaking the truth. Greg is our son and I want him in this family portrait."

The already chaos of wedding portraits erupted worse as she just finished them as parents rushed Matt and herself each hugging and giving congratulations to them.

Greg watched his mother, waiting for her approval. Knowing that she was out numbered, especially when Matt spoke, she nodded at him. Instantly, he was on his feet, standing in front of Matt and Randy.

Greg beamed a huge smile to Sam, who watched with interest. "Isn't it awesome Grand pap Sadler? I really am your grandson! Hey, someone needs to take a picture with mom with us too!" Greg added.

During the reception, Stacy patiently stood nearby as the guests lined for the traditional bridal dance. Her thoughts kept drifting back to that episode at the church and relief filled her. All was happy to finally know the truth and she mentally kicked herself for never telling anyone. Greg brought happiness and joy into all of their lives and now, with the knowledge that he was really their grandson seemed to heighten the love that was felt.

She breathed a light sigh, gently holding her camera in her hands and waited for, as she instructed Randy and Amy, to nod their heads when they wanted a particular photograph taken with someone special. One by one, as the grandparents approached then the parents, Stacy snapped off the demanded pictures.

Matt was busy pouring shots as Sandy held the bag for the gift of money. His gaze never strayed far from Stacy as once again his eyes roamed over her lithe figure in those black pants and black camisole top with cream lace overlay. Ou, she was looking mighty fine this evening, he thought. His grin broadened. He was making some major plans for her but this evening, he noticed a sudden strained look on her face.

It was true. Stacy had grown solemn. This seemed to happen at every wedding she took. She imagined a wedding, her own that she believed she would never have. Sure, even with the acceptance of Matt wanting the responsibility of being Greg's father, nothing else was ever spoken about.

Looking around, she noticed how everything was decorated so perfectly beautiful. The well-wishers were abundant, constantly going to the happy couple whose love showed on their faces when they would look at one another. Even earlier, from across the room, when Randy would gaze in Amy's direction, the love was there.

God, how she wanted that too!

A sigh slipped from her pink painted lips. She would get over it. It was only the atmosphere, she kept telling herself. She was fine until she came to a wedding then the thought her own would fill her. With a sniff, she brought her camera up to snap off a picture when one more time, Matt's intense gaze met hers through the lens. Soon it was time to throw the bridal bouquet. The music began and on the count of three Amy was set to toss it. Stacy held her camera up ready for the shot when suddenly Amy walked towards her, handing her the beautiful rose and calla lily bouquet.

"Amy, what?" she managed before Amy gave her a hug. Turning, she looked to find Matt walking towards her.

Her mouth slightly dropped open when she watched him approach with a most intense look on his face. He swooped down on her so fast and stood so close that she had to take a step away as he reached for her camera. She permitted him to take it out of her grip. He handed it to Amy who laughingly took it.

A scowl of wonder formed on Stacy's face. "Matt, I'm doing a job. What are you doing?"

Matt remained silent. The intense look changed to that of a most serious look was on his face. He gazed long and hard into her dark eyes.

"Matt?"

Randy motioned for the Disc Jockey to stop the music as Matt gently grasped both of her hands in his. Slowly he fell to his knee, his other leg bent as he looked into a now, stunned, beautiful face. Gasps and cries were joined with loud applause.

She could feel the trembling in his hands as he held onto hers. "What are you doing?" Stacy asked, her voice barely above a hoarse whisper.

"Isn't it obvious?"

"But in front of people?"

He nodded. "Darling. This should have been said to you twelve years ago."

"What? What are you."

"Don't interrupt me. I'm on a roll."

A few snickers met their ears with those words.

Smiling, he continued. "Back then I fell in love with you and now whenever I'm with you I fall deeper in love, I feel complete. Whole. My life has more meaning with you in it, and of course, Greg," he whispered, giving her a grin.

She returned with a grin of her own before her teeth began to nervously bite at her lower lip.

His brows furrowed as he looked at their hands. His thumbs rubbed across her knuckles, feeling the softness of her skin as he fumbled for more words, the right words. He looked up.

"Um. Stace, you have my heart. You have had it since high School and earlier. Others have tried but, no one else could ever claim it. It kept calling out your name."

"Oh Matt," she whispered as her eyes filled with tears to slide down her round cheeks.

"I want you next to me forever. I want to wake with you in my arms. With you by my side. I need you."

With his eyes locked onto hers, he released a hand to reach towards Randy who promptly placed a tiny box in it. With his thumb, he flicked it open. God, he couldn't believe how badly he was shaking. He never shook this much fighting the enemy. He looked at Stacy when he heard a sharp intake of her breath. Her eyes were wide, frozen onto the ring that glittered as it was nestled in its black velvet cushion.

Stacy believed she was in shock with Matt's words but when her eyes fell onto the ring; she went beyond words. The sight of the carat squared cut diamond with blue baguettes on the sides filled her vision.

It's true! It's really happening!

Her free hand trembled in front of her opened mouth as she kept looking back and forth to the ring and Matt, who was now looking back at her with all the love he felt.

"Stacy Cannon."

"What?" Came the weak reply.

"Would you please do me the honor and become my wife? There's nothing more I could ask for than a yes."

"Tell him yes mom!" Greg excitedly screamed out, receiving more laughter.

"Oh!" Slowly she fell to her knees to look him in the eyes. "Yes! Oh my but yes!" She squealed as he stood, pulling her up with him.

He caught her trembling hand in his to place the ring on her finger. When he looked into her beaming face, he was surprised to find her looking at him, not at the ring. And he saw nothing but love and happiness in her eyes.

"I love you, Stace," he whispered.

"I love you more, Matt."

His hands dove into her hair, bringing her to him as his mouth covered hers in a long, passionate kiss among the cheers that erupted throughout the hall as flashbulbs lit the room.

CHAPTER 27

Eight Months Later

Matt anxiously glanced to his wristwatch then to the cloudless blue sky beyond. He had received the call thirty minutes earlier that Stace was in full labor and to hurry. Seems the little guy was coming a week before her due date. With permission from his Chief, he borrowed transportation. He radioed in for permission to land the Black hawk helicopter at one of the life flight landing areas of the hospital and got full encouragement. The propellers were still spinning as he jumped out, running up the parking lot to the Emergency Room.

"It's time Stacy."

"No. Please, can't you make it wait?"

She saw the corner of his eyes crinkle from his grin, hidden behind the mask, "I can't do anything like that. Are you ready?"

"No. Matt isn't here yet. I promised him that he'd be here this time..." she stopped as a contraction cut through her swollen stomach. "Oh my God."

"Relax. Breath," he ordered as he checked her.

"Mom, tell him to make it wait."

Beth giggled as Marge held her hand. "He's doing the best he can do and besides, this baby is ready to come. Greg is waiting with Dad and Sam. All you need to do is deliver."

"I can't yet," Stacy argued.

The doors burst opened as Matt rushed in, surrounded by hospital staff helping him with his scrubs over his flight suit. The nurses followed behind, hastily tying the robe closed behind him.

"I'm here!" he loudly stated, immediately going to her side. Marge stepped back as he rushed next to the bed. His hand tightly gripped onto Stacy's, a grimace forming on his face at the strength of her hand clutching onto his seeming to cut the circulation from his fingers.

"Good girl. It won't be long now. Stacy at the next contraction I want you to push. Got that?"

She nodded.

"And Matt, you listen to my commands to help your wife along and watch the miracle God has given to you." At the silence, he looked at Matt, seeing the paleness of his face. "Are you going to be all right?"

"Yeah, yeah. I'll watch."

Stacy giggled as he looked into her face. "I don't believe you," she gasped.

"I'll watch."

Tears streamed from his eyes as not long after he watched his daughter arrive into the world, promising to be as beautiful as her mother.

ABOUT THE AUTHOR

R.E. Laurel is born and raised in Kittanning, Pa. where she lives with her husband, Tim and four pets. A Jack Russell is constantly at her side as she diligently works in her office. Also is one of the three rescue cats, Bella Donna who is either bird watching from her cat scratcher or lounging at her feet. The other two are usually sleeping in one of the other rooms in her house.